From the Library of
Dianne Saxon

Behavioral Systems for the Developmentally Disabled:
I. School and Family Environments

Other books from Banff International Conferences on Behavior Modification available from Brunner/Mazel

Behavior Modification and Families (Banff VI)

Behavior Modification Approaches to Parenting (Banff VI)

The Behavioral Management of Anxiety, Depression and Pain (Banff VII)

Behavioral Self-Management: Strategies, Techniques and Outcome (Banff VII)

Behavioral Systems for the Developmentally Disabled: II. Institutional, Clinic and Community Environments (Banff IX)

Behavioral Systems for the Developmentally Disabled:
I. School and Family Environments

Edited by
L. A. Hamerlynck, Ph.D.

Coordinator,
Mental Retardation
State of Montana

BRUNNER/MAZEL, *Publishers* • New York

Library of Congress Cataloging in Publication Data

Banff International Conference on Behavior Modification, 9th, 1977.
Behavioral systems for the developmentally disabled.

Includes bibliographies and indexes.
CONTENTS: [1] School and family environments— [2] Institutional, clinic, and community environments.
1. Behavior therapy—Congresses. 2. Behavior modification—Congresses. 3. Developmentally disabled children—Congresses. I. Hamerlynck, Leo A., 1929- II. Title. [DNLM: 1. Behavior therapy—Congresses. 2. Handicapped—Congresses. W3 BA203 9th 1977b / WM425 B215 1977b] RJ505.B4B37 1977 618.9'28'914 78-21562 ISBN 0-87630-193-6 (v. 1)

Copyright © 1979 by Brunner/Mazel, Inc.
Published by
BRUNNER/MAZEL, INC.
19 Union Square West
New York, New York 10003

Distributed in Canada by BOOK CENTER
1140 Beaulac St., Montreal, Quebec H4R 1R8

All rights reserved. No part of this book may be reproduced by any process whatsoever, without the written permission of the copyright owner.

MANUFACTURED IN THE UNITED STATES OF AMERICA

Dedicated to
my family,
Marilyn, Mark, and Erik,
and Pat Boedecker, our extended family.

Preface

This is one in a continuing series of publications sponsored by the Banff International Conferences on Behavior Modification. The conferences are held each spring in Banff, Alberta, Canada, and serve the purpose of bringing together outstanding behavioral scientists to discuss the present data related to emergent issues and topics in the field of behavior modification. Thus, the International Conferences, as a continuing event, have served as an expressive "early indicator" of the developing nature and composition of behavioristic science and scientific application.

Distance, schedules and restricted audiences preclude wide attendance at the conferences. Consequently, the publications have equal status with the conferences proper. They are not, however, simply publications of the papers presented at the conference. Major presenters at the Banff Conferences are required to specifically write a chapter for the forthcoming book, separate from their informal presentation and discussion of the topic at the conference itself.

Past conference topics and faculty were:

1969: I. IDEAL MENTAL HEALTH SERVICES

Nathan Azrin
Ogden Lindsley
Gerald Patterson

Todd Risley
Richard B. Stuart

1970: II. SERVICES AND PROGRAMS FOR EXCEPTIONAL CHILDREN AND YOUTH

Loren and Margaret Acker
Wesley C. Becker
Nancy Buckley
Donald Cameron
L. Richard Crozier
David R. Evans
Leo A. Hamerlynck

Ogden Lindsley
Patrick McGinley
Nancy J. Reynolds
James A. Sherman
Richard B. Stuart
Walter W. Zwirner

1971: III. IMPLEMENTING BEHAVIORAL PROGRAMS FOR SCHOOLS AND CLINICS

Joe A. Cobb
Rodney Copeland
R. Vance Hall
Ogden Lindsley
Hugh McKenzie
Garry L. Martin
Jack L. Michael
Gerald R. Patterson
Ernest G. Poser
Roberta S. Ray
Richard B. Stuart
Carl E. Thoresen

1972: IV. BEHAVIOR CHANGE: METHODOLOGY, CONCEPTS, AND PRACTICE

Eric J. Mash
S. M. Johnson and
O.D. Bolstad
K.D. O'Leary and
R. Kent
K. Skindrud
R. Jones
L. A. Hamerlynck
G.C. Davison
G. R. Patterson
H. Hops and J. A. Cobb
J. B. Reid and
A.F.C.J. Hendriks
R.B. Stuart
Lee C. Handy
H.M. Walker and H. Hops
J. LoPiccolo and W.C. Lobitz
D.L. Fixsen, M.M. Wolfe and
E. L. Phillips
L. L. Weiss, H. Hops and
G. R. Patterson

1973: V. EVALUATION OF BEHAVIORAL PROGRAMS IN COMMUNITY, RESIDENTIAL AND SCHOOL SETTINGS

Richard R. Jones
Siegfried Hiebert
Bryan C. Smith
Aldred H. Neufeldt
Peter D. McLean
Robert Paul Liberman,
William J. DeRisi,
Larry W. King,
Thad A. Eckman and
David Wood
Srinika Jayaratne,
Richard B. Stuart and
Tony Tripodi
William B. Neenan
Michael F. Cataldo and
Todd R. Risley
Robert L. Kahn and
Steven H. Zarit
Rosemary C. Sarri and
Elaine Selo
H.S. Pennypacker, Carl H. Koenig and
W. H. Seaver
William W. Cooley and
Gaea Leinhardt
James R. Barclay
Charles Windle and
Peter Bates

1974: VI. BEHAVIORAL MODIFICATION AND FAMILIES

Frances Degen Horowitz
Todd R. Risley,
Hewitt B. Clark and
Michael F. Cataldo
Elaine A. Blechman and
Martha Manning
L. Keith Miller,
Alice Lies,
Dan L. Pettersen and
Richard Feallock
John B. Conway and
Bradley D. Bucher
Stephen M. Johnson,
Orin D. Bolstad and
Gretchen K. Lobitz
Sander Martin,
Stephen Johnson,
Sandra Johansson and
Gail Wahl
Martha E. Bernal,
Leo F. Delfini,
Juell Ann North and

Preface

Susan L. Kreutzer	Gerald R. Patterson
Paul M. Rosen	John A. Corson
Lief Terdal,	Victor A. Benassi and
Russell H. Jackson and	Kathryn M. Larson
Ann M. Garner	Robert F. Peterson

AND
BEHAVIOR MODIFICATION APPROACHES TO PARENTING

Donald R. Green,	Virginia Tams and
Karen Budd,	Sheila Eyberg
Moses Johnson,	Karen E. Kovitz
Sarah Lang,	Barclay Martin and
Elsie Pinkston and	Craig Twentyman
Sara Rudd	Wallace L. Mealiea, Jr.
Barbara Stephens Brockway and	Martin E. Shoemaker and
W. Weston Williams	Terry L. Paulson
Edward R. Christophersen,	Joe H. Brown
James D. Barnard,	A.M. Gamboa, Jr.
Dennis Ford and	John Birkimer and
Montrose M. Wolf	Robert Brown
Buell E. Goocher and	Margaret Steward and
David N. Grove	David Steward
Merihelen Blackmore,	Peter D. McLean
Nancy Rich,	W. Doyle Gentry
Zetta Means and	Allison Rossett and
Mike Nally	Todd Eachus

1975: VII. THE BEHAVIORAL MANAGEMENT OF ANXIETY, DEPRESSION AND PAIN

Donald Meichenbaum and	Peter Lewinsohn,
Dennis Turk	Anthony Biglan and
Ernest G. Poser	Antonette M. Zeiss
Peter McLean	Wilbert E. Fordyce

1976: VIII. BEHAVIORAL SELF-MANAGEMENT: STRATEGIES, TECHNIQUES AND OUTCOME

Frederick H. Kanfer	Richard R. Bootzin
Todd R. Risley	Carol Landau Heckerman and
G. Alan Marlatt and	James O. Prochaska
Janice K. Marques	Richard B. Stuart
Richard M. McFall	Frances Phillips,
Peter Suedfeld	Jackie Hooper,
Lynn Buhler and	Cathy Batten,
Reta McKay	Molly Dexall,
Albert J. Stunkard	Dave Beamish,
Gary E. Schwartz	Tom Pollok and
Marvin R. Goldfried	Gordon McCann
William R. Miller	

Many people have donated their energies and talents to the continued success of the Banff Conferences on Behavior Modification.

Primarily, of course, we must acknowledge the guest faculty who develop, present and discuss topics found in this volume.

The Banff Conferences have been more than places at which theories and research data are presented and discussed. The Conferences have stimulated planning and research in selected areas and have helped to bring together policymakers, program administrators, researchers and clinicians in an effort to stimulate adoption in practice settings of many of the programs that have been discussed during its proceedings. The success of this effort has been aided in great measure by the material support and the technical guidance of the University of Calgary's Division of Continuing Education and by the staff and resources of the Banff School of Fine Arts, which has been the site of the Conferences since their inception.

L.A.H.

Contents

Preface vii

Introduction xiii

Contributors xix

I. SCHOOL ENVIRONMENTS
   1. Advances in School and Classroom Learning
      By R.L. Schiefelbusch 3

   2. Reducing Hyperactive Behavior in the Classroom by Photographic Mediated Self-Modeling
      By Kern A. Olson and Max W. Rardin 23

   3. Interaction Effects of Medication and Classroom Contingencies on Verbal Tics and School Performance
      By Stephen I. Sulzbacher and Kathleen A. Liberty 32

   4. PEERS: A Program for Remediating Social Withdrawal in School
      By Hyman Hops, Hill M. Walker and Charles R. Greenwood .. 48

II. FAMILY ENVIRONMENTS
   5. An Intensive, Home-Based Family Training Program for Developmentally-Delayed Children
      By Edward R. Christophersen and Bobby W. Sykes 89

6. The Insular Family: A Deviance Support System for
      Oppositional Children
   By Robert G. Wahler, George Leske and Edwin S. Rogers 102

7. The Early Education Project
   *By Gerald M. Kysela, Kathleen Daly, Martha Doxsey-Whitfield,
   Alex Hillyard, Linda McDonald, Susan McDonald and Julie
   Taylor* 128

8. A Behavioral Analysis of the Home Environment of
      Autistic Children
   By Sander Martin and Bruce Graunke 172

Index 193

Introduction

Both this volume and its companion volume, *Behavioral Systems for the Developmentally Disabled: II. Institutional, Clinic and Community Environments*, are directed at the design and construction of socio-behavioral environments to accelerate the development of the developmentally disabled. In general, they are not books about the developmental disabilities. Rather, the editor and contributors have directed their efforts at examining, refining or changing the environments in which handicapped children and adults might live and learn. This is not to discount the significance of the unique behavioral repertoires of the developmentally disabled, but represents the habilitative process. As a consequence, the populations described in this book include the usual range of developmental disabilities (mental retardation, autism, epilepsy, cerebral palsy) but also several other populations not currently included within the definition (aggressive, withdrawn, developmentally delayed). The unifying dimensions in terms of the handicapped described are:

1) Behavioral deficiency
2) Behavioral excess
3) Inappropriate behaviors

This book represents one of the most significant developmental stages in the growth of behavior modification: the behavioral ecology stage.

THE BEHAVIORAL ECOLOGY STAGE

This is a stage of maturity involving the analysis of all salient environments. An earlier stage was the Whoopee Stage vividly described by Patterson (Patterson, 1969) where we impressed ourselves and some observers with clinical evidence of the Law of Effect and which passed too rapidly according to some aspiring assistant professors. The Whoopee Stage was followed by the more subtle Methodology Stage where the scientific basis was extended and the derived technology developed. The Behavioral Ecology Stage will answer old questions while posing new design problems.

Behavioral Ecology

Behavior modification as a label or descriptor has a significant flaw or deficiency. It accents description of the dependent variable or output and leads to the inference that the means justify the end, i.e., changed behavior. In a completely free operant world, counter-control would reduce concern about abuses. The counter-controlling behavior of the client would protect the changee from pain control. However, too often human interactions are in settings which may preclude counter-control, i.e., institutions, prisons, classrooms, the family. The result is the widespread development of advocacy, human rights committees, and the general establishment of counter-controls through codes of ethics, peer reviews, etc.

Also, the dependent variable (client behavior) accent has too often led to ignoring the factor of the change process. Behavior modification is not "about changing behavior," but its essence is changing the environment to produce behavioral change, or to maintain or strengthen an adaptive repertoire. We must recognize that there is a real interaction between environments which is reducible and changeable. In other words, the contingencies for developing lifelong, self-help behaviors in the repertoire of a profoundly retarded child must include an analysis and design across both time and space. It is not sufficient to design a token economy and curriculum and then train the staff in the conduct of the system. An intervention intended to teach skills to last a lifetime across different environments and to new classes of the handicapped demands strategic study and design.

Behavior modification's initial successes were with the helpless and incurable, in part because the contemporary therapies/therapists were not threatened. Consequently, the work leading to the token economy by Ayllon and Azrin and Lindsley's work with schizophrenics developed. All we, as scientist/practitioners, wanted was a chance to prove what the laboratory said should work could work.

Introduction

But it is now a different age, and the questions have changed from *Will it work?* to *How long will it last? Will the skill generalize?* These questions obviously involve complex answers—but within scientific parameters. The earlier solution of "give us a chance to demonstrate" can be analogous to the initial step in a backward chain. This may, in fact, be a strategic error. Perhaps behavior modifiers should refuse to develop a technology for solving a problem, i.e., underachieving, out-of-control classroom behavior, until the across time and space contingencies have been developed. A reasonable question to ask in the design stages is, *How much counter-control does the student (client, patient) exert upon the supervisors, parents, administration, etc., supporting the teaching and clinical staff?* A clinical observation I have made is that significant others often sabotage interventions, even when client progress is dramatic. This probably is because they are not, in fact, "controlled" by the behavior of the client, student, patient. Reid and Hendriks, colleagues of Patterson in Oregon, report roughly 25% of parents as "diffuse" or unable to carry out their role in interventions with predelinquent children. Given that a forward chain is often slower than a backward chain procedure and that extrapolation to the planning of interventions still must accept the problem behavior, I propose Hamerlynck's conditions for assuring effects across time and space:

(1) *There is an inverse relationship between the severity, frequency, intensity of the behaviors and the probability that client behavior (counter-controls) influences any one other than the temporally-physically immediate social environment.*
(2) *There is an inverse relationship between the number of social environments influenced by the problem behavior/intervention environment and the need to systematically involve other relevant social environments.*
(3) *There is a direct relationship between the time and personnel demands of a program and the requirement to systematically involve all relevant social environments.*

For instance, you have been asked to design and conduct a program to teach a profoundly retarded child how to sign. The child lives with his family and attends a private school which is committed to mainstreaming. Although the child is extremely handicapped, he is well cared for at home and his teachers report that he is no problem in class. "He is an angel—so good-natured and doesn't cause any fuss."

Applying rule one leads to a low probability of the targeted client behavior change influencing multiple social environments.

Rule two application then leads to the need to assure programmatic support from the family, teachers, peers, school.

Rule three would make the assurances of the members involved by rule two an absolute requirement. Without such, the high cost-intensity, low visibility behavior change would prove very expensive and have low probability of being maintained or generalized.

Additional data to support a systems approach are found in the recommendations of Loring McAllister in Minnesota (1977) which accent the extreme importance of planning and acting upon the larger social systems. Thompson and Grabowski (1977) caution behavioral program designers:

> Implementing effective programs to improve the lives of retarded citizens requires the combined and continuing efforts of advocacy groups, scientists, educators and therapists. Recourse to contingencies directly influencing elected and appointed officials is essential.

All of this leads to the absolute requirement that any attempt to apply behavior modification technology should conceptualize the problem and treatment as a system. The system definition can be roughly assessed by applying the rules for prediction of generalization/cooperation. Then, the behavior modifier should design and negotiate time and space assurance contracts before initiating any interventions. It is time that the science and profession recognize the law of supply and demand.

In summary, I am proposing that behavior modification must recognize that although we have the capability for improving the human condition, we have finite resources for such efforts. Although demonstrations of the validity of the procedures is very reinforcing, just as it was in the Whoopee Stage, do we simply build unrealistic expectancies? Getting a chance to replicate without accounting for the long-range controlling contingencies is probably detrimental to the specific program and cumulatively damaging to the science and technology. Every short-term change involving the behavior modifier and a client should be examined as a loss of resources including time.

Introduction

Even the triadic model of intervention involving the specialist, the immediate social environment, and the client is suspect of waste.

Behavior modification has contributed dramatically to the reform and design of the teaching environments and schools and homes. This volume illustrates the complexity of engineering for solid living and learning environments for the handicapped. It is from applications such as these with high risk/problem populations that proof and technology for normal populations will be modeled. Again, the problems and benefits of behavioral ecology are described.

L.A.H.

REFERENCES

Ayllon, T., and Azrin, N. *The Token Economy: A Motivational System for Therapy and Rehabilitation.* Appleton-Century-Crofts, 1968, New York.

Ayllon, T., and Michael, J., "The Psychiatric Nurse as a Behavioral Engineer," *Journal of the Experimental Analysis of Behavior,* 1959, 2, 323-334.

Lindsley, O.R. "Operant Conditioning Methods Applied to Research in Chronic Schizophrenia," *Psychiatric Research Reports,* 1956, 5, 118-153.

Patterson, G.R. Comments at First Banff International Conference on Behavior Modification, 1969.

McAllister, L. "Implementing Behavior Modification Programs: A State Level Perspective," in Thompson, T., Grabowski, J., *Behavior Modification of the Mentally Retarded,* Second edition, Oxford University Press, New York, 1977. Page 52.

Reid, J.B., and Hendricks, A. F. C. J. : "Preliminary Analysis of the Effectiveness of Direct Home Intervention for the Treatment of Predelinquent Boys Who Steal," in Hamerlynck, L. A., et al. *Behavior Change,* Research Press, Champaign, Illinois, pp. 209-219.

Thompson, T. and Grabowski, J. *Behavior Modification of the Mentally Retarded.* Second edition, Oxford University Press, New York, 1977.

Contributors

EDWARD R. CHRISTOPHERSEN
University of Kansas

KATHLEEN DALY
University of Alberta

MARTHA DOXSEY-WHITFIELD
University of Alberta

BRUCE GRAUNKE
North Texas State University

CHARLES R. GREENWOOD
University of Oregon

ALEX HILLYARD
University of Alberta

HYMAN HOPS
University of Oregon

GERALD M. KYSELA
University of Alberta

GEORGE LESKE
University of Tennessee

KATHLEEN A. LIBERTY
University of Washington

SANDER MARTIN
North Texas State University

LINDA MCDONALD
University of Alberta

SUSAN MCDONALD
University of Alberta

KERN A. OLSON
University of Wyoming

MAX W. RARDIN
University of Wyoming

EDWIN S. ROGERS
University of Tennessee

R.L. SCHIEFELBUSCH
University of Kansas

STEPHEN I. SULZBACHER
University of Washington

BOBBY W. SYKES
University of Kansas

JULIE TAYLOR
University of Alberta

ROBERT G. WAHLER
University of Tennessee

HILL M. WALKER
University of Oregon

Section I

SCHOOL ENVIRONMENTS

1
Advances in School and Classroom Learning

R. L. SCHIEFELBUSCH

In seeking an historical perspective on school and classroom research in the education of the handicapped, I deduce three trends of special interest. One trend is the *changing status of the handicapped,* a second is *the emergence of applied behavior analysis* (ABA), and a third is the emergence of *possible designs for a linking science of instruction.* I will treat each of these in turn prior to moving into some projections about future classroom research.

CHANGING STATUS OF THE HANDICAPPED

Maynard Reynolds (1976) has written an excellent historical perspective on special education, in which he divides the history into four periods as follows:

Rough Time Periods	*Modal Programs Format*
1. Late Nineteenth Century	Residential School
2. Early Twentieth Century	Prototype Community-based Programs, the special class and special school.
3. About 1945-1970	Explosion of the simple "special class" model.
4. Beginning about 1970	Negotiations for more inclusive

arrangements: The period of "least restrictive alternative," "mainstreaming," or "progressive inclusion" (p. 2).

Nineteenth Century: Residential Schools

Most states established residential schools for blind, deaf and retarded children during the nineteenth century. However, not all exceptional children could be accommodated in the institutions since they were limited in size and number. The few private ones were too expensive for many families. Also, some parents considered the removal of their children from the homes to be onerous. Further, children with multiple handicaps were often not eligible for admission to any school.

Of course, residential schools are still in existence, but more and more they are being used only for selected, profoundly handicapped individuals who are thought to be better served there.

Early Twentieth Century: Community Prototypes

Some distinctive community-based programs for the education of exceptional children began to appear at about the turn of the century—special classes and public day schools. In their earliest forms these programs were dependent upon residential schools for leadership, curriculums, and teacher preparation. At their best these early community programs never more than tolerated these exceptional children, and the movement developed slowly. For the first half of the twentieth century most handicapped children were forced to repeat grades until they became embarrassingly oversized in comparison with their classmates. When "special classes" or "opportunity rooms" were instituted for handicapped children, the labels often took on derogatory connotations.

Until comparatively recently, of course, public schools had never seriously tried to serve all children, and especially not those who were difficult to teach. Indeed, most children attended school only long enough to acquire a basic education during the first decade of this century. Consequently, school systems were not prepared physically, philosophically or financially to operate far-reaching programs for exceptional children.

1945-1970: Explosion of Simple Models

As if to make up through one large effort the neglect of centuries, the remarkable surge of activities in behalf of handicapped children began shortly after World War II. Many states launched programs to serve the handicapped in the public schools on a broad scale, and numerous colleges and universities organized programs to train teachers in special education.

It should be noted that the sheer quantitative leap in programming for exceptional children between 1945 and 1970 cannot be attributed to any great technological or ideological advances. Nevertheless, the boundary lines of the categories of exceptional children began to be seriously examined; strong pressures were developed to extend special education services to children who were obviously very much in need of specialized forms of education, but were yet unserved. Overall, one characteristic of the post-war period may be of the greatest importance for the future: For the first time diverse programs of special education were consolidated in single institutions, and for the first time it became possible to look at and to work across all categories and to consider how they might be related to each other. That consolidation began to be reflected in research and training programs in many colleges and universities.

The 1970s: Negotiating for More Inclusive Arrangements

Quite fundamental changes now seem to be in process during the '70s. They involve a renegotiation of boundaries between regular and special education and between community-based and residential institutions. Perhaps the period can be summarized under the rubric "least restrictive alternatives," or "mainstreaming" in a broad meaning, or "progressive inclusion." In a period of less than two centuries, handicapped children have come from total neglect first into isolated residential schools—for just a few—then into isolated community settings—mostly in the form of special classes—and now into more integrated arrangements for many children. At this moment, we are in the midst of what will undoubtedly be recorded in future histories as a remarkable reversal of a negative cascade by which handicapped children were sent off to isolated classes and centers. The agencies of local school boards all across the country in the early '70s reflect the influx to the community of seriously handicapped children earlier sent off to hospitals and residential centers. And on the desk of virtually every school principal are difficult questions concerning accommodation of exceptional children in regular classrooms.

My purpose in giving this brief account of the history of special education is to point up the obvious fact that we are now facing the challenge of teaching *all* handicapped children in school settings. This challenge may place great strain on our teaching formats, our training strategies, and our credibility. Perhaps, too, the current economic crunch will force us to develop teaching systems that can be accommodated into economic feasibility studies of the schools. We will then be forced not only to develop methodological procedures that are effective, but also to make arrangements that can be afforded. I shall come back to these issues again later, but for now I should like to trace another historical development.

Applied Behavior Analysis

The history of applied behavior analysis (ABA) is probably familiar to all of you. You know, of course, that it began in basic science laboratories, building primarily on the formulations of B. F. Skinner (1953). A number of Skinner's contributions are active concepts in behavioral technologies as applied to education. For instance, one of his many contributions was his contention that frequency of responding is a basic scientific datum. Response frequency has become a key measure of applied behavior analysis technology. Another of Skinner's contributions to today's behavioral technology was to establish functional relationships between independent and dependent variables. He established that many behaviors are influenced by various reinforcement contingencies.

From the beginning of operant psychology, several branches of experimentation developed. Some researchers continued, as did Skinner, to use infra-human or lower organisms as subjects. Some conducted laboratory experiments with human beings. Others began to work with adults and children in institutions for the psychotic and the retarded. Although many researchers contributed to applied behavior analysis, this chapter will concentrate only on those known for the development of ABA as it relates to children.

Some of the early work with children using operant procedures was basic research. These studies were conducted in settings not natural to the child's environment. The responses the children were required to emit were not normally in their repertoires. The purpose of these studies was to learn about certain conceptual systems, rather than about the normal behaviors of children. One classic study by Azrin and Lindsley (1956) examined the acquisition, extinction, and maintenance of a cooperative behavior. Baer and Sherman (1964) studied the generalized imitations of children. Bijou (1966) studied the performance of children during extinction phases following various fixed interval schedules. These laboratory studies demonstrated that many of the principles of operant psychology which applied to animals held true with children.

Encouraged by the successes of these laboratory findings, others began to use operant techniques with children in clinical settings. The classic study of this type was done by Wolf, Risley and Mees (1964), who dealt with several behaviors of a young autistic boy in the clinic and the home. Lovaas, Freitag, Kinder, Rubenstein, Schaeffer, and Simmons (1966) used operant procedures in several studies to change various behaviors of schizophrenic youngsters. Several other studies of this type used operant procedures to change and generally to attenuate or decrease the deviant behaviors of children. They had in common the fact that they dealt with one child in a situation where no other children were present.

Operant conditioners then became more venturesome. They entered the classrooms. Many applied research studies were conducted to demonstrate that the techniques were successful when used with an individual or a small group within classrooms.

The work of Harris, Wolf and Baer (1964) and others at the Developmental Psychology Laboratory at the University of Washington is noteworthy for this extension of operant principles to group situations. They demonstrated in a series of studies how isolated play, crying, climbing and other nursery school behaviors were amenable to change by manipulating the contingent praise of teachers. Several other researchers demonstrated how these principles could be used in classrooms with one or more children to attenuate certain troublesome behaviors. O'Leary and his colleagues (1970) did such work as did Becker and his fellow workers (Becker, Madsen, Arnold & Thomas, 1967). The favorite targets of these researchers were children who talked out or left their seats.

Many of these researchers used the term *behavior modification* to describe their methodology. They had taken the vital features of operant conditioning—identification of an observable response, measurement of that response over a period of time, involvement of reinforcement contingencies to affect the frequency of that response—and adapted them to problems of classrooms.

Along with studies which proved that operant or behavior modification techniques can effectively control troublesome behaviors, some researchers also sought to demonstrate that the techniques could change the attending behaviors of pupils. Several investigators have demonstrated that teacher praise is associated with pupil attention; that is, when teacher praise is arranged contingent on the attention of pupils, the amount of time they pay attention is increased. Hall and his colleagues clearly demonstrated in several settings that teacher attention can alter the attending or studying behavior of youngsters, (Hall, Lund & Jackson, 1968; Cossairt, Hall & Hopkins, 1973).

Sherman and Bushell (1975) provide a comprehensive review of behavior analysis as a classroom technique for correcting social, disruptive and attending behaviors. They summarize their discussion by highlighting three issues:

(1) A number of studies have shown that attention and praise from teachers as consequences for student behaviors can increase desirable social behaviors, such as working or studying quietly, and decrease undesirable social behaviors, such as wandering around the classroom and disrupting others.
(2) Occasionally, the use of attention and praise has not been successful. In these cases, and in many others, tokens, exchangeable for prizes and special activities, have been used to increase desirable social behaviors and decrease undesirable social behaviors.
(3) Although it appears that many social behaviors of students can be affected in a desirable way by the use of attention and praise and with token procedures, there is little clear evidence that the academic performance of students is thereby improved (p. 426).

Several researchers using applied behavior analysis techniques have investigated various academic behaviors of children. One of the earliest attempts to obtain academic measures was the work conducted by Birnbrauer, Wolf, Kidder and Tague (1965) at the Rainier School in Buckley, Washington. In their programmed learning classroom, those investigators reported that measures in reading, writing and arithmetic could be obtained continuously. Arthur Staats and his group conducted several studies which related to the effects of reinforcement contingencies on various reading behaviors (Staats & Butterfield, 1965; Staats, Findley, Minke & Wolf, 1964; Staats, Staats, Schultz & Wolf, 1962).

Technology has evolved from operant conditioning in laboratories concerned with conceptual systems to behavior modification which deals with troublesome or attending behaviors in the classrooms. Perhaps the best known of the researchers in this area has been Lindsley (1964), who developed precision teaching emphasizing the measurement of a wide range of classroom behaviors including academic skills.

By the fall of 1971, a variety of behavioral technologies for education had been described in the research literature. However, there was at that time no classroom anywhere in which a single teacher working with an economically feasible program was using the new technology comprehensively. At that time Hopkins and Conard (1976), using school children borrowed from the public schools of Lawrence, Kansas, succeeded in putting together a program that became known as *Super School*, a designation selected by the children themselves. His program demonstrated that it was possible for a single teacher to use a simplified form of applied behavior analysis and to achieve striking results over the course of one- and two-year periods of time.

At the same time, Hall and his associates (1976) developed a distinctive classroom technology to which they gave the name *Responsive Teaching*. Their program focused primarily on the training of teachers already involved in classroom activities. To this date, they have taught hundreds of teachers to use applied behavior analysis techniques and to design practical strategies for teaching children in classrooms. These procedures also have been adapted for parents so that now there is a combination of responsive *teaching* and responsive *parenting* both applied to the combined activities of the classroom and the home. The term *responsive* is applied to these procedures to acknowledge that the content of the courses, the teaching procedures, the trainee projects, and the final training targets are all responsive to the special problems of the special children involved.

Between the years of 1968 and 1969 the Behavior Analysis Follow Through Program at the University of Kansas was developed, along with 20 other sponsoring organizations or educational models under the general rubric of the national Follow Through Program. The behavior analysis program has evolved into a plan to serve approximately 7,500 children in 15 projects distributed around the nation. Although the program operates in many different locations involving a demographically diverse population, the basic model remains relatively constant across all sites. Some of the common components found in all of the behavior analysis (Follow Through) classrooms are: a motivation system, elements of team teaching, a specified curriculum, individualized instruction, and a parent program. A significant feature of the Follow Through Program, which is similar to the results found in the other programs already mentioned, is above average achievement scores of children across the years of instruction. The Follow Through Program also has the advantage of showing information for two additional years beyond the completion of the program. The data indicate that the program is effective both as an on-line program and as a program affecting continued progress of the children (see Bushell & Ramp, 1974).

I also would like to make special mention of the Direct and Individualized Instruction Procedures maintained in the Experimental Education Unit developed by Haring and Gentry (1976) at the University of Washington. This program has a full technological design that involves attention to management, motivation, direct and ongoing evaluation, and selection of targeted behavioral objectives.

Another program which deserves mention is the Applied Behavior Analysis Curriculum Research conducted by Tom Lovitt, also of the EEU at the University of Washington. This program is devoted directly to the teaching of reading, writing, arithmetic, penmanship, spelling and other curriculum activities. The curriculum as defined by Lovitt (1976) includes the many teaching procedures that assist in the development of academic skills. His system includes five primary ingredients: direct measurement, daily measurement, replicable teaching procedures, individual analysis, and experimental control.

It is interesting to note that these applied behavior analysis programs present a full-blown technology for teaching children. However, in order to qualify as a model, a teaching program must present a systematic, replicable set of teaching functions. Only then is there a science of instruction. In this light it should be interesting to observe and to judge how ABA compares to the game plan that is alluded to by Glaser (1976a, b) (discussed in the next section) in his call for a linking science of instruction.

A Possible Linking Science of Education

Those of us in special education who are not students of the history of American education might be surprised to learn that John Dewey maintained a laboratory school at the University of Chicago from 1896 to 1904. His enterprise was an attempt to work out practical development and demonstration techniques. At the central point of his laboratory school effort, Dewey made a presidential address before the American Psychological Association (1900) in which he expressed concern about developing a linking science between psychological theory and practical work. "Do we not lay a special linking science everywhere else between the theory and practical work? We have engineering between physics and the practical working men in the mills; we have a scientific medicine between the natural sciences and the physician" (p. 110).

Unfortunately, this clear perception of the importance of a science of instruction and the practices in Dewey's laboratory school failed to match up. For all of Dewey's pragmatism it is not clear that he was seeking objective evidence of the strengths and weaknesses of new education proposals that he raised. In analyzing the history of Dewey's school, Tyler (1976) has concluded that it did not carry on disciplined inquiry and did not produce well substantiated results. In fact, it seemed to presage the promotional emphasis that marked later laboratory schools.

Dewey founded his school as an act of faith, and his failure to develop a science of classroom experimentation is likely attributable to the success of his proposals. His ideas had wide appeal, and he was therefore deprived of the stubborn and articulate opposition that may push a man to collect solid evidence. There is also evidence that Dewey did not have the technology to collect and analyze the information to validate and refine his ideas. Issues such as programming, prescription teaching, behavioral objectives, formative measurement, and needs analyses were not part of Dewey's lexicon of issues. Also, if we put Dewey's period in perspective, the educational leaders then barely tolerated exceptional children. General educational practices excluded or derogated such children.

The decades between Dewey's school and the 1970s show a gradual increase in the accommodation to handicapped children in the schools, but it seems doubtful that there was the same improvement in the scientific capability for teaching them.

In fact, we might make the same frivolous analysis of the history of educational classroom research that Wohlwill (1963) makes of research on Piaget's system. He was reminded of the hunt for the woozle in Winnie-the-Pooh. In the episode Winnie-the-Pooh and Piglet set about somewhat apprehensively stalking this animal they had heard about, without any idea of what it looks and acts like. Following with increasing alarm a set of footprints (which of course are their own) they wind up merrily going around in circles until Christopher Robin arrives on the scene to rescue them from their predicament.

Like Winnie-the-Pooh and Piglet, researchers on teaching have often gone around in circles. However, unlike their fictional brethren, the educational researchers have had bandwagons to leap on so that they could traverse the circular course more rapidly. Also they have had slogans and buzz words to chant while they plotted interesting, innovative detours along the circular way.

Although we may not yet have a scientific map of the educational terrain of Poohland, we are now at least moving with scientific design toward some known destinations. Nevertheless, we might carry the analogy a bit further and observe that various modern, real-life Winnie-the-Poohs do not yet agree upon what the woozle looks like and where he may be found. Sometimes it appears that they do not want to know exactly what they are searching for. In other words, they seem to want the woozle to remain intriguingly mysterious.

In any event, Dewey and others of that time clearly perceived the importance of research on the process of teaching. Dewey's concern for a linking science has recently been noted and reemphasized by Glaser (1976a, 1976b). He waxes enthusiastic about a psychology of instruction as a practical system for finding a way to educational goals. In discussing his ideas I think we had best abandon the woozle hunt, at least for a time, because I do not think Glaser is a woozle hunter.

Glaser suggests that there are four major components of a Prescriptive Science of Instruction. He also thinks that the same components may be central to a linking science. His listed components are:

(1) description and analysis of competent performance,
(2) description and diagnosis of the initial state,
(3) conditions that foster learning and the acquisition of competence,

(4) effects of instructional implementation in the short and long run.

Description and Analysis of Competent Performance

The problem of task analysis is a central one. Analytical description of what is to be learned facilitates instruction by attempting to define clearly what it is that an expert in a subject matter domain has learned. For example, what is it that distinguishes a skilled from an unskilled reader? When this analysis identifies classes of behavior whose properties as learned tasks are known or can be systematically studied, then inferences concerning optimal instructional processes can be formulated and tested.

Description and Diagnosis of the Initial State

There is an immediate and a long-term approach to this component. The immediate approach is to take seriously the fact that effective instruction requires careful assessment of the initial state of the learner. Glaser advocates that the evaluators have in mind at least an informal hierarchy of increasing competence in regard to the instructional area to be pursued. These hierarchies take the form of structured maps into which a teacher can place a child and thereby direct attention to prerequisite skills that might need to be learned or advanced skills that the child might explore. The hierarchical map is only a guide upon which both the teacher and child can impose their own judgments. Procedures for assessing the current competence and talents of the learner in a way that provides a basis for instruction are generally not available in current educational methods at a level of detail necessary for the effective guidance of individual learners.

The long-term approach is used for purposes of deciding upon instructional alternatives. Initial information does not tell how an individual should be instructed to improve his performance or how instruction might be designed to make the attainment of successful performance more probable. The significant research in this regard is to describe the initial state of learners in terms of processes involved in achieving competent performance. This will allow us to influence learning in two ways—to design instructional alternatives that adapt to these processes and to attempt to improve an individual's competence in these processes so that he or she is more likely to profit from the instructional procedures available.

Conditions that Foster Learning and the Acquisition of Competence

This third component refers to procedures by which one learns and the nature of the environment in which learning occurs. There are at least two directions in this regard that need to be taken.

> The first is to recognize that we do know a little about learning. For example, we know some things about the effects of reinforcement—the contingencies consequent to performance; about the conditions under which discrimination, generalization, and concept performance take place; about the conditions of practice, interference with memory, the nature of attention, the effects of punishment, and how observational learning and modeling can influence new learning, we know these things in terms of descriptive science, but little investigation has been made from the point of view required for the utilization of this information for designing the conditions of instruction. Exceptions to this [are] the work on behavior modification and the work on optimization models described by Atkinson (1976). However, neither of these enterprises have considered complex cognitive performance in any systematic way (p. 309).

The second direction, he suggests, would lead to research on learning cast into the mold of a design science which attempts to maximize the outcome of learning for different individuals. He calls for a new form of experimentation where the tactic is not to develop models of learning and performance, but to test existing models by using them for maximizing the effects of learning under various conditions. He also urges that we need a theory of the acquisition of competence. Such a theory would be concerned with how an individual acquires increasingly complex performances by assembling the present components of his repertoire and manipulating the surrounding conditions and events.

Effects of Instructional Implementation in the Short and in the Long Run

The fourth component of instructional design is concerned with the effects of instructional implementation in the short and long run—

effects that occur immediately in the context of instruction and supply relatively immediate feedback, and effects that persist in terms of long-term transfer, generalized patterns of behavior and ability for further learning. For effective instructional design, tests will have to be criterion referenced in addition to being norm referenced. They will have to assess performance attainments and capabilities that can be matched to available educational options in more detailed ways than can be carried out with currently used testing and assessment procedures.

It is apparent that Glaser's operational suggestions are essentially compatible with Applied Behavior Analysis. His emphasis upon task analysis, criterion referenced testing, instructional goals, instructional alternatives, learning models and generalized patterns is remarkably similar to the technological keynotes of ABA. However, his frequent illusion to "complex cognitive performance" may seem to vary greatly from ABA. Nevertheless, in the area of language intervention, commendable efforts have been undertaken to create a rapprochement between cognitive and behavioral science (see Staats, 1974; Mahoney, 1974) and to work out effective designs combining linguistic and other descriptive cognitive systems with behavioral tactics of instruction.

Some remarkable efforts at designing a full language curriculum with accompanying instruction for teaching them have been published (see Bricker, Ruder & Vincent, 1976; Miller & Yoder, 1974; and Guess, Sailor & Baer, 1978). Nevertheless, these researchers report difficulty in finding the cognitive codes and short-cuts required for teaching such complex curricula. This observation emphasizes that even in a relatively advanced instructional area educational specialists cannot yet draw upon an evolved linking science in designing their most difficult and complex educational programs. This realization must be acknowledged as we consider a further range of possibilities for teaching handicapped children.

Glaser (1976a, b) further poses a challenge for the educational researcher in delineating four levels of competence which our instructions must be designed to accomplish. He observes:

(1) Variable, awkward and crude performance changes to performance that is consistent, relative, fast and precise. Unitary acts change into larger response integrations and overall strategies.
(2) Contexts of performance changes from simple stimulus patterns with a great deal of clarity to complex patterns in which

relevant information must be abstracted from a context of events that are not all relevant.
(3) Performance becomes increasingly symbolic and covert. The learner responds increasingly to internal representations of an event to internalized standards and to internalized strategies for thinking and problem solving.
(4) The behavior of the competent individual becomes increasingly self-sustaining in terms of his skillful employment of the rules when they are applicable and of his subtle bending of the rules in appropriate situations. Increasing reliance is placed on one's own ability to generate the events by which one learns and the criteria by which one's performance is judged and valued (Glaser, 1976b, p. 306).

When some combination of cognitive and behavioral sciences has led to effective method based curricula for teaching all dimensions of this hierarchy, we may claim to have a linking science of instruction. Since we may not yet have such a complete design, let us look at the designs we have. An interesting dimensional analysis is provided by comparing current ABA based program components with the components recommended by Glaser (Table 1).

In making the comparison we should remember that Glaser intentionally had set up a design to accommodate a broad set of instructional operations. The first component relates to the general issue of competence; the second relates to initial assessment; the third, to instructional conditions; and the fourth, to implementation and generalization. The last three of these general points are also consensus points across the ABA programs. Lovitt, Bushell, Haring and Schiefelbusch each have a design for two and three and both Bijou and Schiefelbusch explicitly list the generalization component. There seems to be a fourth component (usually the first or second in the sequence) listed by the ABA designers—the setting of goals or objectives. Lovitt, Bushell, Haring and Bijou each list such a component.

The component that most clearly cuts across each design is the "conditions that foster learning." The ABA terms that acknowledge this issue are (1) "replicable teaching procedures" (Lovitt), "arrange incentives" and "consequence management" (Bushell), "systematic management programs," "individual instructional materials," "instructional procedures," and "motivational factors" (Haring), "program maintenance" (Schiefelbusch), and "arranging the teaching situation" (Bijou). This is a component of strong agreement across programs.

An obvious area where the ABA designers part company with

Advances in School and Classroom Learning

TABLE 1

Glaser (Linking Science)	Lovitt (Curricular Research)	Bushell (Follow Through)	Haring (Direct Teaching)	Schiefelbusch (Language Intervention)	Bijou (Applied Behavior Analysis)
1. Analysis of Competent Performance	1. Direct measurement	1. Define instructional objectives	1. Assessing performance	1. Initial evaluation	1. Specifying goals in observable terms
2. Assessment of the Initial State	2. Daily measurement	2. Determine initial status	2. Setting goals, objectives and aims	2. Program development	2. Beginning teaching at child's level of competence
3. Conditions that foster learning	3. Replicable teaching procedures	3. Arrange incentives	3. Systematic management programs	3. Program maintenance	3. Arranging the teaching situation
4. Effects of Instructional Implementation short and long term	4. Individual analysis	4. Consequence managment	4. Individual instructional materials	4. Continuing evaluation	4. Monitoring learning progress
	5. Experimental control	5. Adapt curriculum	5. Instructional procedures	5. Program extensions	5. Practices that generalize, elaborate and maintain the acquired behaviors
		6. Continuous progress assessment	6. Motivational factors		
			7. Evaluate pupil progress		

R. Atkinson, Elements of an Instructional Situation [Computer Program], 1) Set of instructional actions, 2) Instructional objectives, 3) Measurement scale of costs and achievements, 4) A model of the learning process.

Glaser is in the area of *formative evaluation* (Bloom, Hastings & Madaus, 1971). This component includes the design for "continuing evaluation" (Schiefelbusch), "monitoring learning progress" (Bijou), "evaluate pupil progress" (Haring), "continuous progress assessment" (Bushell), and "individual analysis" (Lovitt).

Analysis of competence is a component objectified by Glaser that is not specified by the ABA designers. The importance given to this issue by Glaser probably reflects his emphasis upon cognitive psychology. Conversely, the emphasis placed upon continuous evaluation by the ABA designers reflects an emphasis upon explicit units of behavior. The surprising fact is not that these different emphases exist but rather that there is such a strong agreement across several parameters of the instructional design. One can conclude that for the most part the continuing quest for a science of instruction will come primarily from improvements in the designs and the technologies that are already staked out. However, there may be one area for ABA researchers in which a somewhat altered design may be indicated. This emphasis is suggested by Glaser's focus upon competence.

It is difficult to see how ABA scientists and their colleagues in experimental analysis of behavior (EAB) can diversify their designs in order to explicitly scale the hierarchy of competence described by Glaser. In the same sense it is apparent that Premack (1974, 1977) is attempting to better delineate a hierarchy of cognitive functions which might subsequently enable us to design for new instructional outcomes. Perhaps we may agree that if we do not know the dispositions (Premack's term) of the student, we do not know (or will not know) the optimal design for teaching the operations that can be taught. The critical instructional variable may be suggested by "a scale of costs and achievements" (Atkinson, 1976). The enormous range of tasks that must be taught if a learner is to achieve a high level of competence suggests that codified short-cuts must be found if the instructional goal is to be achieved. The strategy followed by Atkinson (1976) involves a measurement scale of costs and achievements. He searches for the maximum achievements with minimum costs. This procedure may eventually yield an elegance of instructional design in which instructions achieve optimal effects. The importance of this point emerges from many high cost programs where progress is apparent, but where time and expense factors simply rule out long range continuations. There is obviously a critical issue of "costs" in instructional programming. There usually are not enough time and resources to teach a competence program linearly.

Advances in School and Classroom Learning

SPECULATIONS AND PROJECTIONS

In considering the progress of research in school and classroom learning, one should not stop with instructional designs. There are also significant gains in educational technology. A few examples serve to illustrate this line of progress.

(1) Sensory aids to enhance communication for the blind, deaf and cerebral palsied,
(2) Systematization of instruction (i.e., packaging of mediated instruction, software and programs for teaching machines) and systems-oriented instructional prototypes,
(3) Computer assisted remedial instruction, and
(4) Time-shared, interactive computer controlled information systems.

Although technology based programs are still in experimental stages of development, the prospects do indeed seem promising—especially for information storage, retrieval and dissemination; for the development of conceptual, reproducible models for teaching; and for systems designing so that complex educational problems may be solved. Since most educational technology is in an early stage of development we may expect significant progress in the years ahead.

Recently Schiefelbusch and Hoyt (1978) prepared a futuristic statement under the title "Three Years Past 1984."* Their purpose was to project certain lines of educational research and the improvements in educational technology ahead ten years. Following is a quotation from a section labeled "A Summary (Optimistic)."

> A number of successful pilot programs featuring individualized instruction, designed learning environments, and cooperative educational arrangements have proved to be successful. Also, we are developing a technology for disseminating and replicating programs in areas remote from the parent experimental programs. Then too, we are improving our technology for teaching and training so that we have better educational programs and training sequences for teaching our teachers to be competent with all levels of childhood instruction. Finally, we are building our educational programs upon a more enlightened policy of community involvement so that support programs for the handicapped aid the schools in developing open systems of edu-

---

*A paper presented at a conference on "Issues Relating to the Future of Special Education" in Minneapolis, Minnesota, April 26-28, 1977. Copies available from the Leadership Training Institute, 253 Burton Hall, University of Minnesota, Minneapolis, Minnesota 55455.

cation that extend beyond the physical confines of the school and utilize the parents, citizen groups, and community agencies and settings. We seem at last to have a strong foundation for long-term growth in appropriate educational programs for handicapped citizens.

As a further extension of our optimistic view, we may assume that the needed changes can largely be effected by further investments in educational research and development. After some early confusion, we are now pooling and providing computerized access to successful program results on a nationwide basis. This access to the investments in better programming should enable any school district to have accessibility to program innovations for virtually any kind of handicapped child or for any arrangement in learning.

It is apparent that the authors predict a major role for educational technology. It is equally true that they predict a successful collaboration between schools and the community, between teachers and parents, and between science and humanism. Perhaps most important of all they predict that handicapped people will be given a place of dignity in educational environments—a "normal" status without labels, without rejection and with appropriately designed, individualized learning programs.

Although the authors did not single out Applied Behavior Analysis as the enabling science in these developments it should be said that in many school and community environments today ABA is providing the techniques and the common data that enable teachers, parents, retired volunteers and scientists to work together in planning improved environments for learning and improved dissemination of information to many instructional agents who need them. It should be clear from this brief projection that ABA will contribute greatly to educational outcomes during the next ten years.

REFERENCES

ATKINSON, R. C.: Adaptive instructional systems: Some attempts to optimize the learning process. In D. Klahr (Ed.), *Cognition and instruction,* Hillsdale, N.J.: Lawrence Erlbaum Associates, 1976.

AZRIN, N. H., and LINDSLEY, O. R.: The reinforcement of cooperation between children. *Journal of Abnormal and Social Psychology,* 1956, *52,* 100-102.

BAER, D. M., and SHERMAN, J. A.: Reinforcement control of generalized imitation in young children. *Journal of Experimental Child Psychology,* 1964, *1,* 37-49.

BECKER, W. C., MADSEN, C. H., ARNOLD, C., and THOMAS, D. R.: The contingent use of teacher attention and praise in reducing classroom behavior problems. *Journal of Special Education,* 1967, *1,* 287-307.

BIJOU, S. W.: Application of experimental analysis of behavior principles in teaching academic tool subjects to retarded children. In N. Haring and R. Whelan (Eds.), *The learning environment: relationship to behavior modification and implications for special education.* Lawrence, Ks.: University of Kansas Press, 1966.

BIRNBRAUER, J. S. WOLF, M. M., KIDDER, J. D., and TAGUE, C. A.: Classroom behavior of retarded pupils with token reinforcement. *Journal of Experimental Child Psychology,* 1965, *2,* 219-235.

BLOOM, B. S., HASTINGS, J. T., and MADAUS, G. F.: *Handbook on formative and summative evaluation of student learning.* New York: McGraw-Hill, 1971.

BRICKER, D., RUDER, K., and VINCENT, L.: An intervention strategy for language deficient children. In N. G. Haring & R. L. Schiefelbusch (Eds.), *Teaching special children.* N. Y.: McGraw-Hill, 1976.

BUSHELL, D., JR., and RAMP., E. A.: *The behavior analysis classroom.* University of Kansas Support and Development Center for Project Follow Through, Department of Human Development, Lawrence, Kansas, 1974.

COSSAIRT, A., HALL, R. V., and HOPKINS, B. L.: The effects of experimenter's instructions, feedback and praise on teacher praise and attending behavior. *Journal of Applied Behavior Analysis,* 1973, *6,* 89-100.

DEWEY, J.: Psychology and social practice. *The Psychological Review,* 1900, *7,* 105-124.

GLASER, R.: Components of a psychology of instruction: Toward a science of design. *Review of Educational Research,* 1976, *46,* 1-24. (a)

GLASER, R.: Cognitive psychology and instructional design. In D. Klahr (Ed.), *Cognition and instruction.* Hillsdale, N. J.: Lawrence Erlbaum Associates, 1976. (b)

GUESS, D., SAILOR, W., and BAER, D.: Children with limited language. In R. L. Schiefelbusch (Ed.), *Strategies of language intervention.* Baltimore: University Park Press, 1978.

HALL, R. V., COPELAND, R., and CLARK, M.: Management for teachers and parents: Responsive teaching. In N. G. Haring and R. L. Schiefelbusch (Eds.), *Teaching special children.* N.Y.: McGraw-Hill, 1976.

HALL, R. V., LUND, D., and JACKSON, D.: Effects of teacher attention on study behavior. *Journal of Applied Behavior Analysis,* 1968. *1,* 1-12.

HARING, N. G., and GENTRY, N. D.: Direct and individualized instructional procedures. In N. G. Haring and R. L. Schiefelbusch (Eds.), *Teaching special children.* N.Y.: McGraw-Hill, 1976.

HARRIS, F. R., WOLF, M. M., and BAER, D. M.: Effects of adult social behavior on child behavior. *Young Children,* 1964, *20,* 8-17.

HOPKINS, B. L., and CONARD, R. J.: Putting it all together: Super School. In N. G. Haring and R. L. Schiefelbusch (Eds.), *Teaching special children.* N.Y.: McGraw-Hill, 1976.

LINDSLEY, O. R.: Direct measurement and prosthesis of retarded children. *Journal of Education,* 1964, *147,* 62-81.

LOVAAS, O. I., FREITAG, G., KINDER, M. I., RUBENSTEIN, B. D., SCHAEFFER, B., and SIMMONS, J. Q.: The establishment of social reinforcers in two schizophrenic children on the basis of food. *Journal of Experimental Child Psychology,* 1966, *4,* 109-125.

LOVITT, T. C.: Applied behavior analysis techniques and curriculum research: Implications for instruction. In N. G. Haring and R. L. Schiefelbusch (Eds.), *Teaching special children,* N.Y.: McGraw-Hill, 1976.

MAHONEY, M. J.: *Cognition and behavior modification.* Cambridge, Mass.: Ballinger Publishing Co., 1974.

MILLER, J., and YODER, D.: An ontogenetic language teaching strategy for the mentally retarded. In R. L. Schiefelbusch and L. L. Lloyd (Eds.), *Language perspectives: Acquisition, retardation, and intervention.* Baltimore: University Park Press, 1974.

O'Leary, K. D., Kaufman, K. F., Kass, R. E., and Drabman, R. S.: The effects of loud and soft reprimands on the behavior of disruptive students. *Exceptional Children,* 1970, *37,* 145-155.
Premack, D., and Premack, A.: Teaching visual language to apes and language-deficient persons. In R. L. Schiefelbusch & L. L. Lloyd (Eds.), *Language perspectives: Acquisition, retardation, and intervention.* Baltimore: University Park Press, 1974.
Premack, D.: *Intelligence in ape and man.* Hillsdale, N. J.: Lawrence Erlbaum Associates, 1977.
Reynolds, M. C.: *Trends in education: Changing roles of special education personnel.* The University Council for Educational Administration, 29 West Woodruff Avenue, Columbus, Ohio 43210, 1976.
Schiefelbusch, R. L., and Hoyt, R. K., Jr.: *Three years past 1984.* In M. C. Reynolds (Ed.), *Futures of Education for exceptional children: Emerging structures.* Minneapolis: University of Minnesota Press, 1978.
Sherman, J. A., and Bushell, D., Jr.: Behavior modification as an educational technique. In F. Horowitz (Ed.), *Review of child development research.* Chicago: The University of Chicago Press, 1975.
Skinner, B. F.: *Science and human behavior.* N.Y.: Macmillan, 1953.
Staats, A. W.: Behaviorism and cognitive theory in the study of language: A neopsycholinguistics. In R. L. Schiefelbusch & L. L. Lloyd (Eds.), *Language perspectives: Acquisition, retardation, and intervention.* Baltimore: University Park Press, 1974.
Staats, A. W., Findley, J. R., Minke, K. A., and Wolf, M. M.: Reinforcement variables in the control of unit reading responses. *Journal of Experimental Analysis of Behavior,* 1964, *7,* 139-149.
Staats, A. W. and Butterfield, W. H.: Treatment of nonreading in a culturally deprived juvenile delinquent: An application of reinforcement principles. *Child Development,* 1965, *4,* 925-942.
Staats, A. W., Staats, C. K., Schultz, R. E., and Wolf, M. M.: The conditioning of textural responses using "extrinsic" reinforcers. *Journal of Experimental Analysis of Behavior,* 1962, *5,* 33-40.
Tyler, R. W.: *Prospects for research and development in education.* Berkeley: McCutchan Publishing Corporation, 1976.
Wohlwill, J. F.: Piaget's system as a source of empirical research. *Merrill Palmer Quarterly,* 1963, *9,* 252-253.
Wolf, M. M., Risley, T. R., and Mees, H.: Application of operant conditioning procedures to the behavior problems of an autistic child. *Behavior Research and Therapy,* 1964, *1,* 305-312.

2
Reducing Hyperactive Behavior in the Classroom by Photographic Mediated Self-Modeling

Kern A. Olson
and
Max W. Rardin

The purpose of this study was to investigate a theoretical extension of social learning as applied to the classroom in reducing hyperactive behavior. Specifically, the findings of Bandura (1969, Bandura et al., 1963), Mowrer (1960), Dilley and Paivio (1968), Johnson (1969), Stotland (1969), and Patterson et al. (1965) provided the foundation for the present research in photographic mediated self-modeling. The principles of social learning theory have become increasingly important as the theoretical basis for procedures used to modify children's behavior. Bandura and Walters (1963), in their study of a social learning theory, have stated that learning phenomena can occur on a vicarious basis through observation. An important aspect in Bandura's basis of vicarious learning is the role of retention and delayed reproduction. The reproduction of discrete matching responses requires representational mediation of modeling stimuli. Bandura, Ross and Ross (1963) substantiated the above assumption by using photographic techniques as mediators of effective modeling and disclosed the influential role of symbolic representation in observational learning. In

---

The authors wish to thank Mr. Charles Griffen, Principal of Stanton School and Mrs. Lela Eicher who exhibited patience and understanding while the study was carried out in her classroom. Also, special thanks are due to Mrs. Gail Richardson and Miss Nancy Stewart, who ably assisted in compiling the observational data.

addition, Bandura et al. (1963) observed that verbalizing the model responses as they were performed by the model resulted in significantly more matching responses than did a viewing only condition. This technique of verbalization was observed to be effective by the first author in a previous study (Olson & Kelley, 1969), where the subject was conditioned to verbal cues.

The studies of Paivio and others have further substantiated the effectiveness of pictorial mediation as proposed by Bandura, Ross and Ross (1963). Dilley and Paivio (1968) found that picture-word pairs were associated with more correct anticipations than picture-picture pairs, word-picture and word-word pairs. They favored an interpretation of the results which argues that the preferred mode of storage for children is imagery; pictures are more likely to evoke imagery than words. They concluded that pictures are easier to remember than words but only when the verbal labels for the pictures are stored with them. Rohwer and Levin (1968) found similar results: In their study pictures were superior to words in promoting learning and pictures evoked imagery at all the age levels they assessed. Also, Rohwer and Levin (1968) proposed that the ability to profit from stored images is contingent upon the subject's ability to store an appropriate verbal representation of the object along with its image. In his presentation of the principles of behavior modification, Bandura (1969) concluded that a large amount of social learning is fostered through exposure to behavioral modeling cues in actual or pictorial forms.

The reinforcing property of viewing color slides exhibiting attending and non-attending behaviors is derived from Mowrer's sensory feedback theory of imitation. Mowrer (1960) suggested that if certain responses have been repeatedly positively reinforced, proprioceptive stimuli associated with these responses acquire secondary reinforcing properties and thus the individual is predisposed to perform the behavior for positive feedback. Similarly, if responses have been negatively reinforced, response correlated stimuli acquire the capacity to arouse anxiety which in turn inhibits the occurrence of negatively valenced behavior. Congruent with the foregoing assumptions of Mowrer, this study confronted the subjects pictorially with attending behaviors and positively reinforced the behavior immediately, which enhanced the secondary reinforcing properties. Conversely, the subjects were confronted with pictorial non-attending behaviors and negatively reinforced by the absence of the reward and by verbal cueing that this form of behavior is not appropriate. Mowrer (1960) would then conclude that this situation would arouse enough anxiety to inhibit the occurrence of future similar behaviors.

In more recent investigations, Johnson (1969) and Johnson and Martin (1970) hypothesized that training in the self-administration of a contingent reinforcement may have lasting effects on an individual's tendency to self-regulate his own behavior. This research suggests that when positive self-evaluation has been functional in obtaining reinforcement, it can subsequently serve to enhance the accuracy of the self-evaluated response. Johnson and Martin (1970) concluded that simple self-observation of approved or disapproved behaviors might serve as a powerful clinical tool in behavior change programs.

The hypothesis of self-modeling is an effective extension of the investigations conducted by Stotland (1969), who found that perceived similarity enhances vicarious arousal. Stotland (1969) suggested that the strongest empathetic responsiveness would be expected to occur under conditions of high observer-model similarity and analogous consequences.

In the present study, it was predicted that pictorial mediated self-modeling would significantly reduce specific hyperactive behaviors in the classroom.

Method

Subjects

Experimental subject I was a 12-year-old male with a long history of unmanageability, restlessness, distractibility, inattention and hyperactivity. During the screening observation this subject moved continuously about the classroom distracting the class and constantly demanding attention from his teacher and other members of the class.

Experimental subject II was an 11-year-old male who also had a long history of unmanageability, restlessness, distractibility, inattention and hyperactivity. During the screening observation, Subject II stayed mostly at his desk, but exhibited a large amount of hyperactive behaviors and constantly demanded attention from his teacher and other members of the class.

Subject III, the control subject, was an 11-year-old male who also was placed in the same classroom. Unlike the experimental subjects, this boy did not exhibit excessive non-attending behaviors during the observational periods. Instead, this subject was placed in the special education classroom because of an apparent learning disability. The control subject was selected by the assistant teacher who compiled the baseline observations.

Procedure

The experimental setting was a special classroom for children who were management problems and had exhibited various learning disabilities. After an initial screening observation and consultation with the teacher, the subjects were selected on the basis of excessive activity and non-attending behavior. The assistant teacher for the class was instructed in the use of the observation form adopted from Patterson (1956). The seven categories of hyperactive behavior for which observational data were collected were:

(1) Movements in chair: e.g., shuffling of chair, sliding back and forth in chair, twisting of body in chair, or leaning clear out of chair so that buttocks no longer rested on it.
(2) Movements directed toward the body: e.g., wringing of hands, rubbing eyes, swinging arms, leaning forward in the chair, scratching, or stretching.
(3) Distraction: e.g., looking over toward a noise, toward someone who has just entered the room (unless teacher also looks up), out of the window, or off into space.
(4) Gross movements of legs and feet: e.g., pumping of legs, wiggling of feet, or crossing of legs, or other shift of their position.
(5) Fiddling: arm and hand movements directed toward objects; activities of the hand(s) that interfered with schoolwork or assigned activities, e.g., stroking the desk, fingering the box of color crayons.
(6) Communicative or quasi-communicative activity interfering with schoolwork: e.g., talking to self, pointing, laughing, attempting to attract someone's attention, talking to someone without permission.
(7) Walking or standing that was not encouraged or subsequently approved by the teacher.

Training on the observational form was terminated after a 100% reliability was achieved. A two-week baseline was completed in the fall. This baseline observation consisted of 60 10-second observations on each subject that were completed over a period of two weeks with four observation periods per week. Observations were collected throughout the school day, avoiding concentration of observation on any particular activity.

After this phase was completed, a repertoire of 35mm colored slides was compiled depicting the experimental subjects exhibiting a wide variety of behaviors. This was accomplished by using a 35mm single lens reflex camera and a 105mm lens. The versatility of this camera and lens allowed the experimenter to remain reasonably unobtrusive in the classroom. A total of 125 slides were selected as best depicting the seven categories of non-attending behavior. Also, two observations were completed on the experimental subjects to determine if the presence of the experimenter taking photos affected the rate of their non-attending behavior.

After the slides were compiled, each experimental subject was excused from the class and accompanied to a small room, large enough to accommodate a projector and screen, by the experimenter. The subject was seated before the screen with a red and green light discrimination box which he operated by depressing one of two switches. The experimenter was seated behind the subject and operated the projector by remote control. Upon presentation of a slide the subject was instructed to depress the button (green for attending, red for non-attending) and verbally label the behavior he was exhibiting in the slide. If the subject completed the task correctly and if the behavior being presented was attending (green) the experimenter then rewarded the subject verbally and concretely with M & M candy. Upon presentation of a non-attending behavior (red) the subject was simply asked to describe the behavior he was exhibiting and no reinforcement was given. Each experimental session lasted approximately 10 minutes, while 20 slides were presented. As each experimental session progressed, slides requiring finer discriminations in behavior were presented and rerun until the subject correctly labeled each behavior he was exhibiting. The total experimental phase lasted five sessions, comprising approximately a total of 50 minutes.

Upon completion of the experimental phase, a follow-up baseline was compiled using the same procedure as in the initial baseline. A second observer was also trained to the 100% reliability level. The second observer was introduced as a control so that the subjects would be less aware that the observations were related to the experimental procedure.

FIGURE 1

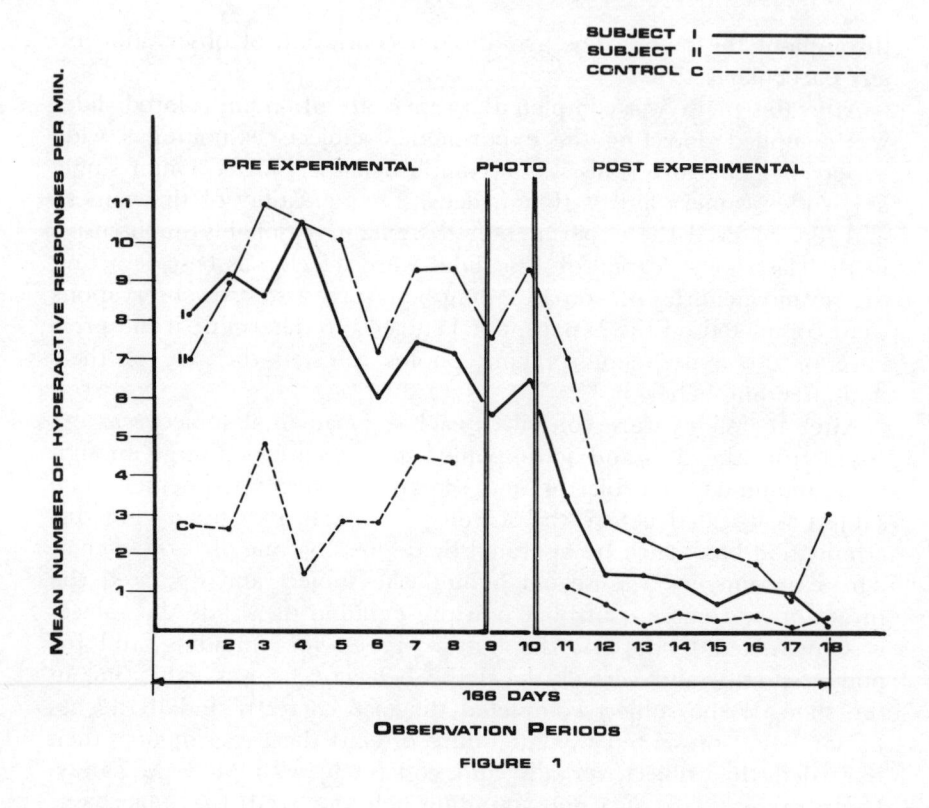

Results

Figure 1 presents the average number of hyperactive responses emitted per minute by the three subjects. The level of activity for experimental subjects I and II is relatively parallel throughout the entire observation period. All three subjects showed a decrease in variability after treatment. Also, a small reduction in the hyperactive response rate can be observed in Figure 1 during the first photographic session. The effectiveness of the experimental technique is represented by the observed reduction in the hyperactive response rate.

Figure 2 presents the pre- and post-experimental response rate of the seven individual hyperactive categories. Certain categories were more influenced by the experimental technique (i.e., the range for experimental subject I was a high of 100% reduction to a low of 77% reduction; the range for experimental subject II was a high of 93% reduction to no reduction for category three).

FIGURE 2

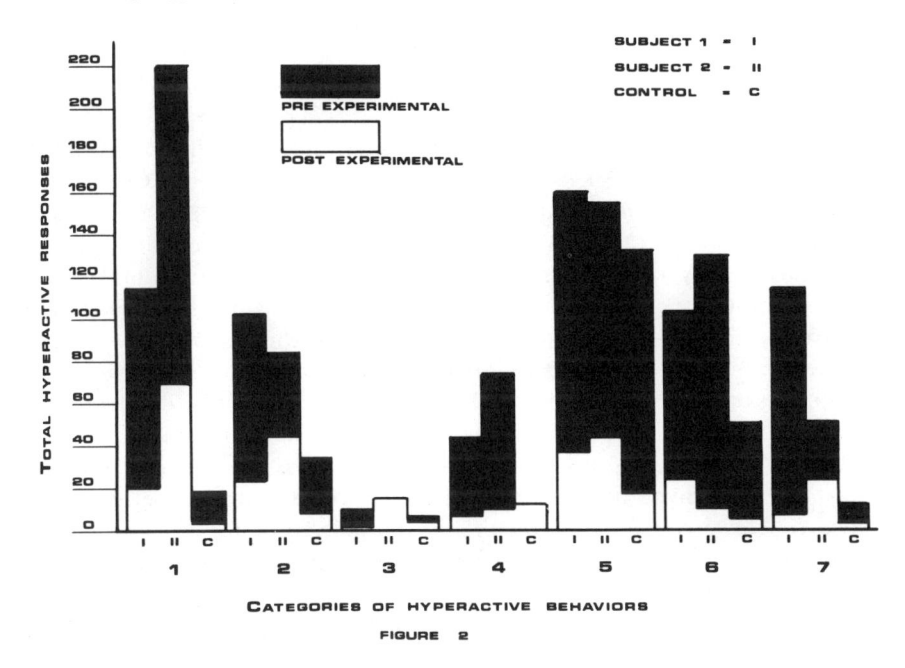

Discussion

The results indicate that pictorial mediated self-modeling is an effective technique in reducing hyperactive responses in the classroom. Also, the comments from the teacher suggest that the two experimental subjects are receiving more positive social reinforcement from their classmates. This observation was also made by Patterson (1965), who concluded that the conditioning procedure initiated a chain of events which was of greater social significance than the decrease in nonattending behaviors.

The importance of peer reaction was evident when, as each experimental subject returned to the classroom, he was asked immediately by other children if the class was going to receive their reward. These findings strongly support the assumption that positive peer response can act as an effective consequence in shaping socially adaptive behaviors.

This study incorporated many of the suggestions offered by Patterson (1956) with the exception that the control subject was not selected from a different classroom. As can be observed in Figure 1, the control subject's response rate decreased in the post-experimental baseline. This finding is similar to Patterson's observation and in future applications will be examined by using more than one control in various situations.

The different baseline behavior makes it difficult to assume adequate homogenity of experimental and control subjects. Comparison between experimental and control subjects and the decrease in the control's response rate remain open to several interpretations. One explanation may be that the two extremely active experimental subjects functioned as catalysts for the class and decreasing their response rate removed powerful disrupting stimuli from the classroom. Or the teacher may have improved her management procedures for the rest of the class as less attention was devoted to the two active children. It seems likely that a combination of these two events occurred.

The different categories of hyperactive behavior are not totally mutually exclusive, and some categories represent competing behaviors. These category characteristics may account for the differential decrease in the hyperactive behaviors. While further research is needed to clearly specify the relative contributions of peer responses, self-modeling and verbal discrimination to the observed changes in behavior, the general procedure appears promising for research and application.

REFERENCES

BANDURA, A., ROSS, D., and ROSS, S. A.: Imitation of film-mediated aggressive models. *Journal of Abnormal and Social Psychology*, 1963, 66, 3-11.
BANDURA, A., and WALTERS, R. H.: *Social learning and personality development.* New York: Holt, Rinehart & Winston, 1963.
BANDURA, A.: *Principles of behavior modification.* New York: Holt, Rinehart & Winston, 1969.
DILLEY, M. G., and PAIVIO, A.: Pictures and words as stimulus and response items in paired-associate learning of young children. *Journal of Experimental Child Psychology*, 1968, 6, 231-240.
JOHNSON, S. M.: Self-reinforcement vs. external reinforcement in behavior modification with children. Unpublished manuscript, University of Oregon, Eugene, 1969.
JOHNSON, S. M., and MARTIN, S.: Self-evaluation as conditioned reinforcement, Unpublished manuscript, University of Oregon, Eugene, 1970.
MOWRER, O. H.: *Learning theory and the symbolic processes.* New York: Wiley, 1960.
OLSON, K. A., and KELLEY, W. R.: Reduction of compulsive masturbation by electrical-aversive conditioning to verbal cues: a case report. *Canadian Psychiatric Association Journal*, 1969, 14, 303-305.
PATTERSON, G. R.: A tentative approach to the classification of children's behavior problems Unpublished doctoral dissertation. University of Minnesota, 1956.

PATTERSON, G. R., JONES, R., WHITTIER, J., and WRIGHT, M. A.: A behavior modification technique for the hyperactive child. *Behavior Research and Therapy,* 1965, 2, 217-226.
ROHWER, W. D., and LEVIN, J. R.: Action, meaning and stimulus selection in paired-associate learning. *Journal of Verbal Learning and Verbal Behavior,* 1968, 7, 137-141.
STOTLAND, E.: Exploratory investigations of empathy. In L. Berkowitz (Ed.), *Advances in Experimental Social Psychology.* Vol. 4, New York: Academic Press, 1969.

3
Interaction Effects of Medication and Classroom Contingencies on Verbal Tics and School Performance

STEPHEN I. SULZBACHER
and
KATHLEEN A. LIBERTY

The purpose of this investigation was to demonstrate the feasibility of using standard behavior analysis methodology to study the effects of medication on clinically relevant behaviors. Such analysis allows for the study of interaction effects with various behavioral contingencies to determine the best environmental as well as dosage arrangements, in order to maximize academic performance while reducing unwanted behaviors. The strategy presented in this study assumes that medications prescribed to change behavior are functionally equivalent with a variety of behavior modification procedures in that: (1) they affect some behaviors but not others; (2) they affect people differently; and (3) the effects on a variety of behaviors can be precisely measured. In other words, effects of medication on classroom behavior can be measured and manipulated in the same way as the effects of changes in curriculum, reinforcement contingencies, and other environmental variables. The basic strategy of operant behavioral pharmacology is discussed in greater detail by Thompson and Schuster (1968), Thompson and Boren (1977), and Sulzbacher (1975), while numerous

---

This research was supported in part by Maternal and Child Health Service (HEW) Project 913 and Bureau of Education for the Handicapped Grant No. OEG-0-70-3916(607). The authors would also like to acknowledge the contributions of Ingrid von Christierson, Lynn McCaffrey, Caroline Rinke, Darcy Walker, Georgia Adams, and Robert Hauck, M.D.

similar applications of the strategy have also appeared in the literature (McConahey, 1972; Sulzbacher, 1974; Shafto & Sulzbacher, 1977).

The clinical behaviors studied in the present investigation were those associated with Gilles de la Tourette syndrome, which is characterized by the emission of various types of tics. Originally described in 1885, this relatively rare syndrome has been studied extensively because of its dramatic symptoms and its theoretical implications for studying the function of the brain stem (DiGiancomo, Fahn, Glass, & Westlake, 1971). The syndrome is characterized by the onset of motor tics at about the age of seven. The first tics to appear are usually small, such as eye blinks and facial tics. As the subject ages, tics in the limbs and torso appear. The tics usually increase in rate and force during the subject's lifetime. At about puberty, existing verbal tics may develop into obscene verbal words (coprolalia). From this age on, most subjects exhibit two or more types of tics. Typically, persons with Gilles de la Tourette syndrome score within the normal range on intelligence tests. Most studies of this syndrome have presented primarily anecdotal information and very few actual data appear in the literature, although there seems to be general agreement on the efficacy of haloperidol in reducing the severity of symptoms (Shapiro, Shapiro, & Wayne, 1973). One study which did provide empirical data (Messiha, Knopp, Vanecko, O'Brien, & Corson, 1971) demonstrated that frequency of ticking decreased as the dosage of haloperidol increased. There seems to be fairly widespread agreement, both in the literature (Challas & Brauer, 163; Healy, 1970) and in general practice, that the tics and involuntary swearing associated with Giles de la Tourette syndrome can be markedly reduced or eliminated through treatment with haloperidol in most cases. Typically, other comparacle medications have not been effective with this syndrome, nor has haloperidol been quite as effective in the treatment of other kinds of tics (Tapia, 1969; Ayd, 1967). Largely because of the known sites of action of haloperidol, it has been theorized that Gilles de la Tourette syndrome is a disorder of the dopaminergic pathways of the limbic mid-brain area and the corpus striatum (Snyder, Taylor, Coyle, & Meyerhoff, 1970).

There have been numerous reports of behavioral interventions to modify ticking (Yates, 1958; Rafi, 1962; Feldman & Werry, 1966; Lahey, McNees, & McNees, 1973), as well as behavioral studies of Gilles de la Tourette syndrome (Clark, 1966), which suggest improvement can also be obtained by these methods. However, no reported study has compared drugs with behavioral interventions designed to control the ticking. Since haloperidol has been shown to affect other behaviors (Jarvik, 1970), changes in other behaviors, especially academic performance, were also important in this study. For example, if ticking were controlled by high dosages, but academic growth suppressed, the "trade-off" might have other unexpected, harmful side effects on the subject's interactions in her classroom and home. The aim of the study was to find an intervention which reduced or controlled the subject's tics while allowing for academic progress.

The present study compares the relative effects of haloperidol with various behavioral interventions to control ticking and presents an analysis of the interaction effects of these treatments and effects on academic performance. Also reported is an unsuccessful attempt to explore the supposed neurological defect underlying Gilles de la Tourette syndrome by measuring the effects of another medication with dopaminergic action (l-amphetamine).

Method

Subject and Setting

The subject was a 14-year-old girl who had been diagnosed as having Gilles de la Tourette syndrome two years prior to this study although she had previously had a variety of treatments, including a behavior modification program, for her tics and coprolalia (involuntary swearing) for some time before this uncommon disease was finally diagnosed. She was enrolled in a secondary level class at the Experimental Education Unit (EEU), University of Washington, which is a demonstration school using behavior modification techniques. She had previously been excluded from a public junior high school because of the severity of her coprolalia.

Experimental Procedures

Data were collected on the following behaviors during the study:

(1) *Verbal tics.* These included two distinguishable, audible utterances: short syllables (e.g., "ut," "it," "uck") and obscene words (most often, "shit"). Both types of verbal tics are "symptoms" of Gilles de la Tourette syndrome (Sweet, Solomon, Wayne, Shapiro, & Shapiro, 1973).

(2) *Yawns.* Haloperidol commonly produces a "feeling of tiredness" (Jarvik, 1970). Data on this behavior were collected to serve as an indicator of the effect of the drug on the subject's body systems.

The data on verbal tics and yawns were collected by an observer seated in an observation room. The subject's desk was placed underneath a microphone, which broadcast into the observation room. The subject was seated within four feet of the observation window, and observers were not visible to the subject. One observer collected data from 9:30 to 10:00 a.m., another observer collected data from 1:30 to 2:00 p.m. Data were collected only on days in which school was in session.

(3) *Academic responses.* Data were collected on the following academic responses to study the effect of the drug on other behaviors. In addition to the work described below, the subject was assigned to other academic work throughout the day. As part of the regular classroom routine, the subject received points which could be exchanged for free time for each academic program. These contingencies, as well as teacher instructions and teacher contacts to the student, remained constant throughout the study. No changes other than those described below were made in the subject's programs. Regular programs for the two observation periods are presented below.

9:30-10:00 a.m.

a) First, a one-minute oral reading sample was taken from *Reading for Concepts, Level C* (Liddle, 1970). The publisher's assigned grade level was 3.2; a Fry readability level was calculated at 3.8. A different story was read daily.
b) Next, the subject completed reading the story silently, and then wrote the letter answers to multiple choice comprehension questions which accompanied each story.
c) The subject practiced for 10 minutes on a worksheet of subtraction problems of the type

$$\begin{array}{ccc} 873 & 880 & 94 \\ \underline{-629} & \underline{-135} & \underline{-59} \end{array}$$

Correction and feedback were then provided, and the subject next worked on a "probe" of the same type of problems for five minutes. During the probe, no instructions were provided. Numbers of digits written, correct and incorrect, were recorded.

1:30-2:00 p.m.

a) The afternoon session began, as did the morning, with an oral

reading sample of one minute from *SRA Power Builders IIb* (Porter, 1969); publisher's assigned grade level 3.5, Fry readability calculated at 3.3. A different story was read each day.
b) After reading silently the remainder of the story, the subject wrote letter answers to multiple choice comprehension questions which accompanied each story.

The subject's 9:30 to 10:00 a.m. schedule was consistent throughout the study. However, afternoon sessions were not held on Fridays; also, other "special events" (e.g., movies) interfered with the afternoon programs.

During the second phase of the study ("Easy Work"), the difficulty level of the work in the morning was decreased. A comparison between verbal tics and yawns during the easy work and previous "regular work" phases was planned to show the effects of reducing possible sources of anxiety, or of manipulating one stimulus event in the subject's environment. Accordingly, the morning schedule was revised as follows, beginning with the 133rd calendar day.

a) The oral reading sample and comprehension questions were taken from *Reading for Concepts, Level A* (Liddle, 1970), with a publisher's grade level of 1.9 and a Fry readability level calculated at 1.5.
b) Subtraction problems were changed from those which required borrowing to the class of $\begin{array}{r}11\\-8\end{array}$ $\begin{array}{r}18\\-9\end{array}$ $\begin{array}{r}13\\-5\end{array}$. Both the practice sheet and the probe were of the same problem type, as in phase 1.

The afternoon work and all other procedures remained identical to those in the first phase.

Reliability

Periodic checks on observer reliability were made by having both observers collect data during one time period. Percentage agreement between observers was calculated by dividing the smaller behavior count by the larger and multiplying by 100. Checks were calculated for each five-minute period within the 30-minute observation time, as well as for the entire period. Reliability figures were shared with each observer at the end of the observation period. The following percentage agreements were obtained:

  Day 95: 94% (five-minute range, 85-100%)
  Day 99: 96% (five-minute range, 66-100%)
  Day 110: 100%
  Day 118: 92% (five-minute range, 71-100%)
  Day 119: 100%
  Day 127: 92% (five-minute range, 71-100%)
  Day 140: 92% (five-minute range, 75-100%)

Data on academic behaviors were collected by the subject's teachers as part of the normal routine. No changes were made in the subject's classroom activities during this experiment.

Medication Conditions

A dosage of 15 mg. haloperidol had been prescribed two years previously for the subject, who was to take 5 mg. three times daily, at 8:30 a.m., 2:30 p.m., and 9:00 p.m. During the collection of baseline data, however, it was learned that the subject was not following the prescribed dosage. The drug was taken infrequently, and the estimated dosage ranged from about 12 mg. to 18 mg. daily. Since the subject also reported that she had taken the drug "when she felt she needed it," the actual range probably was more extreme. At this point it was realized that the first "manipulation" must be a stabilization of the prescribed dosage. Therefore, beginning with the 118th calendar day, the subject received daily an envelope containing the correct dosage from the classroom teacher. The drug was in 5 mg. tablets. The subject was given three at the end of each school day (2:00 p.m.) for the subsequent 2:30 p.m., 9:00 p.m., and 8:00 a.m. dosages. The procedure had been carefully explained to the subject's mother, who was to monitor the administration of the drug, as well as to the subject. No attempt was made to monitor the time at which each tablet was taken, but the subject was required to return the empty evelope of the previous day before receiving the next. Packets for the weekend were given to the subject on Friday afternoon. When dosage or medication was changed, the subject still got packets with three identical appearing capsules, although the active ingredients of the capsules were varied according to the treatment schedule.

During the course of this study, the subject was exposed to three medications: haloperidol (Haldol), benztropine mesylate (Cogentin), and levo-amphetamine. Haloperidol, the medication of choice for Gilles de la Tourette syndrome, is a potent butyrophenone tranquilizer which can cause Parkinson-like extrapyramidal reactions, as it had in this subject. To alleviate these side effects, the subject had been taking 1 mg. per day of benztropine mesylate, which was continued during the time of this study. No extrapyramidal reaction was ever noted, although data were kept to detect any of the behaviors such a reaction might cause.

Amphetamine has been suggested as a treatment for this disorder since it affects dopaminergic brain mechanisms in a manner similar to haloperidol. Levo-amphetamine reportedly has fewer side effects than either its d-isomer or haloperidol and was tried in 10 mg. dosage. Trials of other dosages and of dextro-amphetamine were also planned but not administered after consultation with the subject as her symptoms worsened.

Results

Data were collected over a period of about one year during which various intervention phases were applied. Of primary clinical importance was the frequency of verbal tics, which can be seen in Figure 1 to have been occurring at a fairly stable frequency of once a minute. This baseline rate occurred during an academic quarter when the subject was managing her own medication, which was supposed to be 5 mg. haloperidol three times a day.

As a measure of the possible sedation effects of her medication, frequency of yawning was also recorded during the same period of time and can be seen in Figure 2 to have been declining throughout the baseline quarter from an initial rate of .7 per minute to .43 per minute.

The initial phase involved the standard token economy system previously described with her regular classwork and with the subject presumably taking 15 mg. of haloperidol each day as she had been instructed by her own physician. The first intervention was designed to stabilize dosage by having medication dispensed from school each day and resulted in a decline from a median of 1.26 tics per minute to 0.94. There is a declining trend during this phase of ÷1.33. Concurrently, yawns showed an increasing trend of ×1.26, increasing during this phase from a beginning rate of .2 per minute to an end rate of .75 per minute.

Verbal Tics and School Performance

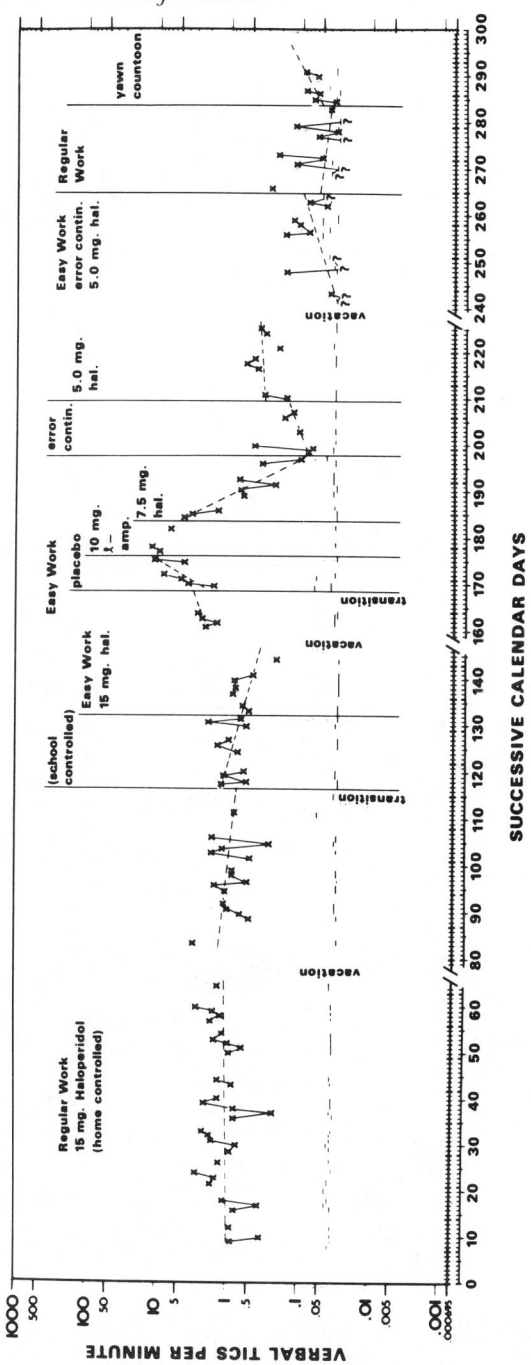

Figure 1. Daily rates of verbal tics.

Figure 2. Daily rates of yawns.

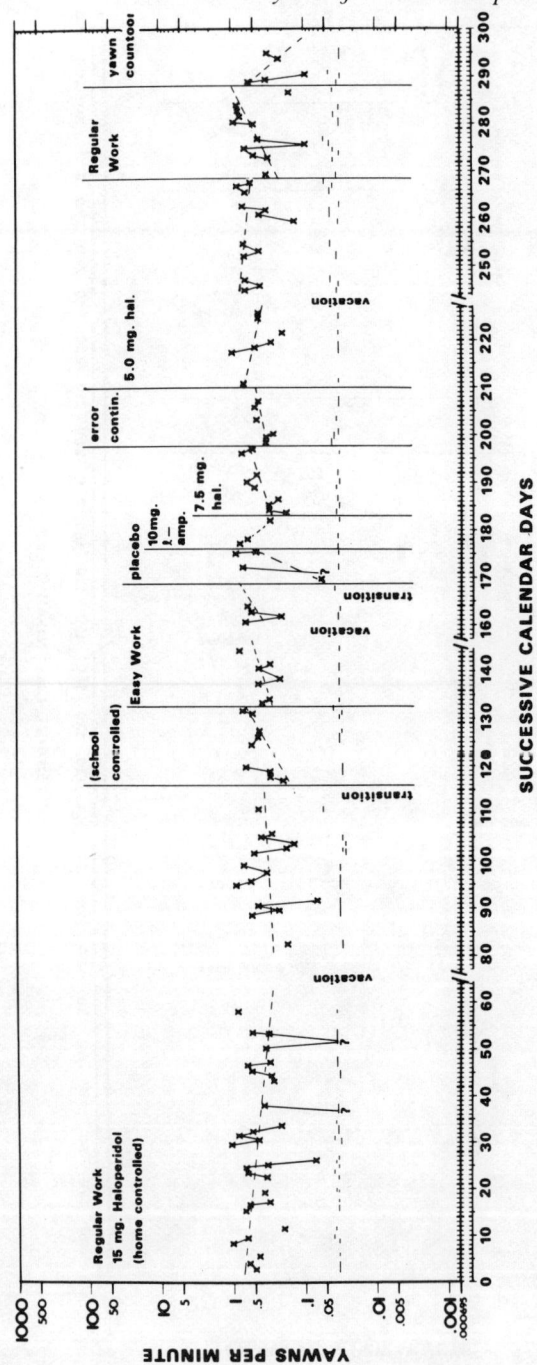

To test the hypothesis that the subject's anxiety might have an effect on her verbal tics, the next phase change was a reduction in the level of difficulty of her schoolwork. As can be seen in Figure 1, this did result in a further reduction of ticking rate to a median of 0.68 per minute. Yawning continued to occur at the same rate, but did show an increasing trend. Following a semester break (during which the subject was again responsible for managing her own medication), the median frequency of verbal tics increased to 2.25 per minute.

At this point in the study, the subject received placebos for a five-day period (to allow for "washout" of medication from her system) and then began a series of seven-day trials on various dosages of the three medications to be investigated (see White, 1972, for the rationale behind seven-day phases and for a detailed discussion of the statistical procedures used in this paper; see also Hersen & Barlow, 1976). Because of increased symptom discomfort and truancy, this part of the experiment was terminated midway through the second phase when the subject requested a return to her former medication. However, by agreement with her mother, we reduced the dosage in half, with the understanding that it would be increased if symptoms did not improve. During the no-medication phase, verbal tics increased at a dramatic rate (trend ×1.5) to a frequency of 12 per minute and remained at about that rate during the three days of treatment with l-amphetamine.

When haloperidol (7.5 mg. per day) was reintroduced, a steep downward trend (÷7.4) reduced the frequency of verbal tics to 0.1 per minute (one every 10 minutes). The next phase change was the addition of an error contingency in which the subject would not receive her normal reinforcement points unless there were no errors in her arithmetic work. Verbal tics showed a slight increasing trend during this phase, but leveled off at a median rate of .33 per minute in the next phase which was a reduction of dosage to 5 mg. haloperidol. Following a semester break, the subject returned to school and received 5 mg. haloperidol each day for the rest of the study. As can be seen in Figure 1, the rate of verbal tics was maintained for the rest of the study at median rates of less than one in 10 minutes with many days on which 0 frequencies were recorded. Returning to more difficult work and the addition of the yawn countoon can also be seen not to have materially increased the rate of verbal tics.

Yawns dropped somewhat during the beginning of no-medication phase, but returned to the previous rate during the l-amphetamine phase. In general, yawns continued to occur at a frequency of about .5 per minute for the balance of the study until a procedure was added to specifically decrease that rate. During the yawn countoon procedure, the subject self-recorded the frequency of yawning. This resulted in a declining trend ($\div 3.2$) to the rate at the end of the study of 0.2 per minute (or one yawn for every five minutes).

Academic Performance

Table I is a summary of the subject's performance during arithmetic probes throughout the study. Figure 3 presents the daily rates of arithmetic performance during the second quarter of the study.

Only the summaries for each phase presented in Table I are available for the balance of the study, since the daily records normally kept in the classroom were inadvertently destroyed when a new teacher

TABLE 1

Subtraction with Borrowing
(digits per minute on 5 minute timings)

	\multicolumn{4}{c	}{Correct Rates}		\multicolumn{4}{c}{Error Rates}
	Start	Trend	End	Median	# Days	Start	Trend	End	Median
Standard contingency-15 mg (home)	25	÷1.25	11	12	9	0.4	x1.0	0.4	0.4
T. sets timer-15 mg (home)	12	x1.25	25	21	18	1.0	÷1.35	0.4	0.6
	\multicolumn{4}{c	}{VACATION}					
T. sets timer-15 mg (home)	12	x1.18	21	16	14	0.8	÷1.14	0.55	0.2
T. sets timer-15 mg (school)	20	x1.0	20	20	11	0.45	÷1.54	"0"	0.2
Easy work-15 mg (school)	15	÷1.39	7.8	9.4	7	0.5	÷1.68	"0"	0.2
Easy work-placebo	24	÷1.8	15	22	7	"0"	x4.0	0.7	0.7
Easy work-1-amphet. then 7.5 mg H.	25	x1.1	30	27	13	1.3	x1.2	1.8	1.5
Error contingency-5.0 mg haloperidol	33	x1.0	33	33	12	1.5	÷1.45	0.3	0.6
	\multicolumn{4}{c	}{VACATION}					
Division facts-I - 5.0 mg halo.	11	x1.66	60	35	10	8.0	÷4.5	"0"	5.5
Division facts-II - 5.0 mg halo.	24	x1.05	32	33	10	8.5	÷1.83	"0"	2.0
Mixed division (Aim x 1.25) - 5.0 mg halo.	5	x2.7	24	14	5	10.0	÷8.0	0.32	3.0
Mixed division (Aim x 1.5) - 5.0 mg halo.	20	x1.6	44	35	8	3.0	÷4.7	0.2	0.7

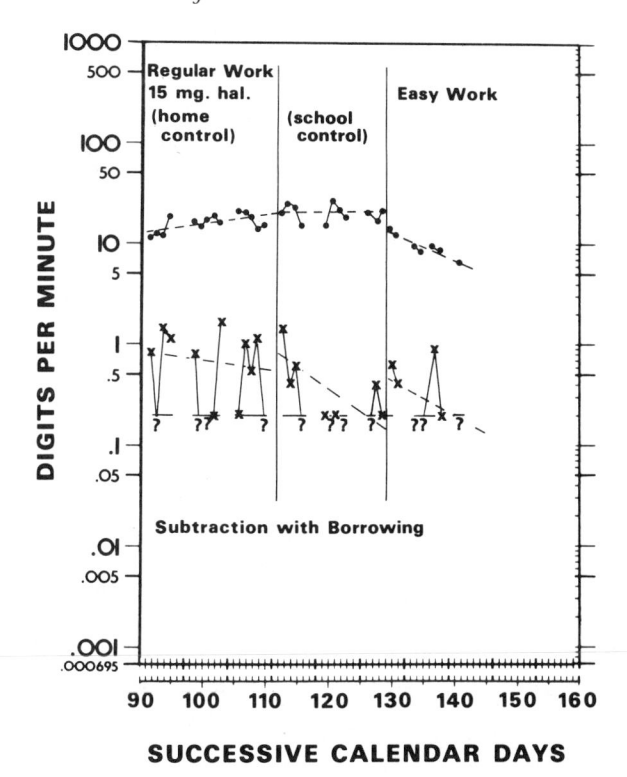

Figure 3. Daily correct and error rates of arithmetic (subtraction digits per minute).

took over the classroom after the present study was completed. The significant features of the data in Table I are a ×1.25 trend when the teacher set the timer starting the arithmetic probe rather than letting the subject do this. Under these conditions, with school control of medication, the subject performed at a very stable rate of 20 digits correct per minute with declining errors, as can be seen in the second phase on Figure 3. When the level of difficulty of the arithmetic work was reduced, there was a paradoxical deterioration in performance to a median of 9.4 digits per minute (trend ÷ 1.4). This decline is apparent in phase 3 of Figure 3. During the next two phases of no-medication and l-amphetamine, the rate of correct digits showed a slight upward trend and so did error rate. With the reintroduction of haloperidol, correct rates remained stable at 33 per minute while errors declined (trend ÷ 1.45) to a median of .6 per minute, this latter decline occurring with the introduction of the error contingency.

During the last quarter of the study, the level of difficulty of arithmetic work was increased by moving from subtraction problems to division facts. It can be seen in Table I that correct rate increased to the highest rates recorded during this study, and errors, while initially quite high, decreased to 0. In the last two phases, the level of difficulty was again increased by providing mixed division problems and adding the contingency so that in order to get any points for her work, the subject had to maintain an upward trend of ×1.25, which she did. In the final phase, the trend requirement was raised to ×1.5 and at the end of the study her rate of correct math digits was 44 per minute with a 0.2 error rate.

Discussion

The goals of this research were (1) to optimize treatment conditions for our patient and (2) to explore more precisely the nature of the disorder and the interaction of drug effects in an attempt to clarify the brain mechanisms which might be affected. In terms of clinical outcome, the subject's verbal tic rate was reduced ten-fold over the course of the study from about one per minute to a rate at the end of the study of less than one every 10 minutes. Academically, the student gained five grade levels in reading and was reading orally at 100 words per minute (proficiency) at the eighth grade level at the end of the study. In arithmetic, the student moved from beginning subtraction through multiplication and division to decimals and fractions, and story problems involving all of these operations. Although less easy to specify on a grade level basis, the subject made similar gains in language arts, social studies, science, and spelling, and her general social behavior and self-confidence also changed dramatically. She was returned to public school at the conclusion of the study at which time she was being maintained on 5 mg. haloperidol, which was one-third the dosage she had been receiving at the beginning of the study.

As with most research, things in this study did not go quite as planned. Nevertheless, there are several features of the data which have potential clinical as well as theoretical implications. Simple stabilization of daily dosage when we switched this subject from home to school controlled medication reduced variability of academic responses and also resulted in a decrease of undesired motor activity—the verbal tics. Particularly dramatic in this phase change was the reduction of errors on subtraction problems to 0. Certainly with a drug as potent as haloperidol, patients should be admonished to resist the temptation to "skip a dose" when they are feeling good or when symptoms seem to be reduced.

We feel it is of utmost importance in any study of the effects of medication that data be kept on an acceleration target behavior. It is philosophically and ethically much easier to argue that a given procedure or medication is being employed *for the patient's good* when it can be demonstrated that the frequency of some positive behavior is increasing. In this case, we monitored the patient's rate of doing arithmetic problems. The effects of varying dosages of medication on arithmetic rates were minimal compared to the rate changes caused by adjusting the level of difficulty of the academic work. Our initial hypothesis had been that making her work easier would reduce anxiety, which Yates (1958, 1970) and Clark (1966) had suggested as a possible cause of the ticking associated with Gilles de la Tourette syndrome. Tic rate did, in fact, decline with the introduction of easy work, supporting the theories of Yates and Clark. Our overall interpretation of the data in this study is that the symptomatology is the result of the interaction of several variables, two of which we were able to successfully manipulate: neurological and classroom environments.

Of more general interest, however, is the surprising decrease in performance from a median correct rate of 20.2 digits per minute to 10.1, when the subject was given an easier class of arithmetic problems. Conversely, later in the study when the level of difficulty in arithmetic was increased, the subject's correct rate went from 11 per minute to 60 per minute, while her error rate went from 8 per minute to 0. Since yawns also showed an increasing trend with the introduction of "easy" work, the interpretation of these data made by Ogden Lindsley is probably correct: He suggested that the subject's arithmetic rate declined because she was bored and increased when she was presented with "more interesting" or challenging work.

We agree with Thompson and Boren (1977) that more careful attention must be paid to the interaction of drug treatment and prevailing environmental contingencies if we are to optimize individual treatment. We also believe that much of the controversy and conflicting research reports on the efficacy of medications like amphetamine and methylphenidate with children may be the result of overlooked environmental interactions and imprecise measurement (Sulzbacher,

1973). Furthermore, the methodology used in this study would appear to have considerable potential for directly demonstrating brain-behavior relationships.

REFERENCES

AYD, F.J.: A clinical appraisal of haloperidol. *Medical Science*, 1967, *18*, 55-58.
CHALLAS, G., and BRAUER, W.: Tourette's disease: Relief of symptoms with R-1962. *American Journal of Psychiatry*, 1963, *120*, 283-284.
CLARK, D.F.: Behavior therapy of Gilles de la Tourette's syndrome. *British Journal of Psychiatry*, 1966, *112*, 771-778.
DiGIANCOMO, J.N., FAHN, S., GLASS, J.B., and WESTLAKE, R.J.: A case with Gilles de la Tourette syndrome: Recurrent refractoriness to haloperidol, and unsuccessful treatment with L-dopa. *Journal of Nervous and Mental Disease*, 1971, *152*, #2, 115-117.
FELDMAN, R.B., and WERRY, J.S.: An unsuccessful attempt to treat a tiquer by massed practice. *Behavior Research and Therapy*, 1966, *4*, 111-117.
HEALY, C.E.: Gilles de la Tourette syndrome *(Maladie des Tics)*: Successful treatment with haloperidol. *American Journal of Diseases of Children*, 1970, *120*, 62-63.
HERSEN, M., and BARLOW, D.H.: *Single case experimental designs: Strategies for studying behavior change*. New York: Pergamon Press, 1976.
JARVIK, M.E.: Drugs used in the treatment of psychiatric disorders. In L.S. Goodman and A. Gilman (Eds.), *The pharmacological basis of therapeutics* (4th ed.). London: Macmillan Co., 1970, 170.
LAHEY, B., McNEES, P.M., and McNEES, M.C.: Control of an obscene verbal tic through timeout in an elementary school classroom. *Journal of Applied Behavior Analysis*, 1973, *6*, 101-105.
LIDDLE, W. (Ed.): *Reading for concepts*. San Francisco: Webster Division, McGraw-Hill, 1970.
McCONAHEY, O.L.: A token system for retarded women: Behavior modification, drug therapy, and their combination. In T. Thompson and J. Grabowski, *Behavior modification of the mentally retarded*. New York: Oxford University Press, 1972, 139-177.
MESSIHA, F.S., KNOPP, W., VANECKO, S., O'BRIEN, V., and CORSON, T.A.: Haloperidol therapy in Tourette's syndrome: Neurophysiological, biochemical and behavioral correlates. *Life Sciences*, 1971, *10* (part I), 449-457.
PORTER, D. (Ed.): *SRA power builders IIb*. Chicago: Science Research Associates, 1969.
RAFI, A.B.: Learning theory and the treatment of tics. *Journal of Psychosomatic Research*, 1962, *6*, 71-76.
SHAFTO, F., and SULZBACHER, S.I.: Comparing treatment tactics with a hyperactive preschool child: Stimulant medication and programmed teacher intervention. *Journal of Applied Behavior Analysis*, 1977, *10*, 13-20.
SHAPIRO, A.K., SHAPIRO, E., and WAYNE, H.: Treatment of Tourette's syndrome with haloperidol: Review of 34 cases. *Archives of General Psychiatry*, 1973, *28*, 92-97.
SNYDER, S.H., TAYLOR, K.M., COYLE, J.T., and MEYERHOFF, J.L.: The role of brain dopamine in behavioral regulation and the actions of psychotropic drugs. *American Journal of Psychiatry*, 1970, *127*, 199-205.
SULZBACHER, S.I.: Behavior analysis of drug effects in the classroom. In G. Semb (Ed.), *Behavior analysis and education—1972*. Lawrence: University of Kansas, 1973, 37-52.

SULZBACHER, S.I.: Chemotherapy with learning disabled children. In H.F. Eichenwald and A. Talbot (Eds.), *The learning disabled child.* Bellevue, Wash.: Edmark Pub., 1974, 44-65.
SULZBACHER, S.I.: The learning disabled or hyperactive child: Diagnosis and treatment. *Journal of the American Medical Association,* 1975, *234,* 938-941.
SWEET, R.D., SOLOMON, G.E., WAYNE, H., SHAPIRO, E., and SHAPIRO, A.K.: Neurological features of Gilles de la Tourette syndrome. *Journal of Neurology, Neurosurgery and Psychiatry,* 1973, *36,* 1-9.
TAPIA, F.: Haldol in the treatment of children with tics and stutterers—an incidental finding. *Psychiatric Quarterly,* 1969, *43,* 647-649.
THOMPSON, T., and BOREN, J.J.: Operant behavioral pharmacology. In W.K. Honig and J.E.R. Staddon (Eds.), *Handbook of operant behavior.* Englewood Cliffs, N.J.: Prentice-Hall, 1977, 540-569.
THOMPSON, T., and SCHUSTER, C.R.: *Behavioral pharmacology.* Englewood Cliffs, N.J.: Prentice-Hall, 1968.
WHITE, O.R.: A manual for the calculation and use of the median slope—A technique of progress-estimation and prediction in the single case. *Working Paper 16.* Eugene, Oregon: Regional Resource Center for Handicapped Children, University of Oregon, 1972.
YATES, A.J.: The application of learning theory to the treatment of tics. *Journal of Abnormal and Social Psychology,* 1958, *15,* 175-182.
YATES, A.J.: Tics. In C.G. Costello (Ed.), *Symptoms of psychopathology: A handbook.* New York: Wiley and Sons, 1970, 320.

4

PEERS: A Program for Remediating Social Withdrawal in School

Hyman Hops, Hill M. Walker, and Charles R. Greenwood

Social Withdrawal: The Nature of the Problem

Social withdrawal in preschool and school-age children, having had a historical association with autism and childhood schizophrenia (Lovaas, 1977), has been increasingly recognized as a serious behavior disorder in its own right (Amidon, 1961; Amidon & Hoffman, 1965; Bonney, 1971; Brison, 1966; Guerney & Flumen, 1970; Strain, Cooke, & Apolloni, 1976). The ability to initiate and maintain positive social relationships with the peer group is considered by many to be an essential developmental achievement. Moreover, Mueller and Brenner

---

The work upon which this publication is based was performed pursuant to Contract No. 300-76-0035, with the Bureau of Education for the Handicapped, U.S. Office of Education, Department of Health, Education, and Welfare.

The authors would like to acknowledge the roles of CORBEH personnel who have been significantly involved in the development of the PEERS Program. In the experimental classroom, Nancy Todd played a key role in supervising the implementation and monitoring of the treatment procedures. Through Annabelle Street's insistence the Joint Task procedure became an effective reality. Stan Paine provided the major effort in the preparation of the Social Skills Tutoring component. Diane Fleischman and Jackie Guild served as Program Consultants in the regular classroom, each making substantive contributions to many aspect of the program, not the least of which was demonstrating that the program was indeed effective in the real world. Bobbi Garrett and Tuck Stevens between them trained nearly 100 observers to collect data reliably. Dick Schram provided the expertise in graphics and Lloyd Maxfield in writing computer programs to efficiently handle such complex data sets. Terri Marks provided the reliable typing and preparation of the manuscript.

(1977) have demonstrated that peer interaction produces unique aspects of social skills, independent of parental influence, at the toddler level! Complex social development appears to be a direct function of increased participation in peer interaction itself.

Interdependency and reciprocity characterize the nature of social interaction in child-child as well as in child-adult relationships (Mueller, 1972; Patterson & Reid, 1970; Shores & Strain, 1977; Greenwood, Walker, Todd, & Hops, 1976). A series of studies with preschoolers demonstrated that the amount of positive reinforcement received from peers was positively and significantly related to the amount given (Charlesworth & Hartup, 1967) and that social interaction was positively related to social acceptance as measured by sociometrics (Hartup, Glazer, & Charlesworth, 1967). Further, popular children were more rewarding of their peers than less popular ones (Hartup et al., 1967). In an earlier study, popular children were also found to be more cooperative (Lippitt, 1941), behavior positively influenced by social interaction (Cook & Stingle, 1974).

With the diminishing adult influence in our society as children grow older, the peer group gains increasing prominence. By the sixth grade, children spend twice as much time with their peers as with their parents (Bronfenbrenner, 1970). Several investigators have argued that peer relationships may be more critical than adult-child associations (Bronfenbrenner, 1970; Lewis & Rosenblum, 1975).

Taken together, these studies suggest that the lack of responsiveness by and to the peer group may have profound implications for a child's later social and academic adjustment. Clearly, children learn a great deal, both directly and vicariously, from interacting with their peers. The absence of peer interaction in withdrawn children may, to some extent, explain their low academic performance (Bushwell, 1953; Strain, Cooke and Apolloni, 1976). A study of sixth graders indicated that girls who were concerned with peers' thoughts about them tended to achieve less and withdraw more (Lahaderne & Jackson, 1970). Popularity with peers, as measured by sociometrics, has shown to be not only related to academic achievement but also predictive of early school dropout (Hartup, 1970). Thus, low rates of positive social interaction with peers among socially withdrawn or isolate children can be considered to be a handicapping condition.

Perhaps even more disturbing have been demonstrations of the stability of social behavior patterns. Keasy (1976) noted a relationship between cognitive and social development stable from kindergarten through grade two. Waldrop and Halverson (1975) found that children low in sociability exhibited the same behavior pattern five years later. The frequency of positive social interaction was significantly and positively correlated with the overall sociability index.

The evidence supporting long-term stability of social withdrawal and isolation has been more equivocal. Several reviews (Asher, Oden, & Gottman, 1977; Strain, Cooke, & Apolloni, 1976) have noted studies demonstrating a relationship between low social acceptance in childhood and later adult mental disorders, delinquency, and suicides or attempted suicides. Strain et al. (1976) cautioned against drawing firm conclusions from these retrospective studies because of their methodological limitations. Several follow-up studies have not found such relationships (Michael, Morris, & Soroker, 1957; Morris, Soroker, & Burrus, 1954). Children referred to mental health services because of shy, withdrawn behavior were not found to become psychotic in adulthood; rather, they tended to lead quiet, retiring lives with some restrictions in social contacts.

Methodological problems with both retrospective and follow-up investigations preclude drawing conclusions about long-term relationships between social acceptance and adult behavior disorders. However, the short-term data do suggest that the problem of social withdrawal is certainly serious enough to warrant systematic treatment.

In spite of the availability of data indicating stability in the social status and behavior of children, the child characterized by low rates of social interaction with the peer group has traditionally been ignored by clinicians, educators, and researchers alike. Two factors may help to explain this vacuum. First, child-adult relationships have long been thought to be more important than child-peer interactions in their influence on social development. Only in the last 10 years has a more concentrated research focus on peer interaction been realized (Lewis & Rosenblum, 1975). Secondly, withdrawn children are not disruptive; they display behaviors that avoid interaction rather than attract it. Cast in a behavioral framework, these children rarely initiate interactions with peers and tend to extinguish or punish peer initiations to them. Thus, they systematically increase and maintain the probability of being ignored, or even punished, by their peers as well as adults.

In the last decade, there has been a slow but increasing concern with the development of remediation techniques for the treatment of social withdrawal. The majority of studies reported in the literature have focused upon a precise demonstration of the impact of one or more independent variables on child behavior. Early investigations assessed the effects of contingent adult attention upon the social behavior of low interacting preschoolers (Allen, Hart, Buell, Harris, & Wolf, 1964; Buell, Stoddard, Harris, & Baer, 1968). Subsequent research has examined more complex procedures, including token systems (Clement & Milne, 1967; Walker & Hops, 1973), symbolic modeling (Gottman, 1977; O'Connor, 1969, 1972), desensitization plus shaping (Reid, Hawkins, Keutzer, McNeal, Phelps, Reid, & Mees, 1967), the use of peers as therapeutic agents to facilitate social interaction (Kirby & Toler, 1970; Strain, Shores, & Timm, 1977; Wahler, 1967; Walker & Hops, 1973), coaching (Oden & Asher, 1977), teacher mediated treatment (Weinrott, Corson, & Wilchesky, in press), and the generalization of interaction skills (Cooke & Apolloni, 1976; Strain, Shores, & Kerr, 1976). With few exceptions (Clement & Milne, 1967; Oden et al., 1976; Weinrott et al., 1976), the impact of this research on the total number of children involved has been exceedingly small. Moreover, few replications have been noted across subjects or experimenters. It is clear that more systematic integrative research is required to produce a standardized set of procedures that can be effective with a broad range of withdrawn children. Further, this set of procedures must be packaged so that it can be easily added to the therapeutic repertoire of school district personnel who are in unique positions to deliver these services to the majority of children who require them.

The purpose of this paper is to describe the development of a comprehensive treatment package for use in modifying social withdrawal within regular school settings. The program to be described has been under development for the past five years at the Center at Oregon for Research in the Behavioral Education of the Handicapped (CORBEH). The Center has specialized in the development of field-tested, packaged intervention programs for various types of behavioral excesses or deficiencies frequently encountered in school settings (Walker, Hops, & Greenwood, 1976).

When completed, the Program for Establishing Effective Relationship Skills (PEERS) will contain a set of procedures for identifying and increasing the withdrawn student's positive social interactions with peers in playground and classroom settings. The program will be implemented and supervised by a teacher-consultant, managed in part by a classroom teacher and playground supervisor. In addition, the total package will contain procedures for brief but comprehensive training of teacher-consultants in the use of the interventions, thereby fulfilling the triadic intervention model (Tharp & Wetzel, 1969) for cost-effective use in school settings.

This report will present an account of the step-by-step process of a systematic research and development program designed to produce a functional set of procedures for remediating withdrawn behavior in school-age children. Following a short discussion of behavior management packages and a review of the research strategy, the five-year process will be unfolded using illustrative data.

BEHAVIORAL MANAGEMENT PACKAGES

Recently, the development of a behavioral technology has advanced to a point where it is feasible to develop and evaluate "packaged" behavior management programs intended for use by relatively untrained "mediators," e.g., parents, teachers, in the natural setting. These social agents (Patterson, McNeal, Hawkins, & Phelps, 1967) are in key positions in the social milieu to provide cost-effective direct services to target subjects in need of behavioral change, e.g., students, delinquents, families. Examples of such innovations in behavioral technology are represented by the following recently developed behavior change programs: a) the Achievement Place model—*The Teaching Family Handbook* (Phillips, Phillips, Fixsen, & Wolf, 1972), a program for the residential treatment of children with delinquent behaviors; b) the Oregon Social Learning Center's model for the treatment of the aggressive child in the home and school—*A Social Learning Approach to Family Intervention* (Patterson, Reid, Jones, & Conger 1975); and c) two programs developed at the Center at Oregon for Research in the Behavioral Education of the Handicapped (CORBEH)—the *CLASS Program* (Hops, Beickel, & Walker, 1975), a program for children with acting-out behavior in the school setting, and the *PASS Program* (Greenwood, Hops, Delquadri, & Walker, 1974), a group behavior management program for work and study skills during academic instructional periods.

These "packaged" behavioral programs contain not only the basic intervention procedures required to successfully change the target subjects' behavior, but also procedures for training the mediator in the correct implementation of the treatment program (Tyler, 1973). The programs are often the result of several years of research and developmental work which document their effectiveness (e.g., Cobb &

Hops, 1973; Greenwood, Hops, Delquadri, & Guild, 1974; Greenwood, Hops, & Walker, 1977a, 1977b; Hops & Cobb, 1973, 1974; Patterson, 1974; Phillips, Phillips, Fixsen, & Wolf, 1971; Hops & Beickel, 1975; Hops, Walker, Fleischman, Nagoshi, Omura, Skindrud, & Taylor, 1978).

The development of a cost-effective packaged program for the treatment of social withdrawal rests upon the solutions to at least three key questions. The first has to do with different types of social withdrawal, the second with the treatment components, and the third with the delivery system.

(1) Will the treatment package be sufficiently flexible to accommodate different types of social withdrawal? For instance, Strain, Cooke and Apolloni (1976) conceptualize a bipolar continuum ranging from the Type I child with a deficient social repertoire, e.g., developmentally delayed, to the Type II child who has the required skills but is deficient in their performance, e.g., selective mutism. Consequently, intervention procedures may have to provide effective treatment for children along both continua.

(2) Can independent variables shown to be effective in component analysis studies with small groups of subjects be combined into a total set of standardized procedures that will be effective across a wide range of isolate children?

(3) Given the recent emphasis on educational mainstreaming, can the program be reduced to manageable proportions and delivered cost effectively to the socially withdrawn child in the regular educational setting?

The Center at Oregon for Research in the Behavioral Education of the Handicapped (CORBEH)

The Center at Oregon for Research in the Behavioral Education of the Handicapped (CORBEH) has as its primary goal the development and delivery of standardized treatment packages for homogeneous subgroupings of behaviorally handicapped children in the regular classroom. In a three-stage development program a) significant treatment variables are identified, operationalized, and functionally analyzed in an experimental classroom setting; b) in a continuing series of experimental studies, these variables are packaged and adapted for use in regular classrooms by teachers working with a

CORBEH teacher-consultant; and finally c) the package is tested in several school districts to evaluate its effectiveness when implemented by local school personnel trained in the role of teacher-consultant. A brief description of this systematic research and development model is provided here. A more detailed description of the experimental and methodological procedures can be found in CORBEH Report No. 35 (Walker, Hops, & Greenwood, 1978).

In Stage I, behavioral assessment instruments, culminating in behavioral observation procedures, are developed for the purposes of (1) identifying and screening subjects and (2) evaluating their responsiveness to specific treatment procedures. Initial investigations are next carried out with children identified as being representative of a specific behavioral subgrouping, e.g., acting-out, social withdrawal. The intensive studies are conducted in an experimental/demonstration classroom setting to determine the relevant variables involved in remediating the problem behaviors and teaching the children more effective and appropriate ones.

In Stage II, the effective treatment techniques are incorporated into treatment packages in the form of procedural manuals and adapted for use within the regular classroom setting. Studies are carried out to clarify issues related to the delivery and implementation of the specific procedures and to fine tune additional treatment variables. At this level, the package is implemented via a teacher-consultant and practical problems associated with the training of teachers, programming maintenance of behavioral changes, and the withdrawal of the consultant are examined.

Research in Stage III answers fundamental questions related to the adequacy of the final package and its utility for widespread use. Reliable procedures are developed to train a variety of consulting school personnel to implement the packages effectively.

The PEERS program for the remediation of socially withdrawn behavior in primary grade school children has now completed the Stage II process. The rest of this report will illustrate the research and developmental process of this behavior management package.

Research and Development of an Intervention Package for the Socially Withdrawn—Experimental Classroom Research

The main objectives of the research conducted in Stage I were twofold. First, a set of procedures for identifying a homogeneous population of withdrawn children and assessing the effects of treatment had to be established. Secondly, a variety of potential treatment procedures had to be evaluated to determine which were the most effective in remediating withdrawn behavior. In meeting these objectives, answers to the following questions were sought.

(1) Are referred children discriminable from their peers in observable behaviors?
(2) Can these differences be socially validated by teacher ratings?
(3) Which treatment variables produce the most effective change?
(4) Which dependent variables are sensitive to the manipulations of the independent variables?

Identification. To insure the selection of children who were clearly socially withdrawn, several criteria were used to reflect both professional judgment and systematic objective observation. Children accepted for treatment were (1) referred by their counselors as deficient in social interactive behavior when compared to their peers, (2) rated high by their teachers on the social withdrawal subscale of the Walker Problem Behavior Identification Checklist (Walker, 1970), and (3) shown to have relatively low rates of social interaction using observation instruments.

A behavioral recording system was developed to obtain both subject and peer interaction data in the classroom setting. The Peer Interaction Recording System (PIRS) (Hops, Garrett, Todd, & Nicholes, 1976) consists of two separate observation codes—the Individual Interaction Code (IIC) and the Peer Tally Code (PTC). The IIC focuses in detail on the interactive behavior of one target subject with interacting partners. The PTC is used simultaneously with the IIC to record the total number of interactions by the subjects' peers during the same observation session. Both codes provide comparable data on interaction rates between the referred child and his respective peer groups. To illustrate the use of this code in the selection process, referral data collected on 14 withdrawn subjects and their peers over a three-year period showed an average interaction rate of .17 per minute for the targets compared to .55 per minute for their respective peer groups.* Percent agreement for the IIC is determined in sequential order for all responses by type and quality. Mean percent agreement for 345 checks carried out during the same time period was .81. For the PTC, a sample of 81 checks produced a mean percent agreement of .92 (Garrett, Hops, Todd, & Walker, 1976).

Delineation of treatment variables. A series of studies designed to assess the effects of several treatments was carried out in our experimental classroom under highly controlled conditions. The classroom is characterized by a) small groups (6 per group) of experimental children, b) a high pupil-teacher ratio, 3 to 1, c) continuous systematic monitoring of student-teacher interaction, and d) feedback to teachers to ensure correct implementation of the independent variables.

The studies were designed to analyze the effects of reinforcing specific topographical components of interaction that appeared essential to initiating and maintaining social exchanges (Walker, Greenwood, Hops, & Todd, in press). Previous studies of social interaction (prior to 1973) had focused on more global measures, e.g., interaction rate and percent time. The components were a) initiating positive interactions (START), b) responding to positive initiations (ANSWER), and c) maintaining social interactions over time (CONTINUE), i.e., beginning with the third reciprocal response in each interactive chain. Three groups of withdrawn elementary students were assigned to the experimental classroom for three to four-month periods each. Each group (N=6 per group) was involved in a different experiment. In Experiment I, each of the three topographic components was reinforced individually during free play activity periods in the following order: a) Start, b) Answer, c) Continue. Experiment II was an intersubject replication of Experiment I. However, to control for possible order effects, reinforcement of the topographic components occurred as follows: a) Continue, b) Answer, c) Start, d) Continue. In Experiment III, all components were reinforced simultaneously within ongoing social interactive behavior.

The results of the three experiments proved extremely interesting. Illustrative data from Experiments I and III are presented in Figures

---

*A test of the comparability between the two coding systems was carried out in one classroom over a six-day period. Mean scores were computed daily for a random sample of five children observed individually (IND), observed as a group (GRP), and for the entire class as a single unit (CLS). No significant differences were found between the the three overall means. Pearson r's computed were 0.70 (IND vs CLS), 0.73 (IND vs GRP), and 0.90 (CLS vs GRP).

1 and 2, respectively. Reinforcement of the components START or ANSWER generally increased the specific response being reinforced *but* did not affect overall interactive behavior as measured by the amount of time observed in social interaction (see Figure 1). In contrast, reinforcement of CONTINUE resulted in more lengthy interactions and large, replicable increases in overall behavior output. When all social responding regardless of topography was reinforced in Experiment III, dramatic increases in interactive time was consistently produced, largely a function of lengthier interactions (see Figure 2). Rates of STARTS and ANSWERS were not affected.

Observations of the experimental periods suggested that the reinforcement of the START and ANSWER components may have been more disruptive of and incompatible with each child's natural interactive style than was the reinforcement of CONTINUE or all three combined. Reinforcing STARTS produced frequent, brief interactions that seemed to be characterized by artificiality of content—similar to cocktail party or table-hopping behavior. Reinforcing ANSWERS produced similar responding but was more difficult for the subjects to produce. This condition was compounded by collateral responding designed to insure that other children would initiate, requiring a skill that few of the children had in their repertoires. Responses used to prompt initiations that could be answered included whispering, facial gestures, and touching. Furthermore, some students could be heard prior to the sessions arranging with peers who would initiate to whom during the session. Unfortunately, this social behavior was not recorded by our observation team. By comparison, the CONTINUE contingency appeared to produce much more meaningful responding with interactions of much longer duration.

When all three components were reinforced simultaneously in Experiment III, no restraints were placed on the topography of social interaction. This contingency produced the clearest effects and seemed to maximally facilitate all children's social interactions. Because of its flexible nature, it was clearly the contingency of choice: a) It allowed all interactive behavior to contribute to reinforcement; b) it was most accommodating to individual interactive patterns; c) it was easiest to implement allowing reinforcement to be delivered, nondisruptively, at various points during an interactive chain; and d) it resulted in the most natural interactive topography.

The implications of these studies suggested the following strategy for intervention. If a child was deficient in either initiating or re-

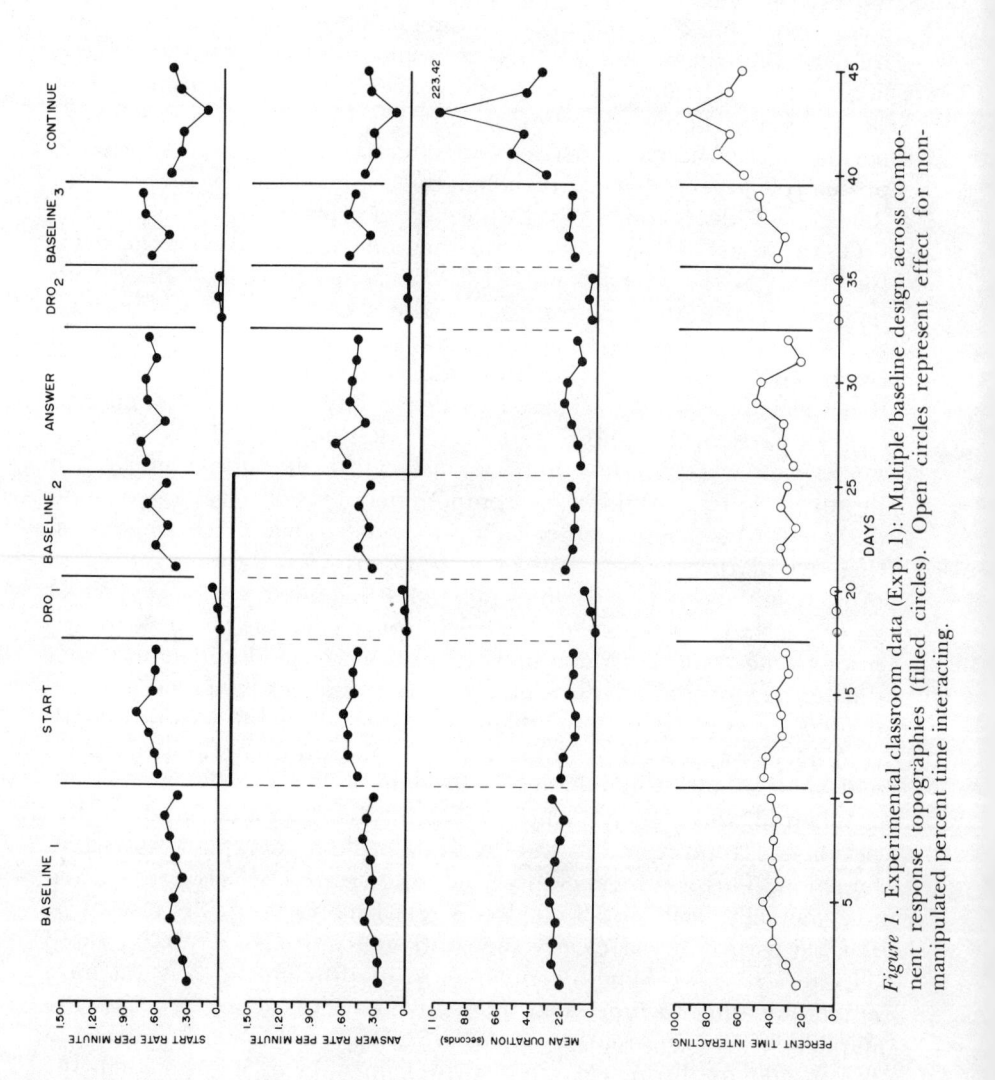

58   Behavorial Systems for the Developmentally Disabled

Figure 1. Experimental classroom data (Exp. 1): Multiple baseline design across component response topographies (filled circles). Open circles represent effect for non-manipulated percent time interacting.

PEERS: Remediating Social Withdrawal

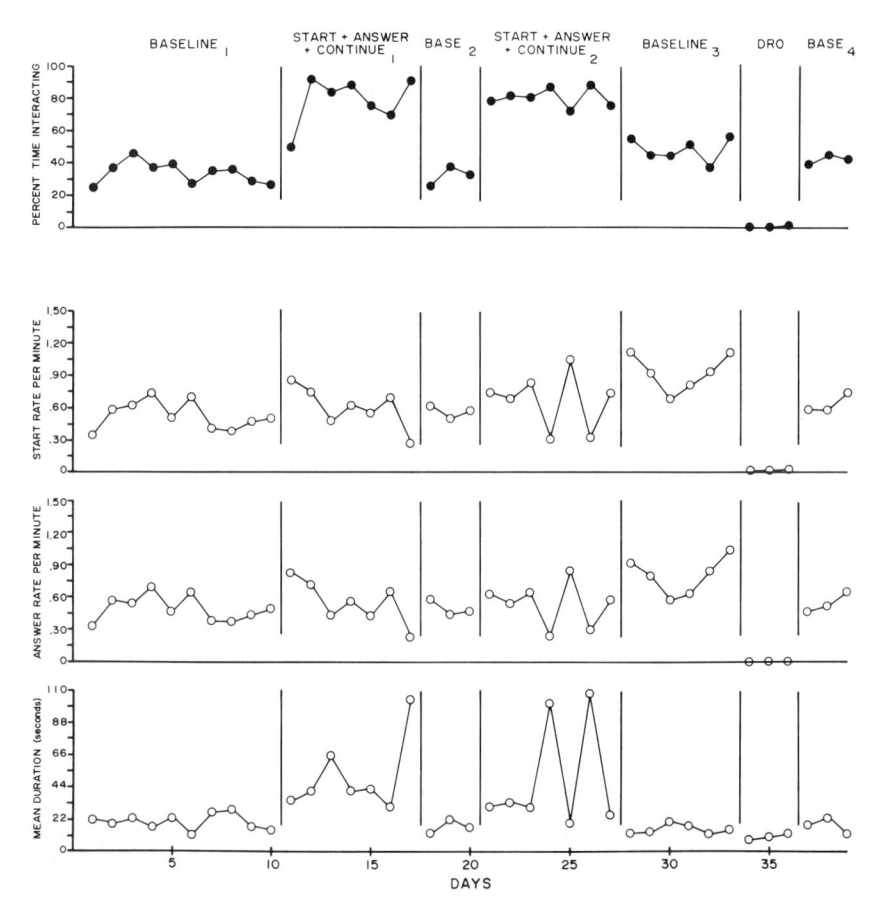

Figure 2. Experimental classroom data (Exp. III): Reversal design with percent time interacting as major dependent variable manipulated. Open circles represent effects for component response topographies.

sponding to others' initiations, the establishment of these skills in the child's repertoire through instruction and/or reinforcement would be considered important. However, as demonstrated, a contingency increasing a single topographic component might place some constraints on the child's overall social interactive behavior and introduce considerable artificiality. The best intervention strategy might be first to reinforce all interactive behavior and only then to determine whether additional instruction and/or contingencies were necessary to correct deficits. If a child increased overall interactive time by interacting with only one peer consistently, then perhaps no further intervention would be required. As will be seen, this strategy is reflected in procedures tested later.

Research in the Regular Educational Setting

At the Stage II level of development, solutions were sought for a series of problems related to conducting intervention programs in the regular school setting with substantially reduced experimental control. New and related variables were studied to test for their potential contribution and possible inclusion in the program.

The foremost addition to the program at this point occurred as the role of teacher-consultants was established and solutions sought for problems related to consultant implementation behavior. For example, in the final PEERS, consultants will be asked to determine the appropriateness of referrals without the aid of a team of observers. Thus, a consultant observation code had to be developed and tested. Secondly, since consultants are considered only temporary change agents, their involvement in the treatment program must be systematically faded out and program control left with the teacher or other involved regular school personnel to carry on and complete.

Problems related to the teacher's participation were of major significance. In our experience, we have found that a teacher is more likely to use a program and follow the procedures carefully where a) there is relatively little response cost, i.e., requiring few major teacher behavior changes, b) systematic support and feedback from the consultant are provided (Cossairt, Hall, & Hopkins, 1973), and c) initial effects of the program demonstrate child behavior change is occurring and change efforts are productive. The issue of maintenance of program gains was also considered and specific programming steps, e.g., systematic fading of controlling variables, was established. There are innumerable issues which were considered and dealt with at each developmental step. For purposes of this report, sample data on select issues of critical importance will be presented.

Consultant observation system. In Year 1 of the second research stage, a relatively easy to use consultant observation system was developed. A six-second interval recording procedure allowed the consultant to record data on the amount of time the referred child was engaged in social behavior, the quality of the behaviors (positive or negative), the form of the behavior (verbal or nonverbal), and the initiator of the interaction (the subject or peer). The code also provided data on rates of interaction.

Previous research at Stage I had used peer normative data (Walker & Hops, 1976) to assist selection of appropriate withdrawn candidates for treatment and to evaluate the magnitude of treatment effects. Attempts to collect data on both targets and their peers by the consultant toward the same ends proved an impossible task. Thus, during Year 2 we decided to build a social behavior normative data base using observations made on "normal" groups of children in playground or recess settings across classrooms and schools which future consultants could use to evaluate their observations of referred children prior to, during, and following treatment.

PIRS II, a new observation instrument, was developed to yield major variables comparable to the consultant's observation code (Garrett, Hops, & Stevens, in preparation). To develop the normative data, five randomly selected peers in each referred child's classroom were systematically observed by a team of trained observers in time-sampling fashion during each recess and lunch period in which the target child was being monitored. To date, data have been collected on over 100 children in grades K-3. Significant differences were found between grades and norms established for each level.

Intervention—Year I. As described earlier, investigations conducted in the experimental classroom examined the effects of a token economy on several components of social interactive behavior, singly and in combination. The results indicated that reinforcement of all forms of social behavior simultaneously produced more powerful effects and more substantial social responding. In Stage II research in the regular classroom which followed, more attention was paid to assessing the effects of different components of the token economy on overall social behavior to determine their adaptability to the regular educational setting. Primary considerations at this point were in the selection of the most cost-effective intervention components—those making the most powerful immediate changes yet practical to implement by the consultant and/or teacher.

In Year 1 of what became ultimately a three-year research program, the effects of one antecedent and several consequent variables on social behavior of children were examined. In Year 2, the treatment variables shown most effective in the first year were combined as a single package and tested on a new group of subjects. In the third year, a second antecedent variable, social skills tutoring, was added to provide direct instruction in social skills, and the package was tested with the additional component.

A series of six single-subject design experiments was carried out in Year 1 (Hops, Fleischman, & Street, in preparation). Five girls and one boy were selected as socially withdrawn; this selection was based initially on teacher nominations and confirmed by at least five days of observation data. Teacher nomination has been shown to be an effective initial screening technique for social withdrawal in preschool settings (Greenwood, Walker, & Hops, 1977; Greenwood, Walker, Todd, & Hops, 1976).

The data for four of the six subjects are presented in Figures 3, 4, 5 and 6 to graphically illustrate the Year 1 results. The baseline data

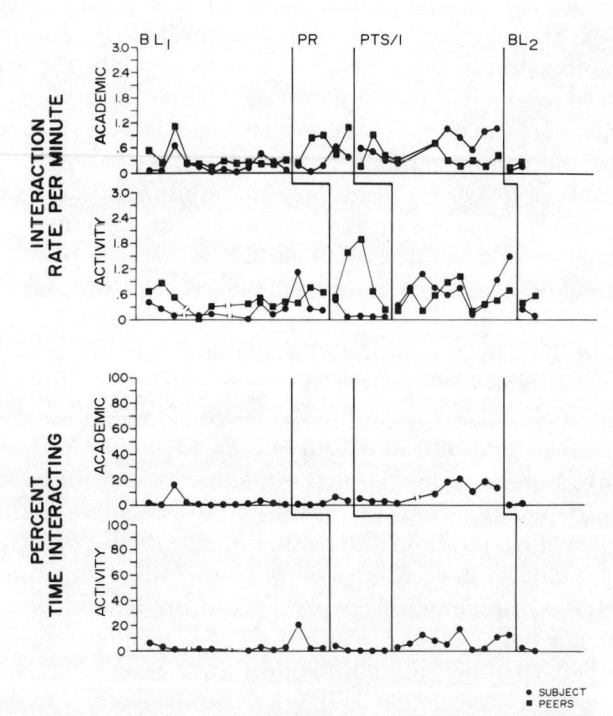

Figure 3. Rate of interaction and percent time interacting for Subject 1 in regular classroom academic and activity periods.

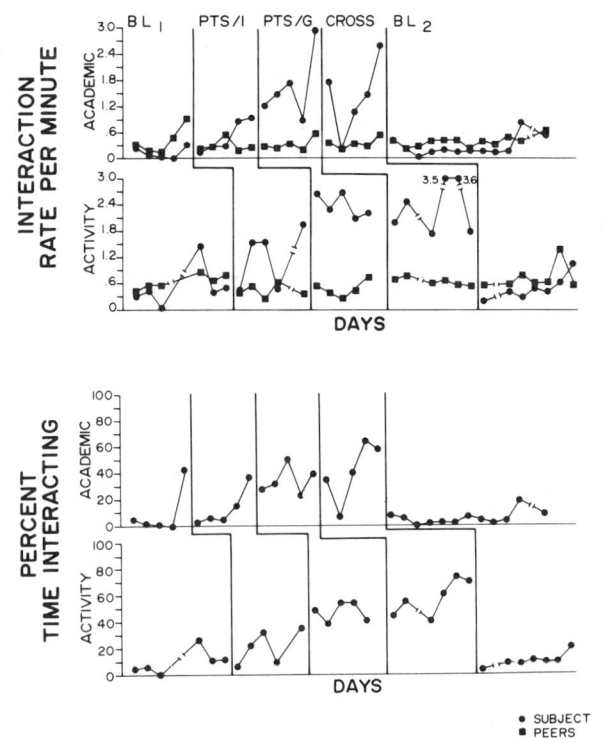

Figure 4. Rate of interaction and percent time interacting for Subject 2 in regular classroom academic and activity periods.

represent the second step in the screening process and show consistent peer/subject discrepancies on interaction rates for Subjects 1, 2, and 3 and on the percent time spent interacting for Subject 4 in the classroom setting.

The initial screening data for Subject 4 did not show discrepancies in interaction rates between the child and her peer group. Informal observation, however, indicated that the child's interactions, although within the peer group range, were relatively brief and insubstantial. An examination of her behavior on the variable time spent interacting indicated that she spent relatively little time in social behavior, although no comparative peer data were available. To test the hypothesis that the child differed from her peers on total interactive time, the PTC section of the PIRS code was modified to obtain comparable peer data. Agreement checks for percent of time interacting for the peer group ranged from .90 to 1.00 with a mean agreement of .95. The correlation between the 14 pairs of scores was .97 (p < .01).

For five of the six children, the experimental procedures were carried out in two classroom periods, a structured academic session and a less structured activity period. For the other subject, treatment was provided in only one in-class period and during recess. The specific procedures tested were a) Joint Task—assignment of the subject and a peer to work at a specific task requiring alternating verbal interaction based on an idea in a paper by Johnson, Goetz, Baer, and Green (1973); b) teacher praise (Allen et al., 1964); and c) three token reinforcement contingencies: (1) individual contingency with individual backups, (2) individual contingency with a backup shared by the entire group, and (3) a crossover contingency in which the subject earned points for group members' initiations to him, the group collectively earned points for the subject's initiations to them, and neither backup was delivered until the subject *and* the group met their respective criteria (Walker & Hops, 1973).

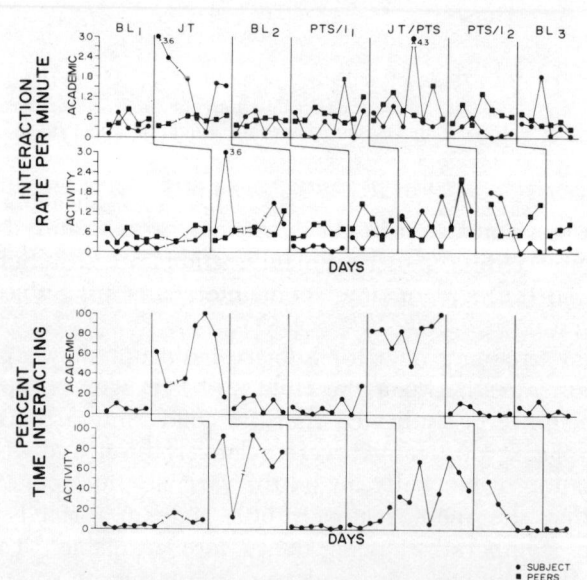

Figure 5. Rate of interaction and percent time interacting for Subject 3 in regular classroom academic and activity periods.

PEERS: Remediating Social Withdrawal 65

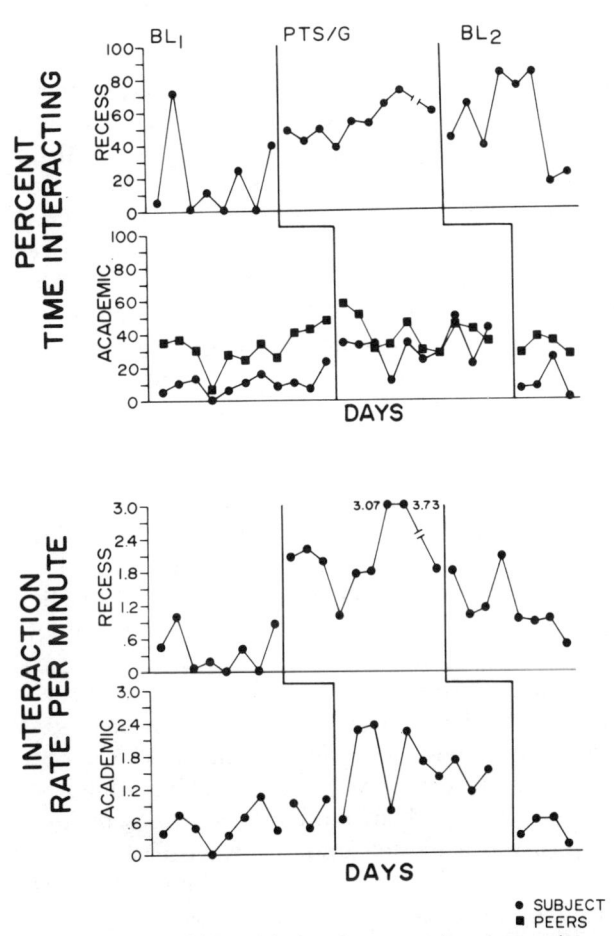

Figure 6. Rate of interaction and percent time interacting for Subject 4 in regular classroom academic and activity periods.

Somewhat surprisingly, teacher praise and individual contingencies for individual backups produced minimal and/or variable effects and were clearly slow to take effect. Increases in social interaction rate under praise conditions for Subject 1, for example (see Figure 3), were noted in the academic period only but not until the fourth treatment day. Her responsiveness to points with individual backups was more marked but quite variable. Similar effects were noted for Subject 2 (see Figure 4) and Subject 3 (see Figure 5) under individual backup conditions. These results are in contrast to the earlier successful findings of Allen et al. (1964) and Buell et al. (1968) with preschool children. The minimal gains achieved in the present studies suggest that our children were more severe cases of social withdrawal and were simply not responsive to these minimal treatments. Lovaas (1977) has noted that reinforcers were frequently difficult to find for autistic children and very often a repertoire of reinforcers had to be developed for individual use. Similarly, our experience with withdrawn children indicates that generally effective social reinforcers, or simple contingencies, are not effective in making substantial changes.

The initial introduction of the Joint Task Procedure with Subject 3 (see Figure 5) produced immediate substantive increases in interaction rates in both periods. Joint Task was an activity assigned by the teacher requiring alternating verbal interaction between the target child and a selected peer. Considering the minimal effects achieved with the individual contingency/individual backup condition and the marked effects produced by the Joint Task Procedure, a new combination strategy was conceived. If Joint Task was paired with the point contingency, interaction rates would be increased (a function of the Joint Task) and the child would receive increased teacher praise and reinforcement. If the Joint Task was then removed, it was hypothesized that the point system and teacher praise alone would maintain interaction rates at a higher level than previously found. Conceptually, Joint Task would be used as an acquisition condition and the individual contingency/individual backup as a maintenance procedure. The results, however, indicated that while the Joint Task/ Points condition did result in moderately increased interaction rates, no maintenance was achieved after the Joint Task to normal stimulus conditions may be required. More work looking at antecedent variables affecting intervention is certainly needed.

Thus, the results indicated that the Joint Task procedure alone was effective in increasing interaction rates of the withdrawn children. In this case, it appears that children, even though withdrawn, come under powerful stimulus control of teacher directives. As the child complied with the teacher command to engage in the task, the structure and demand characteristics of the task insured verbal and social interaction. However, when the controlling features of the task were removed, interactions no longer were under stimulus control.*

---

*More recently, we attempted the same procedure with the most withdrawn child we had encountered during the two years in the experimental classroom at CORBEH. The teacher was asked to instruct the child and a peer to interact on a given academic subject. The child complied as directed.

The individual contingency with group backup and the crossover contingency were found equally effective in producing high rates of social interaction (see Figure 4). These findings replicated the effects noted in the previous study by Walker and Hops (1973). Subject 4 data (see Figure 6) further demonstrate the effectiveness of the group backup condition both in recess and an in-class period.

Contrasting the sensitivity of the two dependent variables, rate of interaction and percent of time spent interacting, several distinct differences become clear. Ignoring peer comparison data, the treatment data for Subjects 1, 2 and 4 generally showed the same effects whether plotted as rate of interaction or percent of time interacting. Within the range of their own variability, the dependent variables were approximately equal in assessing the quantitative effects of the different treatment conditions. For Subject 3, however, the effect of the Joint Task treatment is seen more clearly as percent of time spent interacting (see Figure 5). Interaction rate was more variable and more likely to be dependent on the type of task assigned each day. On specific days, the two dependent variables were inversely related.

To illustrate the specific effect of the task on the dependent variable, consider an alternating flash card activity. Increases in interaction rate would probably occure as the children continuously initiated new interactions. The continuous interactions would also show up as increased time spent interacting. On the other hand, a task which required less frequent alternation, for example, reading paragraphs to one another, would be reflected by lower interaction rates but would be as high in percent of time interacting.

It seems clear that both variables provide both common and unique data on treatment effects. The continued use of both variables would more accurately reflect the total impact of each treatment condition. However, since it was not feasible to collect peer data on both variables, a decision had to be made based upon both economic and practical efficiency. Percent of time spent interacting was chosen as the primary dependent variable based on the following rationale.

First, it appeared more consistent across different treatment conditions. Secondly, to meet the goals of the PEERS program, it more accurately represented the general purpose of the independent variables, i.e., to increase the overall social responding of withdrawn children. Thirdly, it was more clinically reliable as consultants could observe durations of interactions more effectively than rate. Fourthly, as previously shown for Subject 4, it may be a more generally sensitive screening variable for withdrawn behavior. Comparative peer/subject data are not currently available on the same children for both variables to test this last hypothesis. In fact, it may be possible for children to be accepted on the basis of one variable but rejected on the other. Further research is necessary to evaluate the comparative effects of each.

Although maintenance of treatment effects was not actively programmed or expected, some maintenance appeared in the recess data for Subject 4 (see Figure 6). The child's responding during the return to baseline condition maintained at treatment levels for six days as measured by interaction rates and percent of time interacting. This was clearly not the case in the classroom academic setting where marked decreases in social responding occurred. Based on our experience to date, maintenance of social behavior seemed more probable in recess settings than in classroom settings. In recess, social behavior is the norm, less likely to be affected by reinforcement for competing behaviors, e.g., academic independent seatwork; also, in recess the child's peers are more likely to become powerful discriminative stimuli for such behavior.

Overall, the results of Year 1 suggested that a) recess was a more appropriate intervention setting for increasing social interactive behavior; b) the individual contingency/group backup condition was as powerful and more cost-effective than any of the other contingencies; c) the Joint Task procedure could be used to program teacher approved interactive behavior within the regular classroom setting without interfering with more academic objectives; and d) percent of time spent interacting for the purposes of the program was selected as a more useful dependent variable for screening withdrawn children and evaluating all forms of treatment.

Intervention—Year 2. The goals of the second year's investigations were a) produce a package combining cost-effective program components on the basis of previous studies, and b) test the combined set of procedures on a new group of socially withdrawn children. The package would consist of those components found to be maximally effective to this point in producing behavior change and lowest in response cost to social agents implementing the procedures. The nature of the intervention procedure now was matched to the setting and the function of the social agent directly responsible for its implementation. In addition, the package would contain components especially designed to program maintenance of gains.

In the previous section, we made a strong case for using percent time interacting as the primary dependent variable for further assessment of the developing package. However, while the research and development process may so far appear to have evolved in well ordered, predictable fashion, in reality that does not happen. As Kuhn (1962) has so eloquently argued, it is only the historian who creates a linear model out of a continuing series of unpredictable events.

Having made the case for conducting our major intervention procedures during the recess period, we were suddenly confronted with an additional problem with respect to the primary dependent variable. It became obvious to our observers and consultants after conducting increased recess observations that children's social behavior was both interactive *and* noninteractive. The noninteractive component arose out of social involvement in game playing that did not require continuous social interaction. A child may initiate an interaction in order to become involved in a baseball game, but playing left field does not require social interaction unless the ball is hit to the child. Some games involve simply one or two interactions followed by waiting in line to try again, all part of the game. The goal of the program, it seems, should include such game-playing behavior, whether interactive or not. Game-playing is part of the social skills repertoire a child should have to interact successfully with his/her peers.

Consequently, we decided to reinforce the children for all socially involved behavior. The *new* major dependent variable became percent social behavior, the combination of interactive behavior and all other socially involved noninteractive game-playing behavior. An analysis of the data for the two subjects to be presented in this report indicate that the correlation between the two variables, percent time interacting and percent time social behavior, are $r = .81$, $df = 49$, $p < .001$, and $r = .50$, $df = 56$, $p < .001$, for Subjects 1 and 2, respectively.

The package consisted of the following components:

(1) *Recess intervention.* The individual contingency with the group backup was the basic procedure implemented during a selected recess period. The consultant maintained overall responsibility for this portion of the package, running the program in recess and involving the teacher and playground supervisor when necessary.

Prior to each daily session, a brief "pep talk" was held in the classroom during which the teacher a) discussed the program's goals and purposes and b) explained how the target child earned points, c) then had the class vote on the backup for that day, and d) finally selected three or four volunteer special helpers who were assigned the task of assisting the target child meet the criterion necessary for reinforcement to occur.

Using the observation code described earlier, the consultant recorded the social behavior of the target child each six seconds, delivering loud and clear praise and points contingently to the target child and the involved peers. The "special helpers" played an important role in this procedure. Highly motivated by the group backup and the consultant's praise, they excitedly followed the target child and the consultant around, arranging games, talking to the target, frequently asking about the number of earned points and whether the criterion had been achieved for the day.

The criterion for reinforcement each day was based on the average percent of social behavior exhibited by the target child in recess over the previous three days. The maximum criterion established was 73%. This figure, determined from a preliminary analysis of the peer normative data calculated on 48 peers, represented one standard deviation greater than the mean of social behavior.

After three days at or above the 73% level, the consultant observed the child to assess the ratio of a) verbal to nonverbal behavior, b) positive to negative behaviors, and c) interactions initiated by the target to those initiated by others. This strategy was consistent with Stage I findings. If the child's behavior was markedly out of balance on any of these variables, an additional contingency was introduced to change the ratio.

(2) *Academic intervention.* The Joint Task component described previously was introduced three to five days after the recess intervention had begun. The Joint Task procedure was expanded to include a broader range of tasks from highly structured activities requiring alternating verbal interactions, e.g., flash card responding, to relatively unstructured ones requiring more spontaneous behavior, e.g., discussion of a painting or a magnifying glass. This activity was selected and arranged by the teacher to be suitable for the ongoing classroom lesson.

(3) *Programming maintenance.* Several program components were added to increase the probability of maintaining gains following removal of the program. These included a) the involvement and participation of social agents in the child's normal environment, such as the child's peers, teacher, and playground supervisor, b) systematic fading of all treatment components, i.e., lowering of the reinforcement criterion to 50% (the normative mean), fading the daily pep talk, the special helpers, the consultant—who first trains the playground super-

PEERS: Remediating Social Withdrawal 71

visor to monitor the behavior of the child, and adjusting the reinforcement schedule.

A further addition to the maintenance strategy was the inclusion of a self-report/verbal correspondence procedure. As suggested by Meichenbaum & Cameron (1973), Strain, Cooke and Apolloni (1976) and O'Leary and O'Leary (1976), self-control procedures may enhance the maintenance of gains and perhaps produce generalization to untreated settings. Self-control can include self-recording, self-evaluation, and self-reinforcement. O'Leary and O'Leary (1976) have suggested that the most reasonable form of self-reinforcement for continued maintenance under normal conditions would be to teach the child to make positive comments to himself. A series of recent studies have also indicated that reinforcing a child for reporting accurately on his/her performance may lead to increases in the behavior in nonreinforced settings (Israel & O'Leary, 1973; Risley & Hart, 1968; Rogers-Warren & Baer, 1976).

To facilitate potential maintenance and generalization in the present study, the consultant taught each child to evaluate and report his/her social behavior to the teacher upon returning to the classroom after recess. The consultant monitored the report and praised and corrected the child when necessary. Group reinforcement immediately followed. Thus, each child was taught to accurately report and make positive comments about his/her own social interaction during recess.

Experimental data for a grade 1 boy (Subject 1) and a kindergarten girl (Subject 2) are presented in Figure 7 to illustrate the use of the package as described. The experiment was conducted in multiple baseline fashion to demonstrate the effectiveness of the procedures. The shaded area on the graphs represents ±1 S.D. about the mean percent social behavior for the appropriate grade level in the normative sample. The program can be considered successful if the subjects' level of social behavior increased to within the shaded area. During baseline a considerable discrepancy existed between the percent of social behavior exhibited by each child in contrast to his/her respective peer groups, 17.2% vs. 81.5% for Subject 1 and 10.6% vs. 46.7% for Subject 2. The individual points/group backup had an immediate dramatic effect for Subject 1, increasing social behavior to 81.3%, and a lesser but significant effect for Subject 2, 37.3%, replicating previous findings. The successful addition of the Joint Task procedure in the classroom (not shown here) may have had an additional impact for Subject 2 in recess as indicated by a further increase in social behavior. While some variability existed over the course of recess inter-

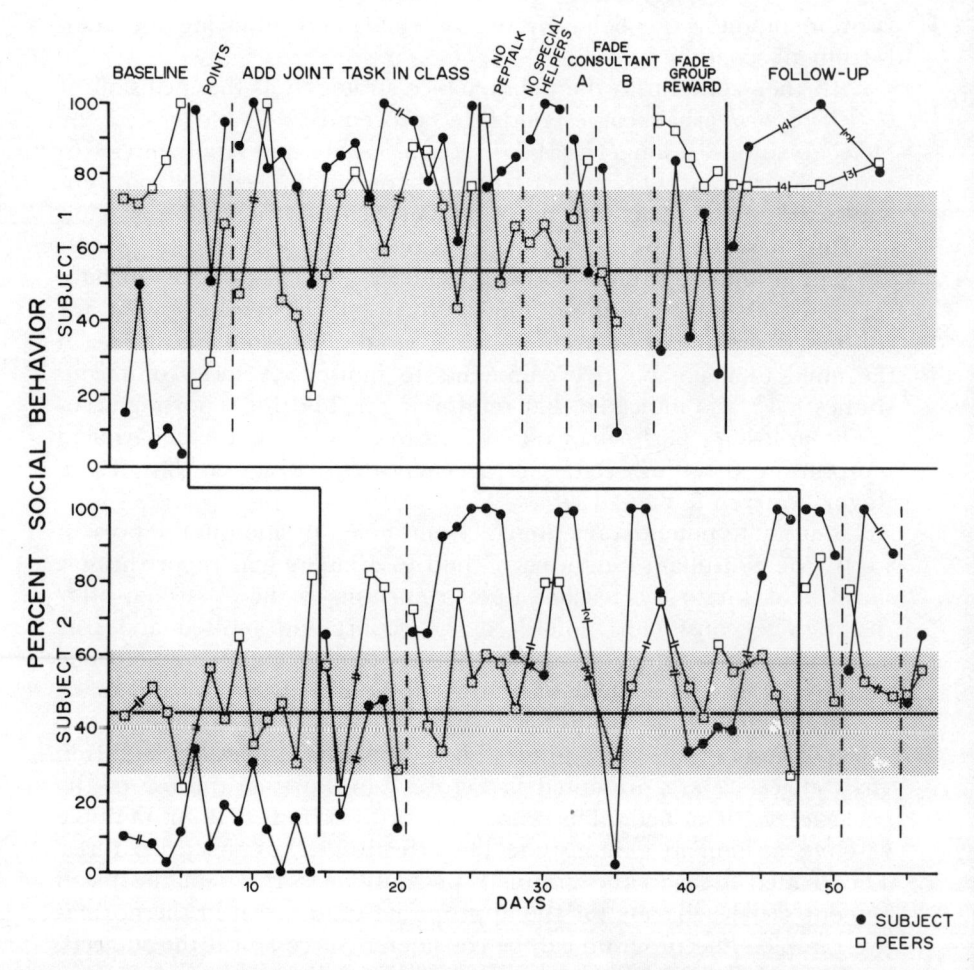

Figure 7. Percent social behavior for Subjects 1 and 2 in Stage II-Year 2 test of PEERS program package. Shaded area includes ±1 S.D. of mean percent social behavior for grade level normative group.

vention, the mean levels of social behavior for both children remained markedly high and above the level of their respective peer groups, 82.8% vs. 64.5% for Subject 1, and 71.9% vs. 55.2% for Subject 2.

Fading the pep talk and the special helpers from the program did not appear to have any discernible effect on either of the children's behavior; if anything, it increased the percent social behavior. However, when the playground supervisor was trained to take over the

PEERS: Remediating Social Withdrawal

program and the consultant removed, a decrease in the amount of social interaction occurred for both children, although both were within the average ranges for their respective grade levels. This marked the end of the program for Subject 2, coinciding with the end of the school year. A further drop in social behavior for Subject 1 occurred during the time the playground supervisor monitored the child's behavior. While the supervisor had been trained by the consultant, she monitored the child only five times during a 15-minute recess in contrast to the 6-second interval system the consultant used. The reliabilities between the playground supervisor and the consultant were not expected to be high; the monitoring was simply a device to extend the program under minimal response cost conditions. As noted on the second day of this condition, the percent of social behavior dropped to 9% under the "watchful eye" of the playground supervisor.

Fading the group backup maintained the mean level of social behavior at 49.8%, very close to the mean of the normative group. Follow-up data collected during the last month of school, with four spot checks over a three-week period, found the subject to be well above the normative level and slightly above the level of his own peer group. Thus, for the two children the effects of the program to this point appeared to have been highly beneficial. Teachers' ratings and anecdotal data gained through interviews provided additional subjective support. One teacher indicated that she thought the program also provided some unexpected benefits—teaching all of the children to care for and share with one another.

Let us summarize the findings of Year 2 and consider the potential of the PEERS package thus far. As indicated previously, six children were run through the same set of procedures. The results indicated that the package was extremely effective for three of the children. Two were of the Type II variety (Strain et al., 1976), not under effective social stimulus control in the school setting but able to demonstrate social behavior in the home, according to parental reports. The third had minimal social skills which appeared to improve during the intervention as the child observed, modeled the behavior of the other children, and was reinforced by the natural peer group consequences as well as the group backup and teacher praise. The program may have been teaching both the children and their respective peer groups that they were potentially reinforcing to one another, i.e., both were becoming more powerful discriminative stimuli (S^Ds) for each other's social behavior.

The program was found to be less effective for the three children who lacked social skills and/or showed deficits in motor coordination, language, and other skill areas. One child, for example, frequently exhibited negative behaviors after her general social behavior had been increased. For her, a response cost contingency was added to control the aversive quality of her social responding. Another child who had various physical and developmental deficits had trouble because the peer group was not readily motivated to play with her. Reinforcing peers for playing ball with a child whose ball handling abilities are severely underdeveloped may produce conflicting contingencies for the peer group. The peer group may have become an S^D for the child, but the reverse was not true.

In total, the results indicated that more attention had to be paid to developing components that would benefit those children receiving only partial benefits from the program thus far. The package could contain a direct instruction component, to teach some social skills to those children deficient in that area. The developmentally delayed child needing training in motor skills was considered out of the purview of the program. Perhaps, in an ideal situation, the program could be run for such children with younger peers at the same level of development. In the school setting this would require administrative support, plus a specialized motor training curricula. However, suggestions such as these could be contained in the manuals for children who were not able to receive the full potential of the PEERS program under existing conditions.

Intervention—Year 3. Taking into account the findings of the previous year's activities, two new components were added to the program to increase the rate of initial acquisition for children with minimal social skills and to assist in the maintenance and generalization of gains. These were:

(1) *Social skills tutoring.* Based on the direct instruction model (Engelmann, 1970), three lessons were formulated to teach the withdrawn children the basic skills of initiating (START), responding to initiations (ANSWER), and maintaining interactions (CONTINUE) in cumulative fashion. The three lessons involved a withdrawn child and a peer and were designed to provide the child with practice in performing the behaviors and in discriminating between interactive and noninteractive behaviors. The peer was added so as not to single out the target child. It was thought that these lessons would, perhaps, speed up the effectiveness of the reinforcement program for those children who may have deficits in the social skill area. Lessons were to

PEERS: Remediating Social Withdrawal

occur on the first three days of the program for approximately 15-20 minutes immediately preceding the recess period. At the teacher's recommendation, a same-sexed, socially skilled peer was selected to participate in the coaching lessons. After each lesson the consultant suggested to the children that it might be a good idea to go to recess and practice the behaviors they had just learned.

(2) *Recess 2—self-report.* The self-report/verbal correspondence component was slightly modified and extended to a second recess setting. This procedure was designed to produce generalization of behavior gains at little cost, using members of the peer group. Prior to each additional recess period, the teacher selected one peer special helper to play with the target child. The teacher spent several minutes in the following way: a) discussed appropriate behaviors for recess, b) asked the children what they were going to do, c) reinforced indications of play behavior, d) told the target child that she/he would be asked to report back after recess on what they had done, and e) told the peer that she/he would be asked to corroborate the target's verbal report.

A single case is presented to illustrate the additional features of the package. The subject was a first grade girl whose social responsiveness during recess, as indicated in Figure 8, was well below that of her peers in two recess periods. The peers' social behavior was very close to the mean of the normative peer group for grade 1. Examining the data for Recess 1, the three days of social skills tutoring appears to have had an initial impact on the social behavior, mostly due to the involvement of the peer who had participated in the lessons. The individual points and group backup increased the percent social behavior to near maximum limits. After three days of above 73% social behavior, the maximum requirement for reinforcement, an additional contingency was added in Recess 1 to increase the child's verbal behavior. As seen in Figure 9, the child's verbalizations were relatively low and although some increase had been noted with the addition of the tutoring and point system, the new contingency was designed to increase verbals to within the normative range as indicated by the shaded area on the graph. The child now earned "play points" and "talk points" and had to meet the criterion for both before a group backup became available. The criterion for verbal behavior was established in the same way as that of social behavior, generally based on her behavior over the three previous days.

The data in Figure 9 clearly indicate that a marked but variable increase in verbal behavior was realized in Recess 1. However, attempts

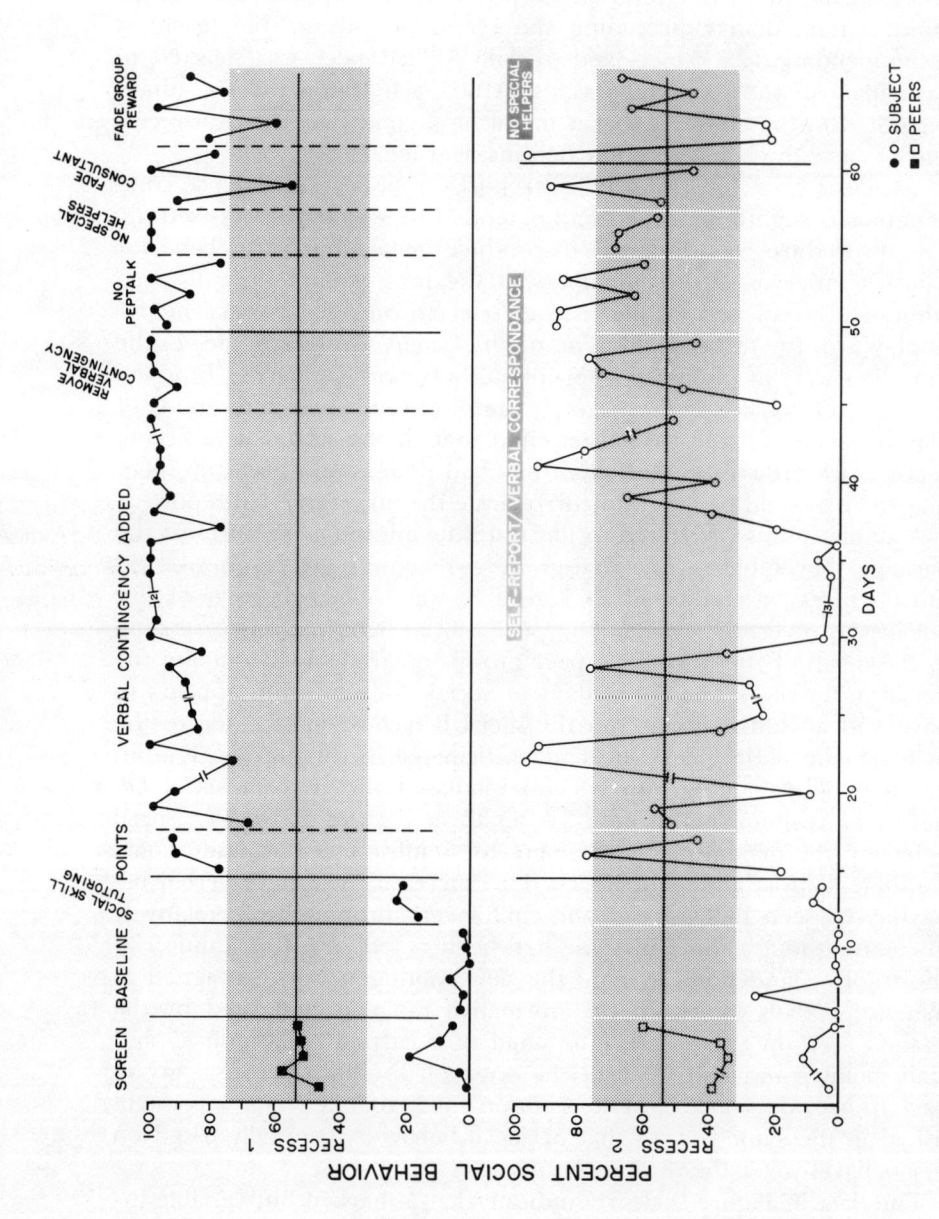

76 Behavorial Systems for the Developmentally Disabled

Figure 8. Percent social behavior across two recess periods for Subject 1 in Stage II-Year 3 test of PEERS program package. Shaded area includes ±1 S.D. of mean percent social behavior for grade level normative group. White lines in Recess 2 represent Recess 1 phase lines.

PEERS: Remediating Social Withdrawal

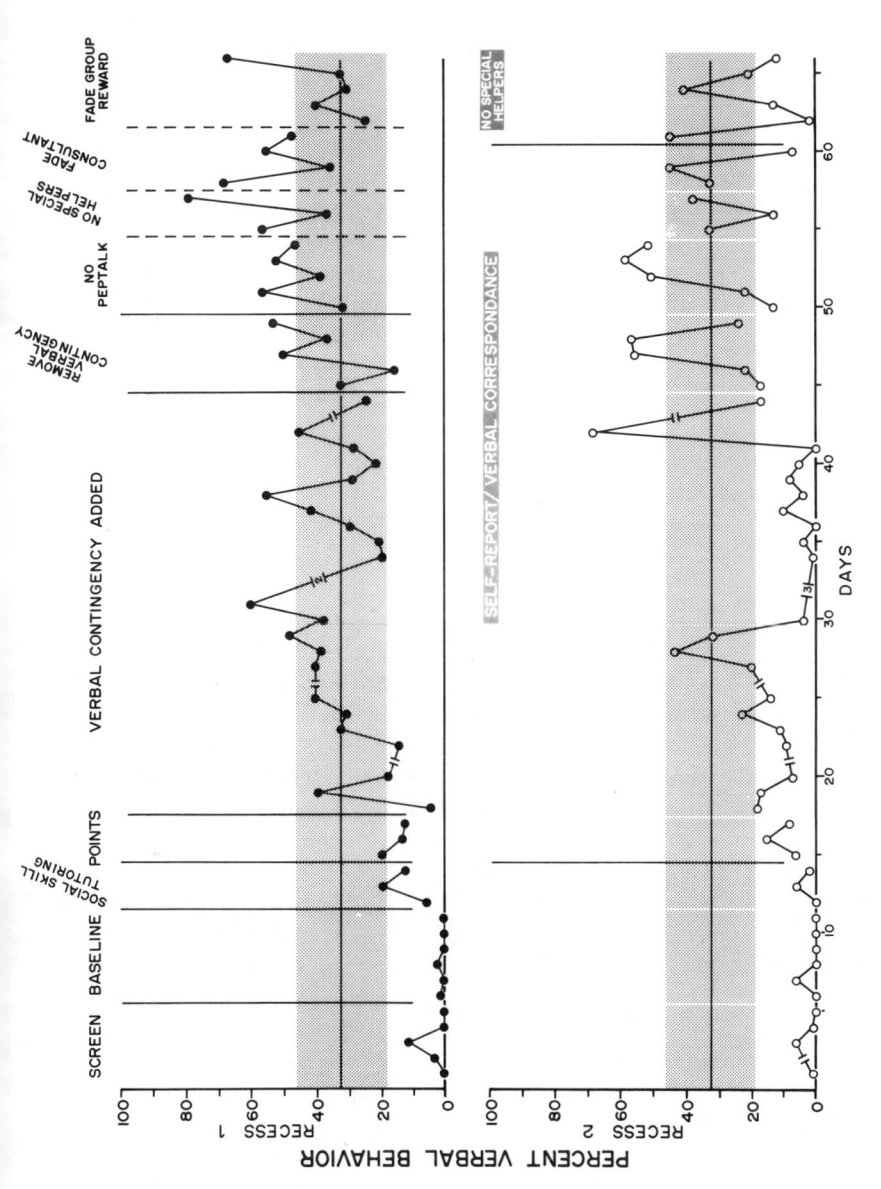

Figure 9. Percent verbal behavior across two recess periods for Subject 1 in Stage II-Year 3 test of PEERS program package. Shaded area includes ±1 S.D. of mean percent verbal behavior for grade level normative group. White lines in Recess 2 represent Recess 1 phase lines.

to increase this level to greater than one standard deviation above the mean of the normative group proved impractical. Since verbal behavior was found to be highly dependent upon the type of game being played, the easiest solution to increasing verbal behavior was to control the type of games being played. However, the repetitious activities were found boring by the children and the child began to balk, refusing to speak. Further, to some degree, the contingency actually built in considerable artificial verbal behavior.

Removing the verbal contingency had no discernible effect on the play or verbal behavior, which maintained at near-intervention levels. In fact, continued fadeout of the other components seemed to have a positive effect on the verbal level of the child. The artificiality induced by the verbal contingency may have initially increased responding, but later suppressed the child's verbal level as the condition maintained. Removing the contingency simply allowed her to interact normally as a function of natural peer shaping and consequences. The level of social and verbal behavior continued markedly above baseline levels with the withdrawal of the consultant and the reinforcement schedule.

The data, graphically describing the effects of the intervention on the social and verbal behavior of the target child during Recess 2, can be seen in Figures 8 and 9, respectively. The intervention procedure in this setting simply involved the pre-recess assignment of one peer "special helper" by the teacher to interact with the target child during recess and corroborate the child's report to the teacher upon their return to the classroom. The social skills tutoring conducted prior to Recess 1 had no effect on the child's behavior in Recess 2 later in the day. A noticeable increase in both social and verbal behavior occurred with the introduction of the verbal correspondence procedure, although some of it may have been due to generalization effects following Recess 1.

The higher levels of social and verbal behavior in Recess 2 maintained during most of the entire intervention phase. (The near-zero levels from Day 30 on may have been due to loss in effect following the Christmas holiday. Social behavior remained at this low level for four days and verbal behavior for nine before the pre-Christmas gains recurred.) Even with the termination of the special helpers on Day 61, the behavior remained well above baseline levels. The major differences between the effects in Recess 1 and Recess 2 were the lowered levels and increased variability in the latter. However, the Recess 2 procedure required minimal effort by the teacher and the results were highly encouraging. The child's behavior remained generally within the normal ranges for her grade level as indicated by the shaded areas on the graph.

The overall results of Year 3-Stage II have been gratifying. The three children tested responded to the packaged procedures similarly. The social skills training was generally enjoyed and had an immediate effect on their behavior in Recess 1. The individual contingency group backup and the Joint Task procedures continued to operate reliably. And the self-report component appears to program generalization to nonreinforced settings at minimal cost to the teacher.

CONCLUSION

This report described the five-year process underlying the development of the PEERS program, a cost-effective standardized intervention program for remediating socially withdrawn behavior in primary-aged, elementary school children in the regular school setting. Within the framework of the CORBEH three-stage research and development process, specific questions related to achieving specific goals at each stage and the ultimate goals at the completion of the package were presented. Studies were designed and results reported describing our attempt to find adequate solutions to these questions. The final result is described in the two manuals for the teacher-consultant (Hops, Fleischman, Guild, Paine, Walker, & Greenwood, 1978) and for the teacher (Hops, Guild, Paine, Fleischman, Street, Walker, & Greenwood, 1978). Each manual describes in detail the daily activities necessary for the correct implementation of the program.

At this point we believe the data indicate that the final package is a viable program which can be used to effectively and efficiently ameliorate the difficulties associated with withdrawn behavior among many school children. For those children with multiple presenting problems, e.g., deficits in motor, language, and other skill areas, the program may work successfully under modified conditions or in conjunction with other skill training. No data are available yet to substantiate this point. For children who lack social skills and who are not under effective stimulus control in social settings, the program appears to have a high probability of being productive.

Baer and Wolf (1970) have conceptualized the social environment as a natural community of reinforcers which shapes a child's social responding and provides the child with a wide variety of skills necessary for successful adjustment in the social community. Unfortunately, there are many children who do not have the skills to make this natural community of reinforcers available to them. Baer and Wolf have argued that simply providing a child with "entry" skills is sufficient. Once the child is admitted, she/he will be "trapped" by the natural consequences that are a function of interaction with the peer group. While the entrapment concept is highly appealing, so far there are very limited data in support of the notion that a withdrawn child simply requires minimal entry skills for entrapment to occur.

The PEERS Program has been designed to ensure that entrapment of the withdrawn child in the natural peer group community *will* occur. The program provides the child with social skills necessary for admittance to the peer group via its social skills tutoring component. Further, it assures that the peer group will accept the child via the group backup reinforcement procedure. Both the Recess 1 and Joint Task in-class intervention techniques provide the child with opportunities to practice interacting both in the free play and academic settings. The self-report/verbal correspondence procedure provides similar opportunities under much less controlled conditions and hopefully programs generalization of the gains made in more structured settings. Fading components and allowing the behaviors to come under the control of the natural community, including adults, enhances potential maintenance of effects.

The final step in the three-stage research process involves testing the delivery of the package to those children who require it within the school setting. A set of procedures developed for training teacher-consultants in the use of the program in two-to-three-day workshops was tested in the 1977-78 school year. The procedures are described in a Consultant Trainer's Manual (Hops, Paine, Fleischman, & Guild, 1978). The program will be evaluated using the child's behavior as the final criterion.

The teacher-consultant model (McKenzie, 1972; Parker, 1975) is thought to be one of the more efficient ways to provide delivery of such services to a wide range of children requiring them. In the past, personnel acting as consultants to regular classroom teachers have included counselors, psychologists, resource room and special class teachers, social workers, principals and other administrative staff, and paraprofessionals working in the classroom. Our previous field tests with the CLASS and PASS programs for acting-out and low academic survival skill children, respectively, have been highly successful at this level of training and implementation, and we anticipate similar results with the PEERS Program.

It has also been our experience that the effect of the program is directly related to the quality of its implementation. Teacher-consultants and teachers who implement the program as designed generally have the greatest impact on the target children. But field-testing by definition results in minimal experimenter involvement with little monitoring of the quality of the intervention. Our experience has shown, however, that if the program structure is sufficiently well developed, and the program manuals describe the procedures in sufficient detail, then the probability of an effective outcome is greater. It appears that a sufficiently structured program can sometimes override the variability encountered in the variety of personnel implementing the procedures under minimal supervision. When the program is effective under these conditions, then it can be said to be truly productive.

A note is required here to deal with the issues of maintenance and generalization of program gains. Most school personnel unrealistically would like to believe and behave as if a good program need be used only once to effect permanent behavior change. However, as Baer, Wolf, and Risley (1968) pointed out a decade ago, and confirmed since in the literature, such effects must be programmed. Behavior and children are variable and subject to the changing consequences extant in the natural community. School personnel must be taught to deal with reversals and their expectations regarding behavior change maintenance made more congruent with the facts. To cope with this reality, our manuals deal with generalization and maintenance issues and contain suggestions on how to achieve these results, e.g., re-establishing some of the conditions necessary to achieve initial gains.

To conclude, we hope that we have been able to impart some of the flavor of the CORBEH research and development process and the evolution of the PEERS program. We are both empiricists and clinicians. Our empirical stance forces us to use data as our primary evaluation tool. Our clinical breeding makes us aware of the many subtle events not recorded by our observation systems and of the problems inherent in the practical delivery of services in real world settings. We believe that this combination of methodologies helped us arrive at a workable program.

REFERENCES

ALLEN, K. E., HART, B. BUELL, J. S., HARRIS, F. R., and WOLF, M. M.: Effects of social reinforcement on isolate behavior of a nursery school child. *Child Development*, 1964, *35*, 511-518.

AMIDON, E.: The isolate in children's groups. *Journal of Teacher Education*, 1961, *12*, 412-416.

AMIDON, E., and HOFFMAN, C. B.: Can teachers help the socially rejected? *The Elementary School Journal*, 1965, *66*(3), 149-154.

ASHER, S., ODEN, S., and GOTTMAN, J.: Children's friendships in school settings. In L. KATZ (Ed.), *Current topics in early childhood education* (Vol. 1). Norwood, NJ: Ablex Publishing, 1977.

BAER, D. M., and WOLF, M. M.: The entry into natural communities of reinforcement. In R. Ulrich, T. Stachnik and J. Mabry (Eds.), *Control of human behavior*. Glenview, IL.: Scott Foresman, 1970.

BAER, D. M., WOLF, M. M., and RISLEY, T. R.: Some current dimensions of applied behavior analysis. *Journal of Applied Behavior Analysis*, 1968, *1*, 91-97.

BONNEY, M. E.: Assessment of effort to aid socially isolated elementary school pupils. *Journal of Educational Research*, 1971, *64*, 359-364.

BRISON, D. W.: Case studies in school psychology: A non-talking child in kindergarten: An application of behavior therapy. *Journal of School Psychology*, 1966, *4*(4), 65-69.

BRONFENBRENNER, U.: *Two worlds of childhood: U.S. and U.S.S.R.* New York: Simon & Schuster, 1970.

BUELL, J., STODDARD, P., HARRIS, F. R., and BAER, D. M.: Collateral social development accompanying reinforcement of outdoor play in a preschool child. *Journal of Applied Behavior Analysis*, 1968, *1*, 167-173.

BUSHWELL, M. M.: The relationship between social structure of the classroom and the academic success of the pupils. *Journal of Experimental Education*, 1953, *22*, 37-52.

CHARLESWORTH, R., and HARTUP, W. W.: Positive social reinforcement in the nursery school peer group. *Child Development*, 1967, *38*, 992-1002.

CLEMENT, P. W., & MILNE, D. C.: Group play therapy and tangible reinforcers used to modify the behavior of 8-year-old boys. *Behaviour Research and Therapy*, 1967, *5*, 301-312.

COBB, J. A., and HOPS, H.: Effects of academic survival skill training on low achieving first graders. *Journal of Educational Research*, 1973, *67*, 108-113.

COOK, H., and STINGLE, S.: Cooperative behavior in children. *Psychological Bulletin*, 1974, *81*, 918-933.

COOKE, T., and APOLLONI, T.: Developing positive social-emotional behaviors: A study of training and generalization effects. *Journal of Applied Behavior Analysis*, 1976, *9*, 65-78.

COSSAIRT, A., HALL, R. V., and HOPKINS, B. L.: The effects of experimenter's instructions, feedback, and praise on teacher's praise and student attending behavior. *Journal of Applied Behavior Analysis*, 1973, *6*, 89-100.

ENGELMANN, S.: The effectiveness of direct instruction on IQ performance and achievement on reading and arithmetic. In J. Hellmuth (Ed.), *Disadvantaged children* (Vol. 3). New York: Brunner/Mazel, 1970.

GARRETT, B., HOPS, H., and STEVENS, T.: *Peer interaction recording system II (PIRS II)*. Eugene: Center at Oregon for Research in the Behavioral Education of the Handicapped, University of Oregon, in preparation.

GARRETT, B., HOPS, H., TODD, N. M., and WALKER, H. M.: *The peer interaction recording system*. In H. Hops (Chair), Systematic analysis of social interaction: Assessments and interventions. Symposium presented at the 84th annual meeting of the

American Psychological Association, Washington, D.C., 1976. (ERIC Document Reproduction Service No. ED 131 937).
GOTTMAN, J. M.: The effects of a modeling film on social isolation in preschool children: A methodological investigation. *Journal of Abnormal Child Psychology*, 1977, 5, 69-78.
GREENWOOD, C. R., HOPS, H., DELQUADRI, J., and GUILD, J.: Group contingencies for group consequences in classroom management: A further analysis. *Journal of Applied Behavior Analysis*, 1974, 7, 413-425.
GREENWOOD, C. R., HOPS, H., DELQUADRI, J., and WALKER, H. M.: *Program for academic survival skills (PASS): Manual for consultants*. Eugene: Center at Oregon for Research in the Behavioral Education of the Handicapped, University of Oregon, 1974.
GREENWOOD, C. R., HOPS, H., and WALKER, H. M.: The durability of student behavior change: A comparative analysis at follow-up. *Behavior Therapy*, 1977, 8, 631-638. (a)
GREENWOOD, C. R., HOPS, H., and WALKER, H. M.: The program for academic survival skills (PASS): Effects on student behavior and achievement. *Journal of School Psychology*, 1977, 15, 25-35. (b)
GREENWOOD, C. R., WALKER, H. M., and HOPS, H.: Some issues in social interaction/withdrawal assessment. *Exceptional Children*, 1977, 43, 490-499.
GREENWOOD, C. R., WALKER, H. M., TODD, N., and HOPS, H.: *Normative descriptive analysis of preschool free play social interactions*. (Report No. 29) Eugene: Center at Oregon for Research in the Behavioral Education of the Handicapped, University of Oregon, 1976.
GREENWOOD, C. R., WALKER, H. M., TODD, N. M., and HOPS, H.: *Preschool teachers' assessments of student social interaction: Predictive success and normative data*. (Report No. 26) Eugene: Center at Oregon for Research in the Behavioral Education of the Handicapped, University of Oregon, 1976.
GUERNEY, B. F., JR., and FLUMEN, A. B.: Teachers as psychotherapeutic agents for withdrawn children. *Journal of School Psychology*, 1970, 8, 107-113.
HARTUP, W. W.: Peer interaction and social organization. In Mussen, P. H. (Ed.), *Carmichael's manual of child psychology*, Vol. II. New York: Wiley & Sons, 1970, 361-456.
HARTUP, W. W., GLAZER, J. A., and CHARLESWORTH, R.: Peer reinforcement and sociometric status. *Child Development*, 1967, 38, 1017-1024.
HOPS, H., and BEICKEL, S. L.: *CLASS: A standardized in-class program for acting-out children. I. Preliminary investigations*. (Report No. 13) Eugene: Center at Oregon for Research in the Behavioral Education of the Handicapped, University of Oregon, 1975.
HOPS, H., BEICKEL, S., and WALKER, H. M.: *Contingencies for learning academic and social skills (CLASS): Manual for consultants*. Eugene: Center at Oregon for Research in the Behavioral Education of the Handicapped, University of Oregon, 1975.
HOPS, H., and COBB, J. A.: Survival behaviors in the educational setting: Their implications for research and intervention. In L. A. Hamerlynck, L. C. Handy and E. J. Mash (Eds.), *Behavior change: Methodology, concepts, and practice*. Champaign, Ill.: Research Press, 1973, 193-208.
HOPS, H., and COBB, J. A.: Initial investigations into academic survival skill training, direct instruction, and first-grade achievement. *Journal of Educational Psychology*, 1974, 66, 548-553.
HOPS, H., FLEISCHMAN, D. H., GUILD, J., PAINE, S., WALKER, H. M., and GREENWOOD, C. R.: *Program for establishing effective relationship skills (PEERS): Teacher-consultant manual*. Eugene: Center at Oregon for Research in the Behavioral Education of

the Handicapped, University of Oregon, 1978.

Hops, H., Fleischman, D. H., and Street, A.: *Manipulating antecedent and consequent events to increase interactive behavior in primary grade socially withdrawn children.* (Report No. 34) Eugene: Center at Oregon for Research in the Behavioral Education of the Handicapped, University of Oregon, 1976.

Hops, H., Garrett, B., Todd, N. M., and Nicholes, J. S.: *The peer interaction recording system (PIRS).* Eugene: Center at Oregon for Research in the Behavioral Education of the Handicapped, University of Oregon, 1976.

Hops, H., Guild, J., Paine, S., Fleischman, D. H., Street, A., Walker, H. M., and Greenwood, C. R.: *Program for establishing effective relationship skills (PEERS): Teacher manual.* Eugene: Center at Oregon for Research in the Behavioral Education of the Handicapped, University of Oregon, 1978.

Hops, H., Paine, S., Fleischman, D. H. and Guild, J.: *Program for establishing effective relationship skills (PEERS): Consultant trainer manual.* Eugene: Center at Oregon for Research in the Behavioral Education of the Handicapped, University of Oregon, 1978.

Hops, H., Walker, H. M., Fleischman, D. H., Nagoshi, J. T., Omura, R. T., Skindrud, K., and Taylor, J.: *CLASS: A standardized in-class program for acting-out children. II. Field test evaluations. Journal of Educational Psychology,* 1978, 70, 647-655.

Israel, A. C., and O'Leary, K. D.: Developing correspondence between children's words and deeds. *Child Development,* 1973, 44, 575-581.

Johnson, T. L., Goetz, E. M., Baer, D. M., and Green, D. R.: *The effects of an experimental game on the classroom cooperative play of a preschool child.* Paper presented at the 5th Annual Southern California Conference on Behavior Modification, Los Angeles, October 1973.

Keasy, C. B.: *A longitudinal study of the relationship between cognitive and social development.* Paper presented at the meeting of the American Educational Research Association, San Francisco, April 1976.

Kirby, F. D., and Toler, H. C.: Modification of preschool isolate behavior: A case study. *Journal of Applied Behavior Analysis,* 1970, 3, 309-314.

Kuhn, T. S.: *The structure of scientific revolutions.* Chicago. The University of Chicago Press, 1962.

Lahaderne, H. M., and Jackson, P. W.: Withdrawal in the classroom: A note on some educational correlates of social desirability among school children. *Journal of Educational Psychology,* 1970, 61(2), 97-101.

Lewis, M., and Rosenblum, L. A.: *Friendship and peer relations.* New York: John Wiley & Sons, 1975.

Lippitt, R.: Popularity among preschool children. *Child Development,* 1941, 12, 305-322.

Lovaas, O. I.: *The autistic child: Language development through behavior modification.* New York: Irvington Publishers, Inc., 1977.

McKenzie, H. S.: Special education and consulting teachers. In F. W. Clark, D. R. Evans and L. A. Hamerlynck (Eds.), *Implementing behavioral programs for schools and clinics.* Champaign, Ill.: Research Press, 1972.

Meichenbaum, D. H., and Cameron, R.: Training schizophrenics to talk to themselves: A means of developing attentional controls. *Behavior Therapy,* 1973, 4, 515-534.

Michael, C. M., Morris, D. P., and Soroker, E.: Follow-up studies of shy, withdrawn children. II. Relative incidence of schizophrenia. *American Journal of Orthopsychiatry,* 1957, 27, 331-337.

Morris, D. P., Soroker, E., and Burrus, G.: Follow-up studies of shy, withdrawn children. I. Evaluation of later adjustment. *American Journal of Orthopsychiatry,* 1954, 24, 743-745.

Mueller, E.: The maintenance of verbal exchanges between young children. *Child Development,* 1972, 43, 930-938.

Mueller, E., and Brenner, J.: The origins of social skills and interaction among playgroup toddlers. *Child Development,* 1977, *48,* 854-861.
Oden, S. L., and Asher, S. R.: Coaching children in social skills for friendship making. *Child Development,* 1977, *48,* 495-506.
O'Connor, R. D.: Modification of social withdrawal through symbolic modeling. *Journal of Applied Behavior Analysis,* 1969, *2,* 15-22.
O'Connor, R. D.: The relative efficacy of modeling, shaping, and the combined procedures for the modification of social withdrawal. *Journal of Abnormal Psychology,* 1972, *79*(3), 327-334.
O'Leary, S. G., and O'Leary, K. D.: Behavior modification in the school. In H. Leitenberg (Ed.), *Handbook of behavior modification.* Englewood Cliffs, NJ: Prentice-Hall, Inc., 1976.
Parker, C. A. (Ed.): *Helping teachers meet special needs.* Minneapolis, Minn.: Leadership Training Institute/Special Education, University of Minnesota, 1975.
Patterson, G. R.: Interventions for boys with conduct problems: Multiple settings, treatments, and criteria. *Journal of Consulting and Clinical Psychology,* 1974, *42,* 471-481.
Patterson, G. R., Reid, J. B., Jones, R. R. and Conger, R. E.: *A social learning approach to family intervention (Vol. 1): Families with aggressive children.* Eugene, Oregon: Castalia Publishing Co., 1975.
Patterson, G. R., McNeal, S., Hawkins, N., and Phelps, R.: Reprogramming the social environment. *Journal of Child Psychology and Psychiatry,* 1967, *8,* 181-195.
Patterson, G. R., and Reid, J. B.: Reciprocity and coercion: Two facets of social systems. In C. Neuringer and J. Michael (Eds.), *Behavior modification in clinical psychology.* New York: Appleton-Century-Crofts, 1970.
Phillips, E. L., Phillips, E. A., Fixsen, D. L., and Wolf, M. M.: Achievement place: Modification of the behaviors of pre-delinquent boys within a token economy. *Journal of Applied Behavior Analysis,* 1971, *4,* 45-49.
Phillips, E. L., Phillips, E. A., Fixsen, D. L., and Wolf, M. M.: *The teaching family handbook.* Lawrence: University of Kansas Printing Service, 1972.
Reid, J. B., Hawkins, N., Keutzer, C., McNeal, S. A., Phelps, R. E., Reid, K. M., and Mees, H. L.: A marathon behavior modification of a selectively mute child. *Journal of Child Psychology and Psychiatry,* 1967, *8,* 27-30.
Risley, T. R., and Hart, B.: Developing correspondence between the nonverbal and verbal behavior of preschool children. *Journal of Applied Behavior Analysis,* 1968, *1,* 267-281.
Rogers-Warren, A., and Baer, D. M.: Correspondence between saying and doing: Teaching children to share and praise. *Journal of Applied Behavior Analysis,* 1976, *9,* 335-354.
Shores, R. E., and Strain, P. S.: Social reciprocity: A review of research and educational implications. *Exceptional Children,* 1977, *43,* 526-530.
Strain, P. S., Cooke, T. P., and Apolloni, T.: *Teaching exceptional children: Assessing and modifying social behavior.* New York: Academic Press, Inc., 1976.
Strain, P. S., Shores, R. E., and Kerr, M. A.: An experimental analysis of "spillover" effects on the social interactions of behaviorally handicapped preschool children. *Journal of Applied Behavior Analysis,* 1976, *9,* 31-40.
Strain, P. S., Shores, R. E., and Timm, M. A.: An experimental analysis of peer-delivered social initiations on the social behavior of behaviorally handicapped preschool children. *Journal of Applied Behavior Analysis,* 1977, *10,* 289-298.
Tharp, R. G., and Wetzel, R. J.: *Behavior modification in the natural environment.* New York: Academic Press, 1969.
Tyler, J. L.: Developing training packages. *Exceptional Children,* 1973, *39,* 405-407.
Wahler, R. G.: Child-child interactions in free field setting: Some experimental

analysis. *Journal of Experimental Child Psychology,* 1967, *5,* 278-293.
WALDROP, M. G., and HALVERSON, C. F.: Intensive and extensive peer behavior: Longitudinal and cross-sectional analysis. *Child Development,* 1975, *45,* 19-26.
WALKER, H. M. The Walker problem behavior identification checklist. Los Angeles: Western Psychological Services, Inc., 1970.
WALKER, H. M., GREENWOOD, C. R., HOPS, H., and TODD, N. M.: Differential effects of reinforcing topographic components of free play social interaction: Analysis and systematic replication. *Behavior Modification,* in press.
WALKER, H. M., and HOPS, H.: The use of group and individual reinforcement contingencies in the modification of social withdrawal. In L. A. Hamerlynck, L. C. Handy and E. J. Mash (Eds.), *Behavior change: Methodology, concepts, and practice.* Champaign, IL: Research Press, 1973.
WALKER, H. M., and HOPS, H.: Use of normative peer data as a standard for evaluating classroom treatment effects. *Journal of Applied Behavior Analysis,* 1976, *9,* 159-168.
WALKER, H. M., HOPS, H., and GREENWOOD, C. R.: Competency based training issues in the development of behavioral management packages for specific classroom behavior disorders. *Behavioral Disorders,* 1976, *1*(2), 112-122.
WALKER, H. M., HOPS, H., and GREENWOOD, C. R.: *CORBEH: An R & D model for the systematic development of behavioral intervention packages.* (Report No. 35) Eugene: Center at Oregon for Research in the Behavioral Education of the Handicapped, University of Oregon, 1978.
WEINROTT, M. R., CORSON, J. A., and WILCHESKY, M.: Teacher mediated treatment of social withdrawal. *Behavior Therapy,* in press.

Section II

FAMILY ENVIRONMENTS

5
An Intensive, Home-Based Family Training Program for Developmentally-Delayed Children

Edward R. Christophersen
and
Bobby W. Sykes

Many families with identified high-risk children are so overburdened with day-to-day responsibilities that they have no opportunity to stimulate their children in the home environment (Haus & Thompson, 1976). The introduction of new stimulation programs through community agencies frequently does benefit those children and families in the program; however, when the program ends, there is rapid erosion of the gains (Jason, 1975; Bronfenbrenner, 1975).

Tjossem (1976) stated that the parents of high-risk children should be the prime target for early intervention because they can be the primary mediators of the intervention technology and they most often bring the child to the attention of services.

In home-based interventions, the participants remain together and the momentum of the program insures some degree of continuity. In addition, when siblings are present in the home, they, too, receive the benefits of a home-intervention program. Bronfenbrenner (1975) emphasized the importance of (1) early screening, (2) intervention aimed at improving the parent-child interactions, since the parent is such an

---

This research was supported by a grant (HD 03144) from the National Institute of Child Health and Human Development to the Bureau of Child Research, University of Kansas. These data are from the Master's Thesis submitted by Bobby Sykes to the Department of Human Development, University of Kansas.

important part of a child's development, and (3) family-centered intervention, carried out in the natural home, with actual parent-child interaction as opposed to simulated interaction.

Christophersen, Barnard, Ford and Wolf (1976) described an intensive, in-home behavior management program for working with families whose children exhibited behavior problems. The present study extends this technology for behavior-disordered children to include children with developmental delays.

METHOD

Participants

Three children were the subjects in this study. Each child resided with his parents in his natural home. All three subjects were essentially nonverbal. Of the three subjects, one (Peter) was diagnosed by a neurologist as being mildly retarded, while the other two (Gene and Andy) were both suspected of having some degree of retardation by medical personnel familiar with their medical histories. Due to the severity of their problems, all three children had experienced great difficulty in finding therapeutic help.

Peter, age five, had been referred to a university medical center for the following problem behaviors: spitting, cursing, throwing objects, slamming doors, always running and general disobedience. The child was mildly retarded and had crossed eyes, the result of which was double vision. Prior to the time of this study, Peter had been rejected from at least three preschools (facilities for both normal and retarded children) because of his uncontrollable problem behaviors and noncompliance.

Gene, age three and one-half, had been referred to a university medical center for essentially noncompliant behavior. In addition, the child had tantrums, was nonattentive and walked with an infantile gait, stumbling constantly. Gene's medical history revealed a partial cleft palate (which was believed to be responsible for his constant drooling) and possible neurological damage as diagnosed by physicians at the medical center. Until the time of this study, the extent of Gene's learning capabilities was almost unknown because of his refusal to comply with instructions and the resulting difficulty in testing him.

Andy was a three-year-old boy who had been referred to a university medical center primarily for nonattentive and noncompliant behavior. He was a withdrawn child who cried a lot and preferred to be left alone. Prior to this study the child was not toilet trained, ate only baby food (which had to be fed to him) and still drank from a baby bottle. Andy also engaged in autistic-like hand clapping behaviors and made almost no attempts to play with toys or roam about the house.

Setting

The treatment and observation techniques used in this study were conducted in the natural home of each subject. Peter lived in a small three-bedroom house with his mother, grandmother and younger brother, age three. Peter's mother was on welfare.

Gene resided with his mother, brother (age 10) and sister (age 12). Their home was a three-bedroom, two-story house which was part of a housing complex. His mother was divorced and held a full-time job.

Andy lived with both parents and three brothers (ages seven, nine and 10) in a low income housing project. The family was on welfare.

Behavior Code and Recording

Since the treatment portion of this study was aimed at increasing the number of appropriate parent-child interactions as well as reducing the number of inappropriate interactions and child behaviors, a simple global rating system was devised.

A positive interaction was defined: "When the parent has a pleasant facial expression and/or talks to the child in a calm manner with no note of agitation or disgust in his/her voice. Included are praise statements and times when there are little or no verbal exchanges but interactions such as playing occur. Instructions followed by praise statements come under this category. An example of such an instruction is, 'John, point to your nose, please; that's a good boy.'"

A negative interaction was defined: "When the parent shows facial signs of agitation and/or disgust and/or shouts at the child or reprimands him in a harsh way. Any interaction not considered positive will be scored negative."

Not attending was defined: "When the parent is not attending to the child in any way, verbally or socially, e.g., ignoring the child."

In addition to the global ratings, parental commands and child compliance were defined: "Commands or requests directed toward the child and compliance in the same time interval. If more than one command is given in one interval, record the first one. Requested verbal imitation by the parent is not to be counted."

Parent-child interactions were recorded during pretreatment and posttreatment phases of this study. All recordings were made in the natural home at prearranged, randomly selected times. The parents were instructed to make no special preparation for the recording sessions. Once a recording session was begun, the video equipment was run continually unless something out of the ordinary but not connected with the study interrupted the session, e.g., the parent or child having to go to the bathroom.

For one subject, Andy, midtreatment observations were substituted for posttreatment observations because the severity of his problems necessitated very lengthy treatment. The maximum time of these videotape recordings was 25 minutes, with the average time being approximately 20 minutes. The scoring of these tapes was done by the experimenter and one other observer, independently of one another. Seventy-five percent of all the observation sessions was subjected to reliability checks with at least the first 20 minutes of the session being viewed and scored by both the experimenter and the second observer.

Each tape was viewed simultaneously with a time tape which played alternately an audible 10-second tone followed by 10 seconds of silence (cf. Quilitch, 1972). Interactions were observed during the tone and recorded during the silence.

Reliability was computed by dividing agreements plus disagreements into the number of agreements.

Design and Treatment

A modified multiple baseline design (Baer, Wolf, & Risley, 1968) was utilized across subjects for recorded problem behaviors. The treatment employed was carried out by the therapist in the natural home (cf. Christophersen, Barnard, Ford, & Wolf, 1976). For each subject, in addition to the treatment conducted in the home, a similar program was instituted in the preschool which he attended.

A complete description of the treatment techniques employed is given by Christophersen, Barnard and Barnard (1977a, 1977b). Since the main objective of the treatment was to increase the number of positive parent-child interactions, an attempt was made to increase those behaviors acceptable to the parents and at the same time reduce or eliminate undesirable behaviors. It was thought that this would cause the parents to react more favorably towards the child. The parents were taught to reward behaviors which they considered appropriate and to punish those behaviors which they considered to be inappropriate. Positive rewards consisted of smiles, hugs, verbal praise, playful touches (e.g., tickles), as well as edible substances such as candy, cookies, ice cream and fruit juices. A brief time-out (two or three minutes) or verbal reprimand served as punishment for these subjects. Occasionally, the parents would have to administer a spanking in addition to the other forms of punishment.

Results

The observation sessions in this study produced 24 videotapes. These tapes were the product of both pretreatment and posttreatment observations (midtreatment observations in the case of Andy).

For the purpose of computing reliability, a number was assigned to every tape (both pre- and posttreatment) of each subject. The numbers for one subject were then mixed together and the order of scoring randomly selected. This was done in an attempt to conceal the treatment phase of each tape from the observer (i.e., to randomize the viewing of pre- and posttreatment tapes). It was hoped that possible observer bias could be kept to a minimum by using this procedure. In principle, this procedure is identical to what Rosenthal (1966) calls "blind contact" (concealment of the treatment condition).

Reliability was computed on the occurrence or non-occurrence of the target interactions and commands and compliance. The range of reliability for data on Peter was between 60% and 100%, with the mean reliability being 88%. These figures are based on the scoring of five videotapes. Reliability was computed on eight tapes for Andy. The range was from 0% to 100%, with a mean reliability of 89%. For Gene, seven tapes were checked for reliability. Reliability estimates ranged from 67% to 100%, with a mean reliability of 86%.

Figure 1 shows the percent of intervals during pretreatment and posttreatment (or midtreatment) which were scored as containing a positive parent-child interaction. As the line drawn through the means of each treatment phase indicates, there was a noticeable increase in the percentage of positive interactions between each subject and his

POSITIVE PARENT–CHILD INTERACTIONS

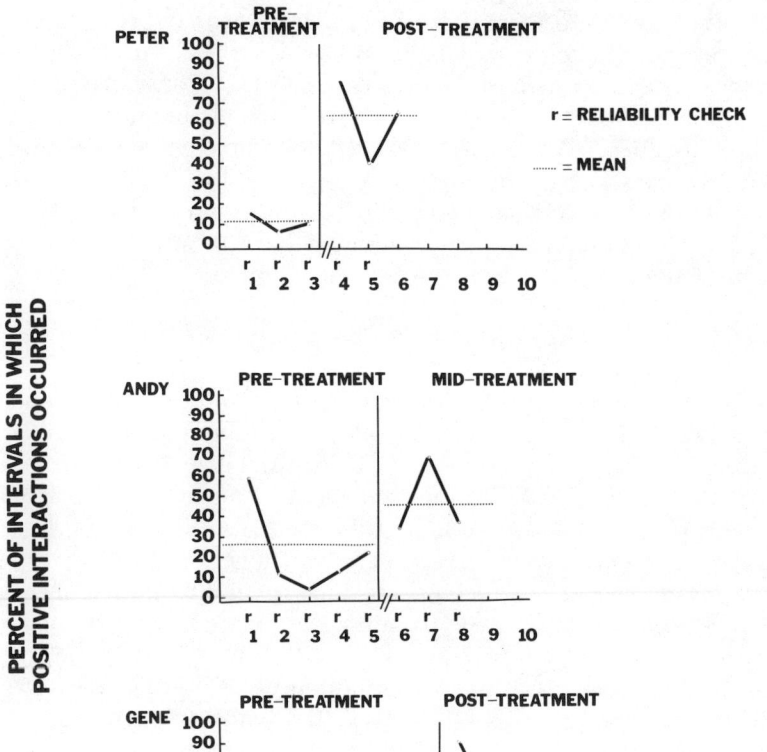

Figure 1. Positive parent-child interactions

parents. For Peter, the mean percentage rose from 11% to 63% (range: pre, 6% to 16%; post, 41% to 83%); for Andy, from 26% to 45% (range: pre, 3% to 59%; mid, 33% to 67%) and for Gene, from 27% to 73% (range: pre, 9% to 45%; post, 59% to 90%).

NEGATIVE PARENT–CHILD INTERACTIONS

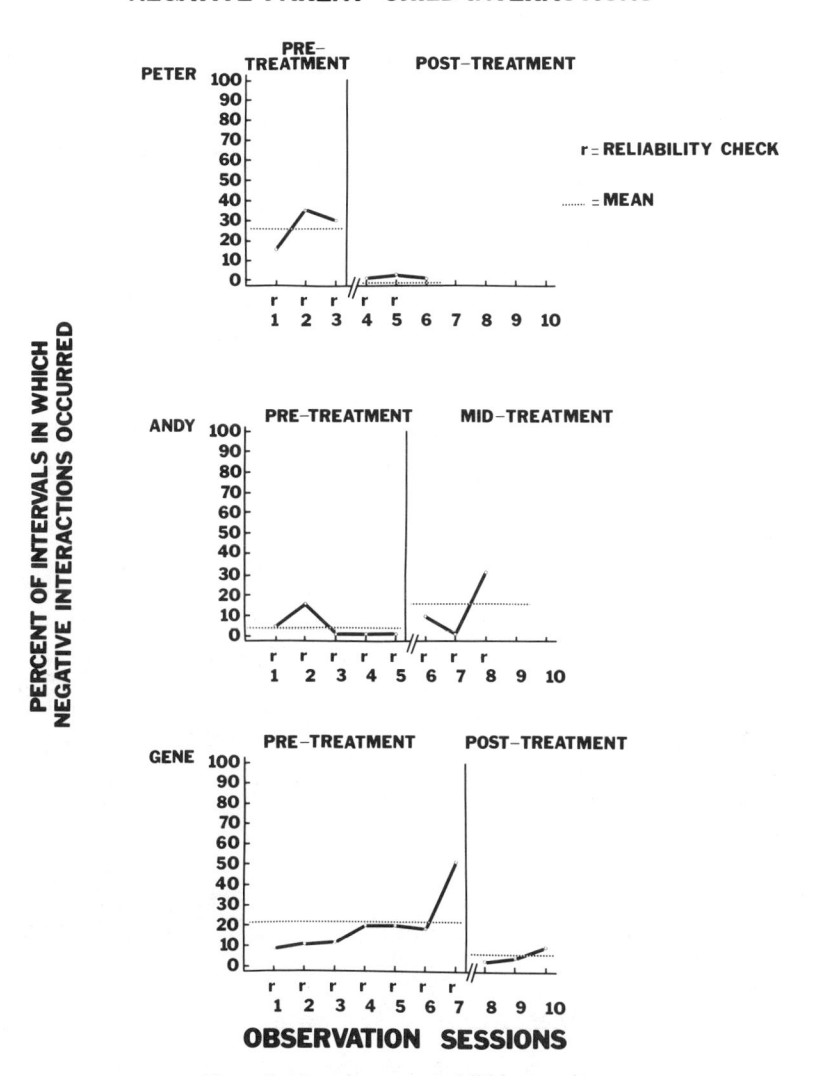

Figure 2. Negative parent-child interactions

Figure 2 shows the percent of intervals which were scored as containing a negative parent-child interaction. For two subjects a trend is shown toward a reduction in the number of negative interactions in the posttreatment phase. Peter's mean percentage dropped from 27%

PARENTAL NON-ATTENDING

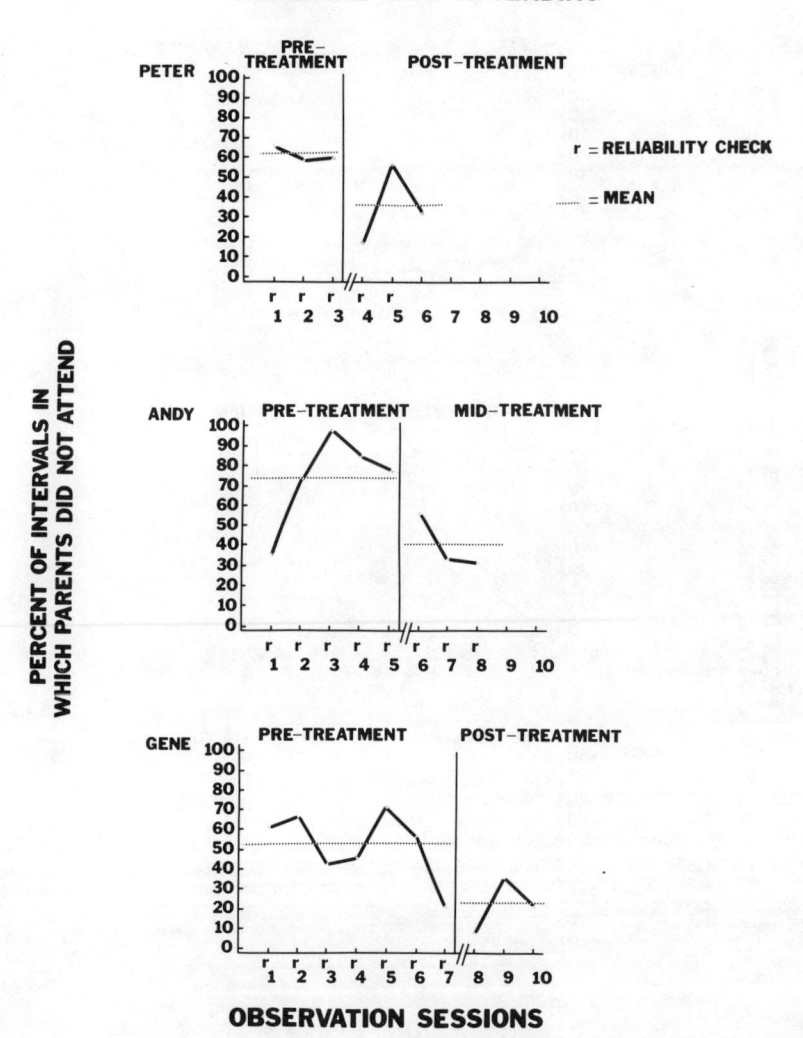

Figure 3. Parental non-attending

(pre) to less than 1% (post) with a range of 17% to 35% (pre) and 0% to 2% (post). Gene's pretreatment mean of 20% for negative interactions dropped to 5% during posttreatment with a range of 9% to 52% (pre) and 2% to 10% (post). In the case of Andy (whose treatment is

COMMANDS

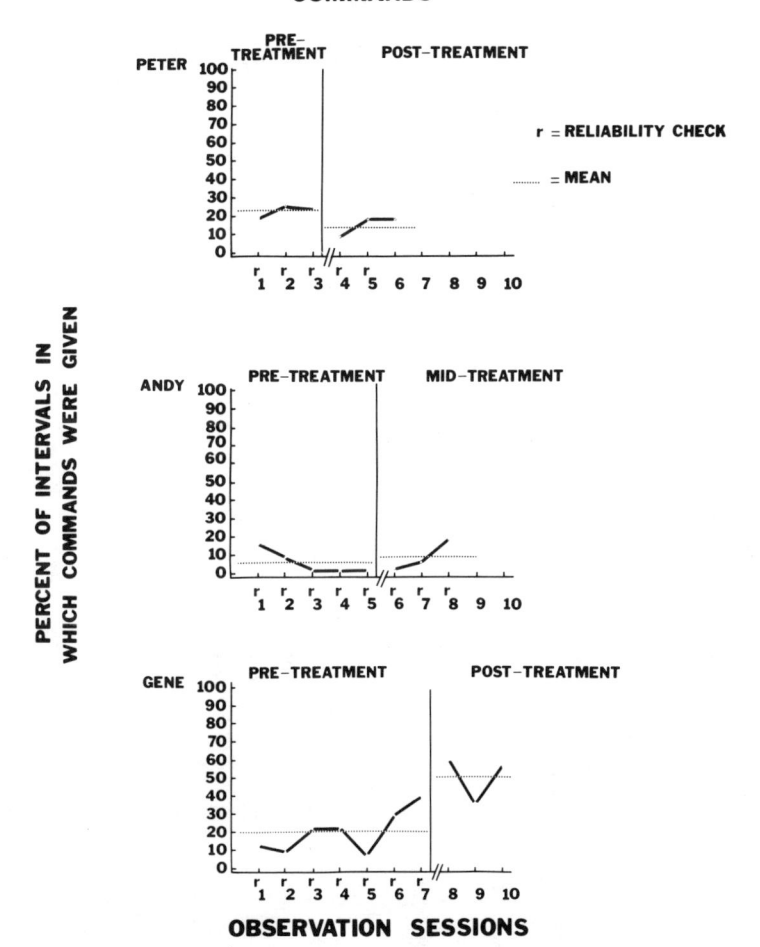

Figure 4. Commands, the percent of intervals in which commands were given

incomplete as of this writing) the data showed an increase in the mean percentage of negative interactions from pretreatment (4%) to mid-treatment (14%). His range was 0% to 13% (pre) and 0% to 32% (mid).

Figure 3 represents the percentage of time during an observation session in which the parent is not attending at all to the subject. As might be expected, each pretreatment session is characterized by a

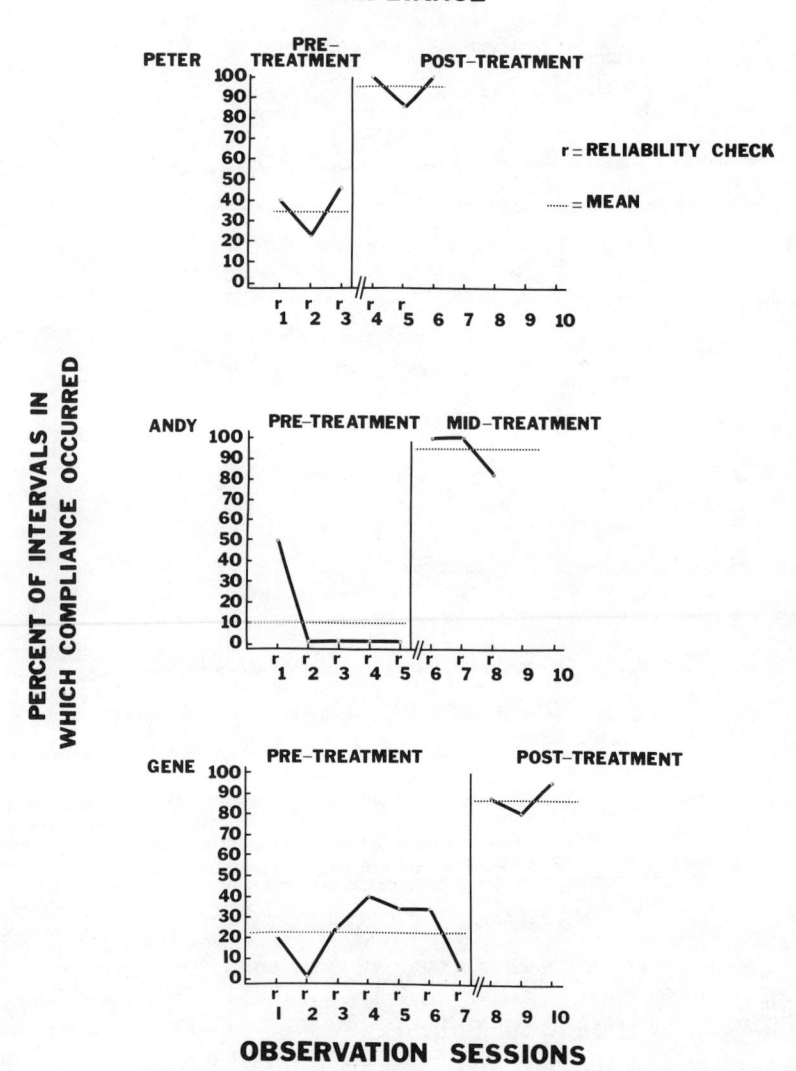

Figure 5. Compliance, the percent of intervals in which commands were complied with

fairly high percentage of nonattending behavior on the part of the parents. During one pretreatment session with Andy, the mother was nonattending 97% of the total observation period. The means for each child were: Peter—62% (pre) (range: 59% to 67%), 36% (post) (range: 17% to 57%); Andy—74% (pre) (range: 36% to 97%), 41% (mid) (range: 32% to 57%); Gene—52% (pre) (range: 21% to 71%), 22% (post) (range: 8% to 37%). Each mother attended more to the subject child in posttreatment than during pretreatment.

The percent of intervals in which commands were given are shown in Figure 4. It was thought that this information might show some relation to parental attending behavior or to the type and degree of dominant interaction (positive or negative). No such relationship could be found. The data are presented to possibly offer more information for comparison with the compliance graphs (Figure 5).

The information on compliance in Figure 5 shows substantial differences between the pretreatment and posttreatment means. For Peter, a dramatic difference of 36% compliance during pretreatment and 95% during posttreatment was shown. The range was 23% to 46% (pre) and 86% to 100% (post). Data on Andy show a mean level of 10% during pretreatment, contrasted with 94% at midtreatment, with a range of 0% to 50% (pre) and 82% to 100% (mid). Gene's data showed a mean of 22% (pretreatment) and 88% (posttreatment) with a range of 0% to 40% (pre) and 80% to 95% (post).

Discussion

The present study is an analysis of the effectiveness of a home-based behavioral intervention program (Christophersen et al., 1976) for use with developmentally delayed children. The intervention was successful at (1) increasing positive parent-child interactions in all three child-parent pairs, (2) decreasing negative interactions in two of the three pairs. (3) decreasing parent nonattending in all three pairs, (4) increasing child compliance to reasonable parent commands, while actually (5) reducing the number of commands given by the parents.

That these procedures were successful with developmentally delayed children is important for two reasons. One is that these results support the extension of the Family Training Program Model (Christophersen et al., 1977a) to include an important clinical population (developmentally delayed children). The Family Training Program Model has already been adapted for use with families referred for abuse and neglect (Christophersen, Kuehn, Grinstead, Barnard, Rainey, & Kuehn, 1976) and for families referred for juvenile delinquency (Barnard, Gant, Kuehn, Jones, & Christophersen, in preparation).

The second reason is that both testing and intervention programs for developmentally delayed children are often hampered by the child's exhibiting behavior problems. Lack of compliance on the child's part can frequently invalidate the results of a testing program and can lead to unnecessary frustration on the part of the change agent (whether parent or other therapist). The authors have noted, from their clinical experience, that behavior problems are frequently much easier and quicker to resolve than developmental delays. Once the therapist has taught the parents how to manage the presenting behavior problems, the parents (1) have much more confidence in the competence of the therapist and (2) find it easier to deal with the delays since they are not confounded by behavioral problems.

The Family Training Program Model follows Bronfenbrenner's (1975) recommendations by dealing directly with the parent-child interactions in the natural home, with a behaviorally based treatment program. Although this model has been demonstrably effective in dealing with behavior problems in the developmentally delayed child, the efficacy of this model for the treatment of the actual delays has yet to be demonstrated.

REFERENCES

BAER, D. M., WOLF, M. M., and RISLEY, T. R.: Some current dimensions of applied behavior analysis. *Journal of Applied Behavior Analysis,* 1968, *1* (1), 91-97.

BARNARD, J.D., GANT, B.L., KUEHN, F.E., JONES, H.H., and CHRISTOPHERSEN, E.R.: Home-based treatment of the juvenile probationer. In preparation.

BRONFENBRENNER, U.: *A Report on Longitudinal Evaluations of Preschool Programs. Vol. II: Is Early Intervention Effective?* Washington, D.C.: DHEW Publication No. (OHD) 76-30025, 1975.

CHRISTOPHERSEN, E.R., BARNARD, S.R., and BARNARD, J.D.: *The Family Training Program Manual: The Home Chip System.* Kansas City, Ks.: University Printing Service, 1977. (a)

CHRISTOPHERSEN, E.R., BARNARD, S.R., and BARNARD, J.D.: *The Family Training Program Manual: The Home Point System.* Kansas City, Ks.: University Printing Service, 1977. (b)

CHRISTOPHERSEN, E.R., BARNARD, J.D., FORD, D., and WOLF, M.M.: The family training program: Improving parent-child interaction patterns. In Mash, E.J., Handy,

L.C., & Hamerlynck, L.A. (Eds.) *Behavior Modification Approaches to Parenting.* New York: Brunner/Mazel, 1976.

CHRISTOPHERSEN, E.R., KUEHN, B.S., GRINSTEAD, J.D., BARNARD, J.D., RAINEY, S.K., and KUEHN, F.E.: A family training program for abuse and neglect families. *Journal of Pediatric Psychology,* Spring 1976, 90-94.

HAUS, B.F., and THOMPSON, S.: The effect of nursing intervention on a program of behavior modification by parents in the home. *Journal of Psychiatric Nursing and Mental Health Services,* August 1976, *14*(8).

JASON, L.: Early secondary prevention with disadvantaged preschool children. *American Journal of Community Psychology,* March 1975, *3*(1).

PATTERSON, G.R. and COBB, J.A.: A dyadic analysis of "aggressive" behaviors. In J.P. Hill (Ed.) *Minnesota Symposia on Child Psychology, Vol. V.* Minneapolis: University of Minnesota Press, 1971, 72-129.

PATTERSON, G. R., COBB, J. A., and RAY, R.S.: A social engineering technology for retraining aggressive boys. In H. Adams and L. Unikel (Eds.) *Georgia Symposium in Experimental Clinical Psychology, Vol. II.* Springfield, Ill.: Charles C. Thomas, 1972.

QUILITCH, H.R.: A portable, programmed audible timer. *Journal of Applied Behavior Analysis,* 1972, *5*(1), 18.

ROSENTHAL, R.: *Experimenter Effects in Behavioral Research.* New York: Appleton-Century-Crofts, 1966.

TJOSSEM, T.D. (Ed.): *Intervention Strategies for High Risk Infants and Young Children.* Baltimore: University Park Press, 1976 (NICHD-Mental Retardation Research Center Series).

6
The Insular Family: A Deviance Support System for Oppositional Children

ROBERT G. WAHLER, GEORGE LESKE
and
EDWIN S. ROGERS

Strategies for helping troubled families have seen considerable growth in the field of behavior modification. Typically focusing on the children of such families, a good many empirical studies of the helping process have yielded encouraging results. We now know that a most feasible means of dealing with the problem is to "re-educate" parents (see Patterson, 1976). That is, if the parents of disturbed children can be taught to employ some principles of operant learning theory (à la Bijou & Baer, 1961), desirable changes will occur in the children and in child-parent relationships (e.g., Hawkins, Peterson, Schweid & Bijou, 1966; Wahler, 1969).

The re-education model of family intervention has been primarily concerned with child referral problems that might be classified as *oppositional behavior* (Wahler, 1968). And with good reason since children whose behavior problems constitute refusals to comply with parent and community rule systems (e.g. noncompliance, stealing, fighting) are today's most common referrals to mental health centers (Taplin & Reid, 1975). In addition, several follow-up studies of childhood behavior disorders reveal that chronic oppositional behavior in the pre-adolescent years is a good predictor of adolescent and adult prob-

---

The research data reported in this paper were generated by support from grant MH 18516 from the National Institute of Mental Health, Crime and Delinquency Section.

The Insular Family

lems (Robins, 1966; Roff, 1961). Thus, the focus on oppositional children in family treatment might be expected.

Re-education as a parent intervention strategy has been refined to the point that the parameters of intervention are now well mapped out with respect to the oppositional child. Several variables have emerged as factors important to the success of most such treatment programs.

(1) *Programs should be environment specific.* This variable refers to an emphasis on aiming the treatment program to that environmental setting where the presenting problems have emerged. In reference to a troubled family, this setting would obviously be the home. This is not to say that parent instruction through written presentation of material (Patterson, 1975), modeling (Hanf, 1969) or didactic verbal interchanges (Patterson, Cobb & Ray, 1973) should not occur outside the home. Rather, it means that the content of the instruction must relate specifically to those child-parent interchanges considered deviant in the home. In addition, chances of treatment success are greater if feedback on parent performance is provided in the home setting (Forehand, 1977).

(2) *In reference to the re-education process, it appears important to focus on both the antecedents and consequences of the child's oppositional behavior.* First, consider the importance of antecedent events. The parents of oppositional children commonly note that the child's problem behaviors tend to be specific to certain environmental conditions (e.g., when a parent ignores the child; when the family is getting ready to leave the house in the morning; see Wahler & Cormier, 1970). In fact, Patterson's pioneering work in the objective analysis of antecedent and consequental events supports the need to examine the functional properties of antecedent stimuli. His studies (see Patterson, 1976) indicate that parental cueing behaviors (such as disapproval) account for as much, *if not more,* of the variance in child problem behaviors as do parent dispensed consequences. For example, in one of Patterson's experimental analyses of a mother-son problem interaction (Patterson & Whalen, 1978), the boy's chronic nagging and whining were shown to be most clearly under the stimulus control of a maternal discriminative cue pattern—time periods when the mother was required to ignore her child.

The practical importance of studying parent cue patterns in problem interchanges is seen in studies aimed at altering one such set of parent cues. This set, comprised of parental *instructions,* is a necessary antecedent event for the most common problem behavior of oppositional children—noncompliance (Forehand, 1977). Several investigators have shown it useful to teach parents to reduce the number of instructions they dispense to their children (Mash & Terdal, 1973), and to improve the clarity of the instructions (Forehand, Peed & Roberts, 1975). Such alterations appear therapeutic in the sense that child compliance is more likely to occur.

(3) *A final factor of crucial significance in the re-education process centers on the pattern of parental consequences for the oppositional child's behavior.* It now appears that *punishment,* as well as reinforcement, may be a necessary ingredient in the family treatment program. While the family literature has documented the therapeutic use of reinforcement alone (e.g. Herbert & Baer, 1972), the likelihood that a singular use of this contingency will modify chronic oppositional behavior is bleak. Wahler (1968) trained the parents of five families in the use of differential approval, producing probable reinforcement for the children's non-oppositional behaviors. However, results showed that this procedure was ineffective in modifying the children's oppositional actions. Only when a time-out contingency was applied did desirable changes in oppositional behavior occur. Similar results were obtained by Herbert, Pinkston, Hayden, Sajwaj, Pinkston, Cordua and Jackson (1973) and Budd, Green and Baer (1976).

It is important to note that all three of the above reinforcement-alone treatment failures used parent approval as a hoped for reinforcer. It may be that nonsocial stimuli such as money and television could have produced more desirable outcomes. In the absence of such data, however, punishment has become a "tool of the trade" in family treatment programs. While time-out (with release contingent on quiet behavior; Hobbs & Forehand, 1975) is the preferred tactic, social disapproval also appears to be an effective means of suppressing oppositional behavior (Doleys, Wells, Hobbs, Roberts & Cartelli, 1976).

The Durability of Therapeutic Effects

One of the most important questions to ask of any therapeutic procedure concerns its effectiveness over time. Granted that a treatment package addressing the above three factors can produce desirable changes in troubled families, how long will these changes persist? Unfortunately, answers to this question have been sparsely doled out in the literature. With only a few exceptions (Walker & Buckley, 1972; Herbert & Baer, 1972; Johnson & Christensen, 1975), the bulk of family treatment studies have failed to include follow-up phases in their data collection. And, as Forehand and Atkeson (in press) have concluded in their survey article, there appears to be an inverse relationship between the rigor of follow-up assessment and evidence of treatment durability. Independent, direct assessments of child-parent interactions in follow-up (e.g. Patterson, 1975) indicate that not all families are able to maintain therapeutic changes without continued help. Certainly, at this time the question of treatment durability cannot be considered answered across *all* troubled families.

A rather pessimistic view on the durability issue was recently put forward by Wahler, Berland and Leske (1975). These investigators conducted an evaluative assessment of a highly regarded residential-community intervention program for oppositional pre-adolescent and adolescent children. This behavioral program, called *Riverbend*, emphasized building social and academic skills in the children, and re-education experiences for their parents. Despite the fact that the sample of 30 children made large behavioral gains in residence, most of the sample (82%) regressed back to their initial presenting problems within one year of follow-up.

Because of the unexpectedly poor durability of treatment change in the Riverbend study, the authors began to speculate on differences that might account for the follow-up failure of this program compared to more successful programs (e.g. Patterson, 1975). One obvious difference centered on the amount of consultation time spent in the parent re-education process. Since the bulk of the Riverbend program was residential, little time could be devoted to home-based parent training. Recently, a similar accountability study of residential programs for oppositional children showed follow-up failures strikingly close to the Riverbend program (Residential Community Corrections Programs, 1975).

A second difference between the Riverbend program and other re-education programs might well have been in characteristics of the subject sample. Of interest here was the finding that most of the Riverbend children were referred for treatment by their public school and juvenile court officials rather than their parents—even though the parents also viewed the children as deviant at home. One might thus speculate that parent motivation to change child behavior was lacking. In reference to this point it should be noted that most of these parents were experiencing a good many more problems than those stemming from their children. Many were single parents who were poorly educated, economically disadvantaged, and living in sections of the county noted for a high crime rate, crowded living conditions and poverty.

Clearly, it would appear that residential treatment programs alone are insufficient to insure the maintenance of treatment gains—at least when aimed at children like those in the Riverbend sample. One also wonders about the long-term success of intensive parent re-education programs for such a sample, given the sparsely reported follow-up evidence in the literature. We must close this section with the time-worn conclusion, "Further research is needed."

The Child Behavior Institute: Some New Studies of Treatment Durability

A few years ago, the National Institute of Mental Health, Crime and Delinquency Section, funded the Child Behavior Institute—a group of investigators aimed at examining a variety of generalization problems with respect to oppositional children and their families. Up to that point, the first author of this paper had already begun to accumulate generalization data on oppositional children from families quite dissimilar to those in the Riverbend sample. Essentially, the first author's sample was composed of middle-class families, the parents of which had initiated the help-seeking process. With the recent NIMH funding, generalization questions broaded to include children from more disadvantaged families as well.

The studies presented in this paper are focused on one important aspect of generalization problems: treatment durability or the generalization of therapeutic changes over time. In line with the durability issues discussed earlier, the authors suspected that certain family characteristics of oppositional children would be key determinants of treatment durability. That is, it may be that the maintenance of therapeutic change is a function of family living conditions; the more severe these conditions are, the more unlikely it is that therapeutic change will be maintained over time.

Study I: A Comparison of Treatment Durability in High and Low Risk Families

Several years ago, sociologists documented a correlational relationship between the delinquent behaviors of children and a set of family characteristics the authors term "high risk." According to the sociological studies, oppositional children who attract most of a community's formal agency attention come from families marked by poverty, poor education, single parents, and residence in areas of a city hampered by high crime rates and crowded living conditions (Shaw & McKay, 1969). Now, whether or not the children of such families do, in fact, present more serious forms of oppositional behavior is unclear (Hirschi, 1969; Empey & Lubeck, 1971). It is clear, however, that the bulk of legal agency attention (i.e., police and juvenile court) and helping agency attention (e.g., mental health center) is devoted to the high risk family. It seems reasonable to assume that oppositional children from high risk families are less likely to "outgrow" their rule-violating or oppositional actions. Given this assumption, it is also reasonable to speculate that behavior change programs geared to these families will not have the durability of similar programs aimed at "low risk" families (those having few of the sociological characteristics just presented).

Table 1 presents demographic characteristics of two areas of a single city studied by the Child Behavior Institute. The high risk area fits all of the sociological descriptors of families who are most likely to attract social agency attention. Another important difference between the families in these two communities centers on the source of problem child referrals to the Child Behavior Institute (CBI). In the low risk community, all referrals were initiated by the children's parents. In the high risk community, all referrals stemmed from the concerns of public school officials. Following a school referral, it was up to CBI staff to contact the parents and ask whether or not they perceived home-based problems with the child.

Over a three-year time period, a sample of nine families was accumulated in the low risk community, while eight families composed the high risk sample. It is of interest to note the percentage of referrals in which the parents remained with the CBI program through the intervention or treatment phase. The nine low risk families represent 100% of the initial referrals; the eight high risk families completing treatment, however, were little more than 50% of the initial referrals. About half of those families not completing treatment were "dropouts" at various points in the CBI program. The other half declined to enter the program because the parents did not perceive the children as deviant at home.

Figure 1 depicts the presenting problems of the children as reported by the parents in both community samples. Some differences are obvious. Those behavior problems reported to occur outside the immediate presence of a parent were more commonly noted by parents in the high risk sample. Strangely enough, however, the low risk parents reported three times as many problems with their children within the confines of parent-child interchanges. According to interviewer reports, the absence of noncompliance and temper outbursts in the high risk families may have been due to fewer rules and instructions set by the parents.

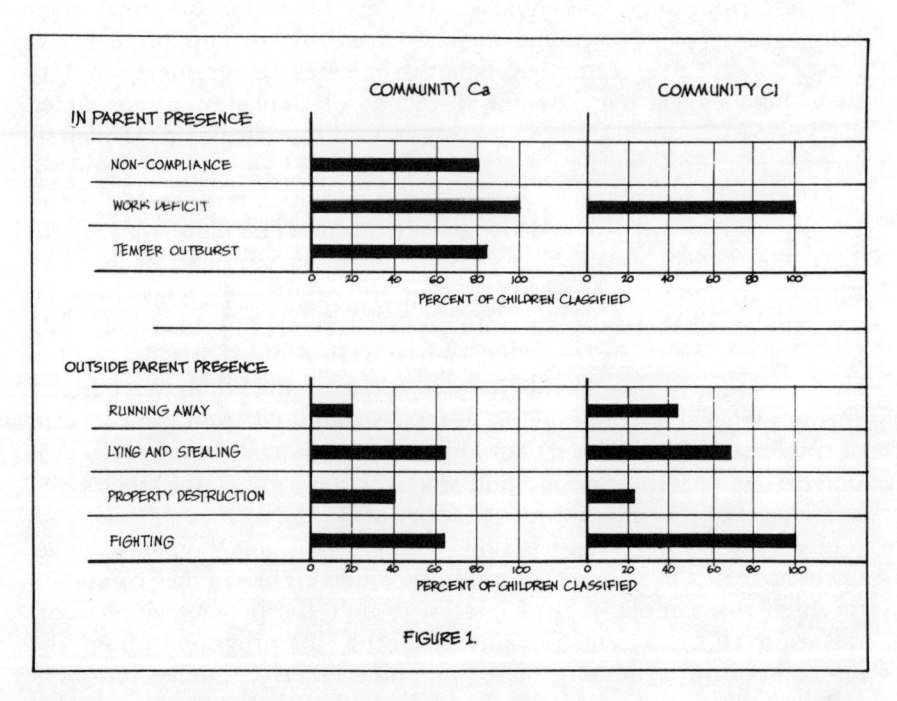

Figure 1. A schematic portrayal of child behavior problems in a low risk (Ca) and a high risk (C1) community. These referral problems were obtained through parent interviews.

Table 1.
Demographic Information for Low and High Risk Communities

	Low Risk Community	High Risk Community
Geographic Area	200 acres	45 acres
Average Yearly Income	$7000.00	$1400.00
Welfare Recipients	None	70%
Average Educational Grade Level Attained	High School	Elementary School
Both Parents in Home	80%	10%
Average Police Contacts Per Day	.2	12
Average Juvenile Court Petitions Per Year	5	20
Average Number of Mental Health Center Referrals per Year	20	200

Baseline assessment procedures were somewhat different for the two family samples. In both samples, direct observations were made of family interactions at home. These were based on a standardized coding system (SOC) developed by Wahler, House and Stambaugh (1976). Families were usually observed three times weekly during that time of the day in which parents reported the most probable evidence of those child behavior problems cited in the top portion of Figure 1. The SOC recording system permits the scoring of multiple child behaviors, as well as stimulus input provided by the child's adult and peer interaction associates.

Child behavior problems listed in the bottom portion of Figure 1 were recorded by the children's parents. Since these behaviors were unlikely to occur during the relatively brief SOC observations (30 minutes), parental recording was deemed necessary. Unfortunately, a technique for obtaining consistent parent reports was available only for the later studied high risk families. This technique, called episode report data (ERD), requires the SOC observer to prompt the parents' recall of problem episodes following the completion of a SOC observation. Parents are expected to provide recall in yes-no fashion only for that portion of the day preceding the SOC observation.

A final portion of the assessment package was devoted to the measurement of parent attitudes toward their children. Since negative attitudes (e.g. dislike, guilt) are often stumbling blocks in the re-education process, it was deemed important to at least measure these events. Following Wahler, Leske and Berland (1977), parent attitudes were conceptualized as summary reports. These were then scaled on a 7-point dimension in which 7 summarized a maximally negative report and 1 a maximally positive report. At the end of each SOC session, observers asked the parents to provide a scale number summarizing their attitudes toward the children during the half-hour observation session.

Figure 2 presents a summary of SOC baseline observations for both family samples. The congruence between these data and the parent referral problem reports of Figure 1 is striking. First, consider the oppositional cluster of codes. These represent the sum of a child's *complaints, noncompliance* with parent instructions and *rule violations* (e.g., temper outburst). As stated by the low risk parents, oppositional behavior was indeed an obvious feature of the children's in-house behavior. Also in line with the reports of the high risk parents, oppositional behavior was seldom, if ever, observed by the SOC observers. Second, notice the very low occurrences of the work cluster of codes. These represent the sum of *sustained schoolwork* and *sustained work* (household chores). It will be recalled from Figure 1 that both samples of parents reported work deficiency to be a problem with their children. Since ERD findings (samples of child behavior problems in bottom of Figure 1) were gathered only for the high risk sample, these data are not presented in Figure 2. As expected from the high risk parent referral reports, these parents consistently reported an average of 1.42 daily occurrences of the ERD categories representing the sum of fighting, lying and stealing, property destruction and running away.

Parent re-education strategies for the two samples were quite similar, but had different components because of different presenting problems in the two sets of families. In both samples, didactic instruction on principles of social learning theory was conducted in the home setting. This was followed by implementing formal contingency con-

The Insular Family 111

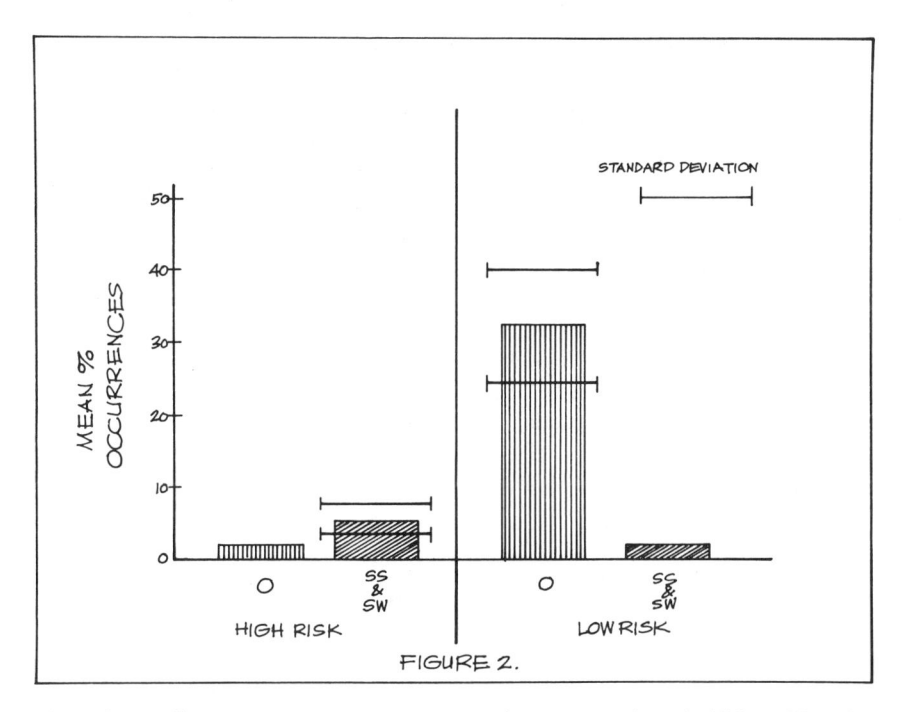

Figure 2. Baseline mean percent occurrences of two categories of child problem behavior as scored by observers in the homes of high and low risk families. Oppositional behavior (O) and sustained work behaviors (SS and SW) were recorded through a format developed by Wahler, House and Stambaugh (1976).

tracts between parent and child. These contracts were limited to those baseline referral problems occurring in the presence of a parent (opposition and work deficiencies). The problems outside parental presence were not included in the contracts because of difficulties in setting immediate contingencies for those behaviors, as well as the authors' interest in the study of possible generalization across treated and untreated behaviors (see Berland, Coe, Resch, & Wahler, 1976).

Parent-child contracts were aimed at providing parent dispensed approval and material rewards for the work behaviors of the children. For the low risk families, the use of a time-out contingency for oppositional behaviors was also included in the contracts. As an added impetus to the success of the high risk family intervention, a home-school checklist was included in the contracts. This checklist allowed parents and teachers to keep track of the children's work production in both home and school settings. In addition, both parent and teacher could reinforce work increments in either setting.

Implementation of the parent-child contracts was under the direction of a trained consultant who provided home-based feedback on parent performance. In the low risk families, about 40 hours of consultation time composed the average intervention phase. In the high risk families, almost 60 hours (average) of consultation time per family was necessary before the consultants were satisfied with parent performance.

Demonstrations of the functional properties of treatment were provided by different experimental designs for the two samples. For the low risk families an intrasubject replication design was utilized, while a multiple baseline across families was employed with the high risk families.

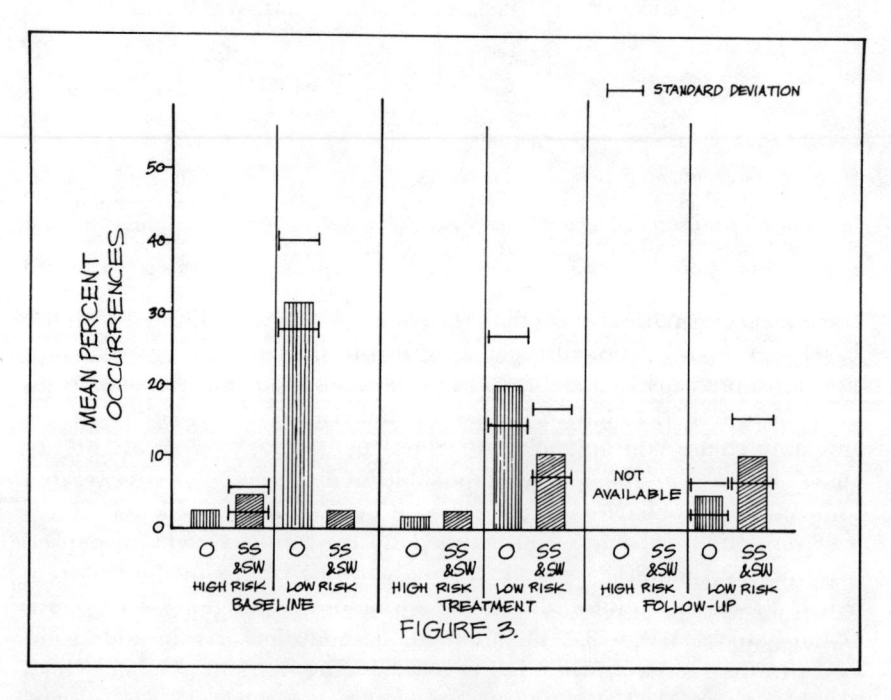

Figure 3. Mean percent occurrences of the Figure 2 categories comparing the high and low risk children over three phases of the study.

The Insular Family

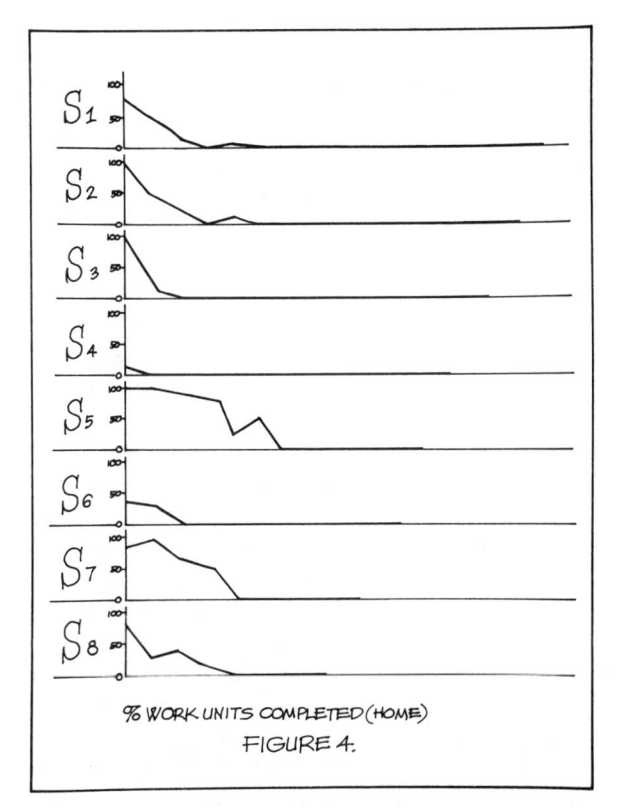

Figure 4. Percent of homework assignments completed by the eight high risk children from the beginning of treatment and extending over the treatment year.

Figure 3 presents SOC data on the two family samples over three phases of this study. In addition to SOC, Figure 4 describes parent-teacher checklist scores on home-based schoolwork for the high risk children. Only those scores in which both parent and teacher agreed on the completion of homework are presented. Thus, the checklist data satisfy the reliability criteria of interobserver agreement.

An inspection of SOC data for the low risk children shows clear improvement in the oppositional and work deficiency problems. In addition, the children's therapeutic gains are sustained in the one year follow-up phase. However, less evidence on the impact of treatment is available for the high risk children. While the parent-teacher checklist data show proof of homework completions, SOC observers reported no changes from baseline through treatment. In addition, an examination of homework scores over the treatment phase indicated that completions tapered off to zero for all eight children. Finally, although a small decrease in parent reported ERD scores (parent records of child fighting, stealing and property destruction) was seen from baseline through treatment, this decrease was statistically insignificant due to a gradual increase in ERD problems toward the end of treatment. Even more dismal proof of parent re-education inadequacies for the high risk sample is seen in the follow-up year. By the end of the first year of treatment, all eight families had dropped out of the CBI program, thus preventing a second year of assessment. The only bright point in the high risk sample is seen in the improved parent attitude scores toward their children during the treatment phase. These shifted from a mean of 4.48 (7 being maximally negative) to a mean of 2.48 during treatment. A t-test for correlated means showed this difference to be statistically significant ($p < .05$).

It seems evident that parent training procedures had functional impact on the low risk children's problems—an impact that was durable for at least one year. Not presented in Figure 3 was a reversal phase in which the contingency contracts were discontinued. In all nine families, the children's problem behaviors returned to baseline levels. In the follow-up phase the parents were free to follow any procedure they wished, and CBI staff were available for "booster shot" consultation. Two of the nine families requested such help, requiring only a few more hours of consultation time. In all families, parent subjective reports (as well as SOC) indicated sustained improvement in the children by the end of the follow-up phase.

Evidence for even a short-term impact of parent training was ambiguous for the high risk children. While all consultants were satisfied that the parents understood the contracts and could implement them, our best data source (SOC) showed no change in child work deficiencies from baseline through treatment. In addition, parent reports on non-targeted problem behaviors (ERD) showed no clear evidence of change when treatment was implemented. Even the homework checklist measures cannot be considered tied functionally to the parent training program. Since homework was rarely assigned during baseline, a functional analysis of parent-child contracts as a causal variable was not possible. Only the parent attitude scores (or Attitude Scale Ratings—ASR) showed baseline to treatment changes. But, because these scores have no possible reliability evaluations, their improvements cannot be clearly assigned to the parent training program.

The Insularity Hypothesis

On virtually every count, parent re-education failed to attain therapeutic results for the high risk families. Certainly there is no shortage of speculation on the reasons for these failures (anywhere from consultant incompetence to biased data sampling). The authors, however, have chosen to follow a lead based on their clinical inferences about the makeup of high risk families. These inferences have led to an hypothesis termed *insularity*. According to the hypothesis, families who possess the high risk sociological descriptors become "insulated" from their surrounding social context. While they may have as many, or more, extrafamily interactions as low risk families, the interactions are *non-functional* with respect to family operations. In other words, family members interact with one another in rather predictable fashion, regardless of social input from outside the family.

Development of the insularity hypothesis stems back to the observational work of Patterson and his colleagues (e.g. Patterson & Reid, 1970). Their studies of the oppositional child's interchanges with family members supported a "coercion" view of how such families operate (see Patterson, 1975). Accordingly, many of the child's parent directed behaviors could be described as "mands"—or, behaviors aimed at obtaining a specific class of reinforcers—namely, parent compliance with the content of the mand (e.g., whining and nagging to the extent that a parent must attend to the child). Keeping in mind that mands are usually aversive to parents, and that successful mands will be temporarily terminated, a set of stable learning conditions can be established within the family: The child's manding actions are positively reinforced by parent compliance and parental compliance is negatively reinforced by child termination of manding.

But, as Patterson and Reid (1970) discovered, the oppositional child and his or her parents both pay a high cost for their reinforcement. The parents, frequently bombarded by whining, nagging and screaming, are likely to couple their typical compliance with retaliation. Thus, with both parties serving as sources of pain for each other, one could readily imagine a gradual dissolution of affectional interchanges between parent and child. As the first author (Wahler, 1968, 1969) discovered, chronically oppositional children are not likely to find parental approval reinforcing. And, on the other side of the coin, it is not unusual to hear the parents of these children offer comments of the following sort: "I love my child but I don't like him."

The above discussed within-family insularity presents a model the authors believe might also produce extrafamily insularity—particularly with high risk families. Given the sociological descriptors defining the high risk family (e.g., crowded, crime-ridden neighborhoods), it is likely that these families are subject to day in and day out harrassment by neighbors and representatives of various community agencies (e.g., police, social welfare, CBI). Thus, the positive reinforcement network linking high risk families and their community subgroups should be sparsely constructed; that is, insularity might well be expected. Therefore, it would seem reasonable to find that community helping programs have little functional impact on high risk families. While the parents of these families might initially comply with helping program mands, other sources of support for family change are lacking. Somehow, a more extensive positive reinforcement network must be established with these families in order to promote therapeutic change. These speculations led the group of CBI investigators into a next step of empirical inquiry.

Study II: A Descriptive Comparison of Family Social Networks in High and Low Risk Communities

The insularity hypothesis leads one to examine relationships between family members and people in that family's community. If high risk troubled families are indeed more insular than low risk troubled families, one would expect differences in the makeup of their extrafamily social networks. A nonfunctional network ought to somehow look different from one possessing stimulus control properties. However, before attempting to tackle the stimulus control issue, it seemed wise to first provide a descriptive study of social networks: Do high risk families display a different pattern of social contacts in their communities from low risk families? Given that differences in network structure do emerge, one could then attempt the more complex task of evaluating the impact of these differing networks on family operations.

Over a period of more than one year, the CBI investigators began the construction of a self-report instrument suitable for the measurement of parent interchanges with members of their social communities. Accordingly, it seemed reasonable to expect that parents could give an accurate picture of their social contacts in the community if the expected picture were simple in nature and if relatively short time spans were involved in parent recall. While it would be difficult to provide a direct means of examining the reliabilities of such measures, one could do so indirectly by constructing other measures of parent-community contact. The degree of convergence between measurement outcomes might provide a rough validity assessment of both systems.

The Community Interaction Checklist (CIC)

The major burden of sampling parent community contacts was carried by the Community Interaction Checklist (CIC). Through this device, it was possible to provide a weekly rate measure concerning a variety of parent social contacts, the duration of these contacts, their distance from home, and the perceived valence of these contacts (painful, neutral, positive).

Use of the CIC required the standard family observer to ask a set of routine questions following the observer's completion of the usual 30-minute direct observation (based on Wahler, House, & Stambaugh, 1976). These observations were usually scheduled three times weekly during the late afternoons or evenings. In all cases, mothers were the respondents on the CIC and were the principal child caretakers in all of the troubled families treated by CBI staff.

Following a family observation, the observer conducted a brief interview with the mother, using the CIC as a guideline. Mothers were asked to recall their extrafamily contacts over the past 24 hours. The community role of each contact member (e.g. friend, kinfolk, helping agency representative) was specified, and the previously noted duration, distance and valence factors were also recorded.

Help-Seeking Interview (HSI)

Just prior to an analysis of the CIC data, all mothers were interviewed to derive a picture of just how they would seek help in the event that their child or children presented a variety of problems. These included "emotional" problems, "noncompliance," "school truancy" and "fighting." This single, open-ended interview was intended to produce another set of community interchange data that could be contrasted with the somewhat similar CIC data. Granted that the CIC rate data would reveal differences between the high and low risk parents, would the Help-Seeking Interview data be congruent with such differences? In essence, this one-shot interview was a means of examining the consistency of maternal self-reports on the CIC checklist.

Following completion of the interviews, all transcripts were examined for maternal report of community members mentioned in the help-seeking process. These members were categorized from the informal agents of help (e.g., kinfolk, minister, friends) to the more formal and extreme agents (e.g., mental health center, juvenile court). The percentages of high and low risk mothers noting these various agents were then contrasted.

Family Samples

The families involved in this second study were quite similar to those seen in Table 1 of the first study. If anything, discrepancies between this second set of high and low risk families were more extreme than those in the first study. Primarily, these larger differences in demographic factors were due to the low risk families: Their income levels and educational levels were higher than was true of the first set of low risk families (average income = $20,000; at least two years college) and all but one were two-parent families. The high risk families, however, were almost identical to the high risk sample of the first study.

As was true of the samples in the earlier study, reasons for the children's referrals to CBI centered on the sorts of oppositional actions depicted in Figure 1. In the present samples, however, the high and low risk children were identical in terms of presenting problems. Once again, initiation of help-seeking by the parents differed for high and low risk families. While all low risk referrals stemmed from parent initiation, all high risk referrals were due to direct action by schools, human services agencies and the juvenile court. In the present samples, six families composed the low risk group and 15 families represented the high risk group. With exception of the Community Checklist (CIC) and the Help-Seeking Interview (HSI), all assessment procedures in this study were identical to those of the first study.

The Insular Family

Figure 5 presents the overall results of mother social contacts outside the family for the high and low risk samples. Dramatic differences in the daily rates of such contacts are obvious. While the low risk mothers reported an average of almost 10 daily social contacts, the high risk mothers revealed less than half that number. Since some consistent differences emerged in subsequent analyses of these high risk mothers, it seemed reasonable to separate them into three subgroups: married or intact families (N=5), single females who were self-supporting (working) (N=5), and single females who were welfare dependent (non-working) (N=5). As Figure 5 suggests, the high risk single, self-supporting mother appears most similar to the low risk mother.

The next four figures present the content features of social interchanges between the mothers and their community contacts. As Fig-

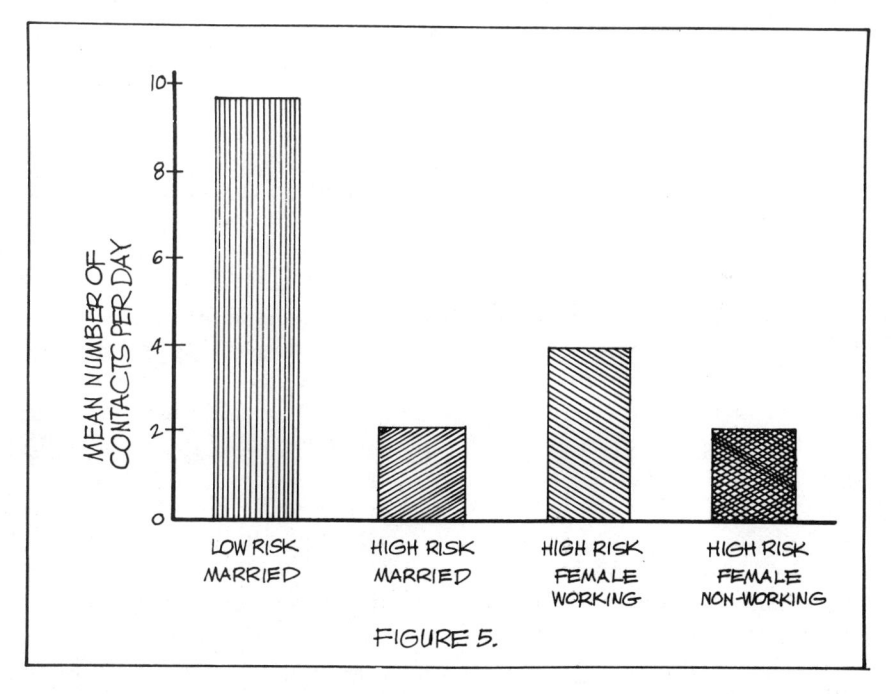

Figure 5. Mean number of social contacts by the mothers of one group of low risk families and three groups of high risk families. All contacts were between the mothers and members of their communities. Contacts were recorded through the Community Interaction Checklist (see appendix).

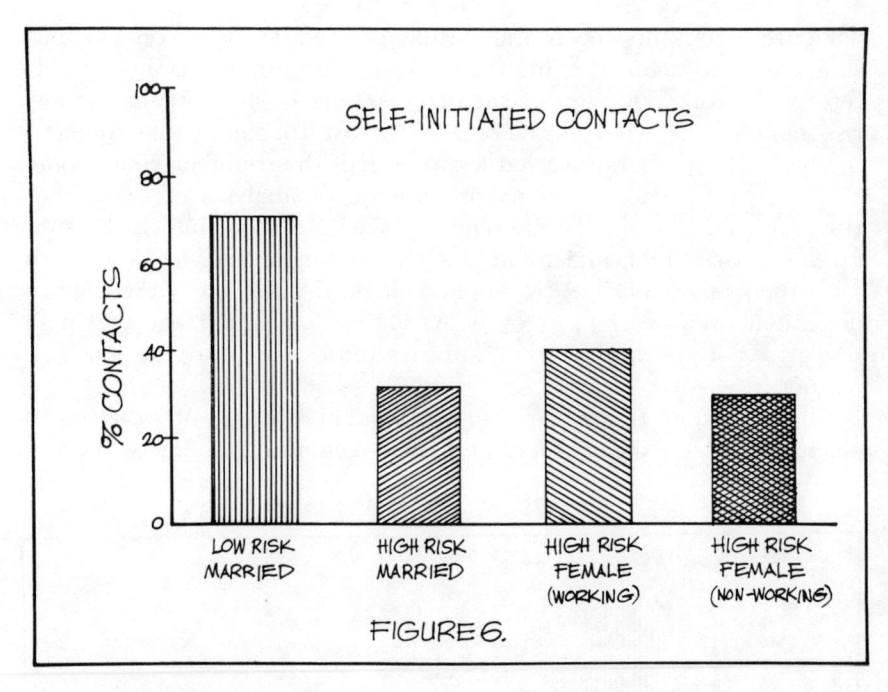

Figure 6. Proportion of the Figure 5 community contacts that were self-initiated by low and high risk mothers.

ure 6 indicates, the low risk mothers were decidedly more instrumental in generating such contacts. On the average, 71% of the low risk mother's social interactions were self-initiated. In contrast, the majority of high risk mothers' interactions were initiated by other parties. Once again, the single, self-supporting high-risk mother resembles the low risk mother.

Figure 7 presents the first of three sizeable differences in the identities of the community member interacting with the mothers. Friendships account for more than half of the low risk mothers' extrafamily interchanges—as they do for the self-supporting high risk female. In contrast, the other high risk mothers are relatively friendless.

In Figures 8 and 9 the bulk of high risk mother contacts are identified. Helping agencies (typically social welfare) were incredibly frequent visitors for the high risk married and non-working single mothers. At this point it is important to compare the valence of social

The Insular Family

contacts as far as the previous two sets of community members are concerned. As expected, friendship contacts are judged to be more positive than agency contacts—in essence, depicting a more extensive reinforcement network for the low risk mothers and the high risk self-supporting mothers.

Another curious, unexpected difference emerged with regard to kinfolk contacts across the four groups of mothers. The functionally similar low risk and high risk working mothers rarely reported interchanges with their extended families. In contrast, the other high risk mothers could recall more than five times as many daily contacts with relatives outside their nuclear family. Clearly, these latter two groups of mothers were closely knit in terms of a more broadly construed family network. However, it is also of interest to note mother comments about the valence of extended family contact. Many of these contacts were judged as "interfering" (manding) by the high risk

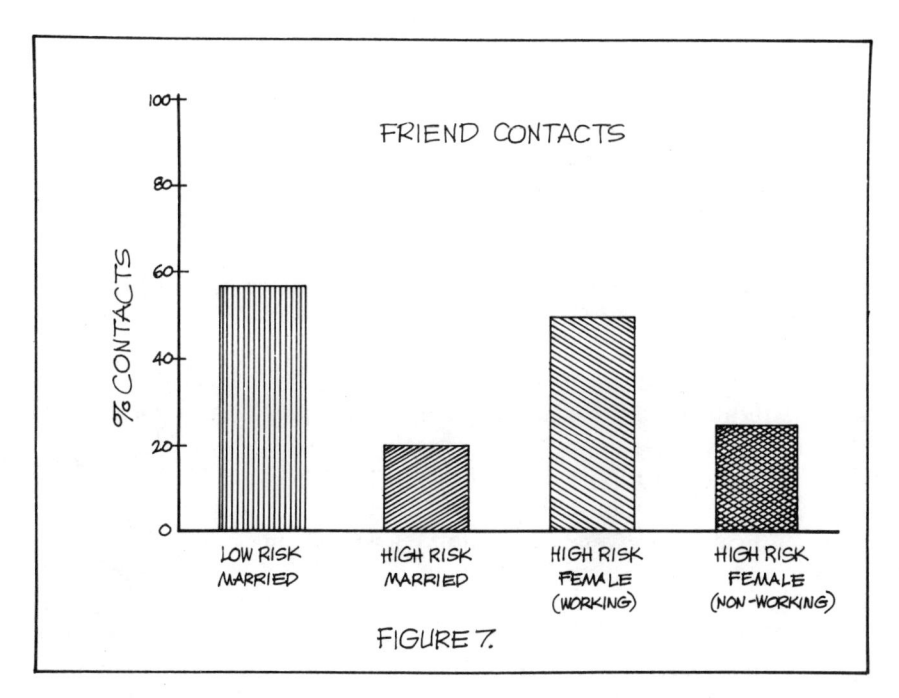

Figure 7. Porportion of the Figure 5 community contacts identified as friends by low and high risk mothers.

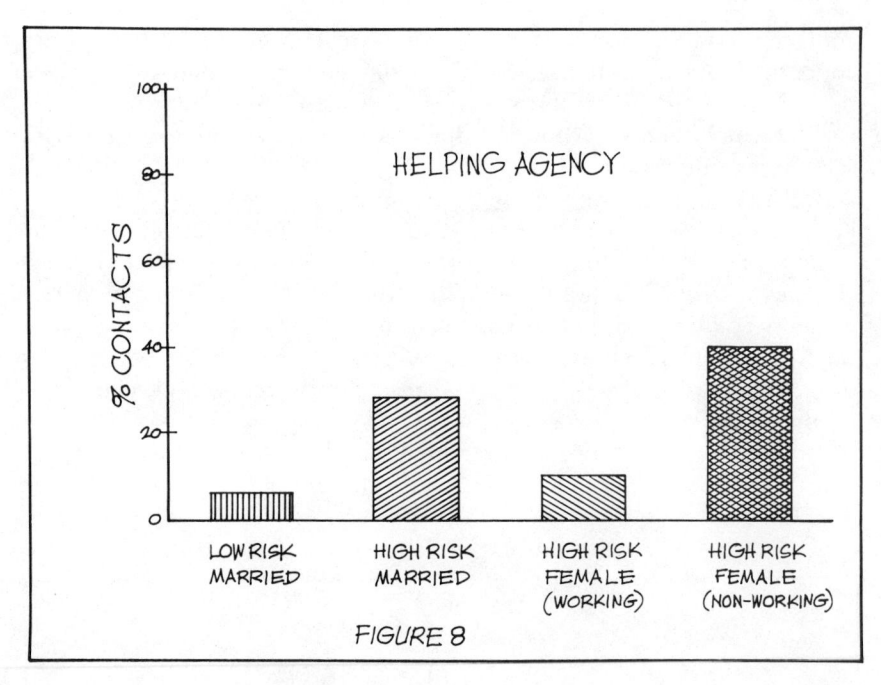

Figure 8. Proportion of the Figure 5 community contacts identified as helping agency representatives by low and high risk mothers.

mothers—quite different from the previously noted friendship interchanges.

We now turn to a rough evaluation of the consistency of mother self-report as based on the Community Interaction Checklist (CIC). It may be recalled from earlier pages that consistency (or the lack of it) was viewed as our only means of assessing the validity of CIC reports. Thus, mother self-report data from the Help-Seeking Interview were contrasted with previously reported CIC data from the same mothers. Figure 10 categorizes maternal interview statements concerning whom they would contact if their children were experiencing "emotional" problems. Notice that friends are never mentioned as help sources by high risk mothers, while more than 25% of the low risk mothers designated this source. The bulk of high risk mother responses centered around agency-professional sources of help. Thus, the low risk mothers' friendship orientation to help-seeking and the high risk

The Insular Family 123

mothers' preferences for more formal sources are rather consistent with their day-to-day CIC reports.

Even more striking evidence of informal versus formal help-seeking solutions emerged when the mothers were asked about childhood problems that specifically characterized their troubled children—opposition to instructions and rule systems. In Figure 11, the low and high risk mothers differ markedly along this dimension. While the low risk mothers would prefer to handle this problem themselves, through library and friendship sources, the high risk mothers turn to the more formal, agency solutions.

INSULARITY: CONCLUSIONS FROM STUDIES I AND II

The literature review presented in this paper, along with the results of Study I, force a conclusion important for future work in applied behavior analysis: Although we currently possess the technology to

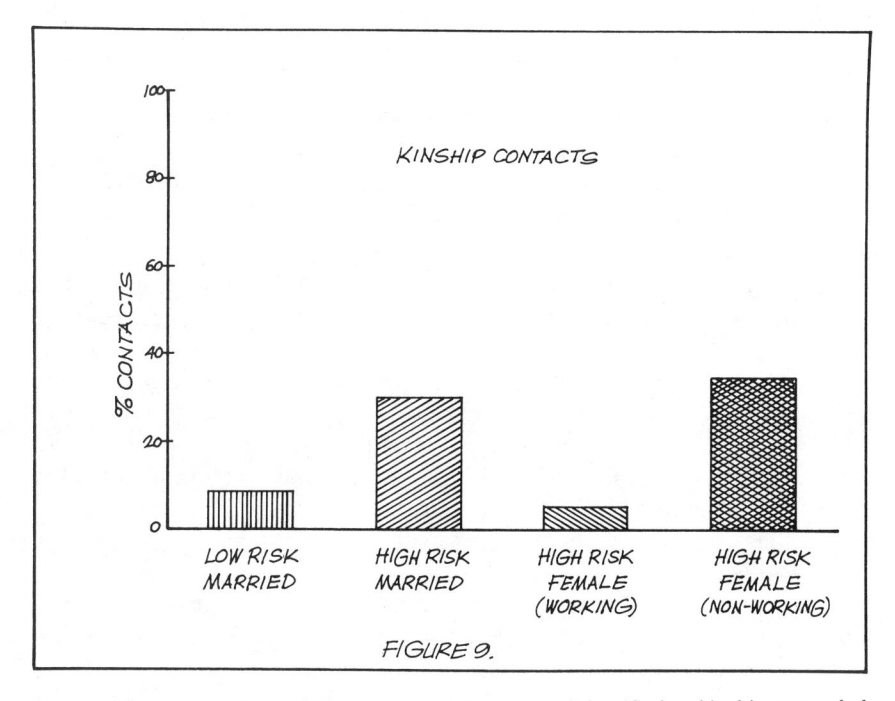

Figure 9. Proportion of the Figure 5 community contacts identified as kinship (extended family members) by low and high risk mothers.

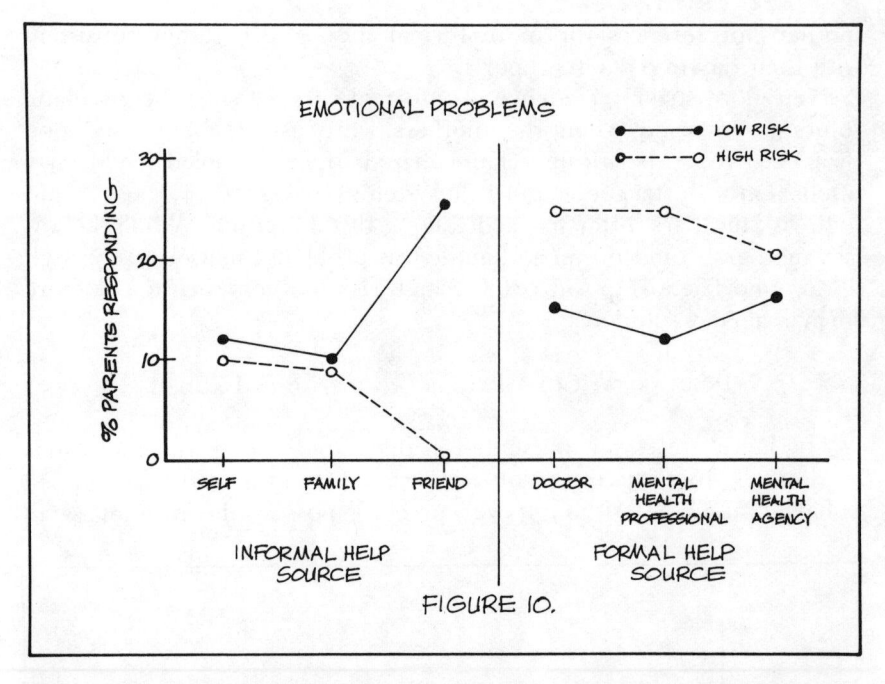

Figure 10. Help sources as identified by low and high risk mothers following the question: "To whom would you go for help if your child were experiencing an emotional problem?" This question was asked as part of the Help-Seeking Interview.

help the children of troubled families, not all children will benefit from that technology. In fact, the results of Study I suggest that we can now specify a population of troubled families that are unlikely to profit from the standard contingency management approach to behavior change. Furthermore, these sociologically defined "high risk" families appear to be more in need of help than is true of other families. Oppositional children from high risk families are apt to continue their rule-violating actions into adolescence and adulthood—to the point that they constitute serious problems to themselves and their communities.

While no solutions are as yet available for the problems of high risk families, it does appear that we are gaining perspective on the nature of these problems. The insularity hypothesis explored in Study II provides some potentially useful notions concerning treatment failures. One of the most obvious differences between high and low risk

The Insular Family

families centers on the content of caretaker interactions within their communities. Low risk mothers are decidedly more spontaneous in the arrangement of such interchanges, and they tend to be in tune with the "old boy" networks of their communities. These informal, friendship-oriented community groups clearly exclude most high risk mothers. Rather, these mothers' principal encounters involved unsolicited, manding sorts of interchanges with helping agencies and members of their extended families. Friendship may be the missing ingredient in effective therapeutic intervention for high risk families.

A next crucial step in evaluating the insularity hypothesis must entail a means of analyzing the stimulus control properties of extrafamily social contacts. If, for example, maternal friendship contacts do affect mother-child interactions, consistencies should emerge between measures of these two sorts of social exchanges. Given that one can demonstrate correlational relationships between extra- and intrafamily

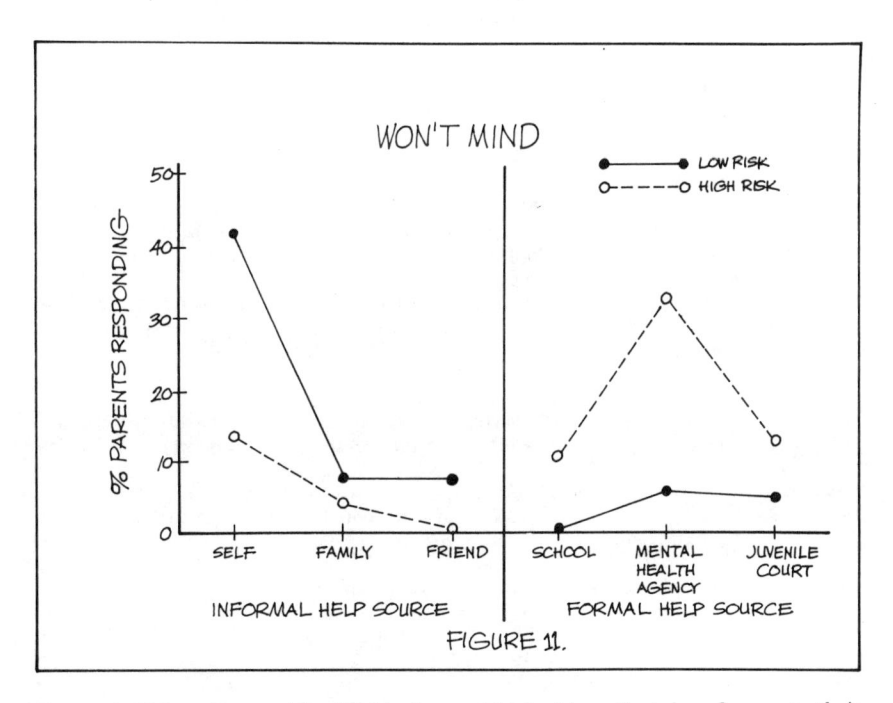

Figure 11. Help sources as identified by low and high risk mothers in reference to their children's oppositional problems. As in Figure 10, the Help-Seeking Interview was the context for this question.

interactions, a pathway to durable treatment procedures might be opened. In addition to the time proven contingency management procedures for within-family treatment, future data could suggest the necessity of contingency changes beyond the family.

REFERENCES

BERLAND, R.M., COE, T.D., RESCH, E.E. and WAHLER, R.G.: Independent toy play: A keystone behavior for oppositional children. Paper presented at the American Association for Behavior Therapy, New York, December, 1976.

BIJOU, S.W. and BAER, D.M.: *Child Development. Vol. I. A Systematic and Empirical Theory.* New York: Appleton-Century-Crofts, 1961.

BUDD, K.S., GREEN, D.R. and BAER, D.M.: An analysis of multiple misplaced parental social contingencies. *Journal of Applied Behavior Analysis,* 1976, 9, 459-470.

DOLEYS, D.M., WELLS, K.C., HOBBS, S.A., ROBERTS, M.W. and CARTELLI, L.M.: The effects of social punishment on noncompliance: A comparison with timeout and positive practice. *Journal of Applied Behavior Analysis,* 1976, 9, 471-482.

EMPEY, L.T. and LUBECK, S.G.: *Explaining Delinquency.* Lexington, Mass.: Heath Lexington Books, 1971.

FOREHAND, R.: Child noncompliance to parent commands: Behavioral analysis and treatment. In M. Hersen, R.M. Eisler and P.M. Miller (Eds.), *Progress in Behavior Modification* (Vol. V). New York: Academic Press, 1977.

FOREHAND, R. and ATKESON, B.M.: Generalization of treatment effects with parents as therapists: A review of assessment and implementation procedures. *Behavior Therapy.* In press.

FOREHAND, R., PEED, S. and ROBERTS, M.: Coding manual for scoring mother-child interactions. Unpublished manuscript, University of Georgia, 1975.

HANF, C.: Facilitating parent-child interaction: A two-stage procedure. Unpublished manuscript, University of Oregon Medical School, 1969.

HAWKINS, R.P., PETERSON, R.F., SCHWEID, E. and BIJOU, S.W.: Behavior therapy in the home: Amelioration of problem parent-child relations with the parent in a therapeutic role. *Journal of Experimental Child Psychology,* 1966, 4, 99-107.

HERBERT, E.W. and BAER, D.M.: Training parents as behavior modifiers: Self recording of contingent attention. *Journal of Applied Behavior Analysis,* 1972, 5, 139-149.

HERBERT, E. W., PINKSTON, E.M., HAYDEN, M.L., SAJWAJ, T.E., PINKSTON, S., CORDUA, G. and JACKSON, C.: Adverse effects of differential parental attention. *Journal of Applied Behavior Analysis,* 1973, 6, 15-30.

HIRSCHI, T.: *Causes of Delinquency.* Berkeley: University of California Press, 1969.

HOBBS, S.A. and FOREHAND, R.L.: Effects of differential release from timeout on children's deviant behavior. *Journal of Behavior Therapy and Experimental Psychiatry,* 1975, 6, 256-257.

JOHNSON, S. and CHRISTENSEN, A.: Multiple criteria in follow-up of behavior modification with families. *Journal of Abnormal Child Psychology,* 1975, 3, 135-154.

MASH, E.J. and TERDAL, L.: Modification of mother-child interactions: Playing with children. *Mental Retardation,* 1973, 11, 44-49.

PATTERSON, G.R.: The aggressive child: Victim and architect of a coercive system. In L.A. Hamerlynck, L.C. Handy and E.J. Mash (Eds.), *Behavior Modification and Families.* New York: Brunner/Mazel, 1976.

PATTERSON, G.R.: Interventions for boys with conduct problems: Multiple settings, treatments and criteria. *Journal of Consulting and Clinical Psychology*, 1975, *42*, 471-481.
PATTERSON, G.R., COBB, J.A. and RAY, R.S.: A social engineering technology for retraining the families of aggressive boys. In H.E. Adams and I.P. Unikel (Eds.), *Issues and Trends in Behavior Therapy*. Springfield, Illinois: Charles C. Thomas, 1973, 139-210.
PATTERSON, G.R. and REID, J.B.: Reciprocity and coercion: Two facets of social systems. In J. Michael and C. Neuringer (Eds.), *Behavior Modification for Clinical Psychologists*. New York: Appleton-Century-Crofts, 1970.
PATTERSON, G.R. and WHALEN, K.: Determining the status of a controlling stimulus. Oregon Social Learning Center, 1978.
Residential Community Corrections Programs. Report by Governor's Commission on Crime Prevention and Control, State of Minnesota, April, 1975.
ROBINS, L.N.: *Deviant Children Grown Up: A Sociological and Psychiatric Study of Sociopathic Personality*. Baltimore: Williams and Wilkins, 1966.
ROFF, M.: Childhood social interaction and young adult bad conduct. *Journal of Abnormal and Social Psychology*, 1961, *65*, 333-337.
SHAW, C.R. and MCKAY, H.D.: *Juvenile Delinquency and Urban Areas*. Chicago: The University of Chicago Press, 1969.
TAPLIN, P.S. and REID, J.B.: Changes in parent consequation as a function of family intervention. *Oregon Research Bulletin*, 1975.
WAHLER, R.G.: Behavior therapy for children: Love is not enough. Paper presented at the meeting of the Eastern Psychological Association, 1968.
WAHLER, R.G.: Oppositional children: A quest for parental reinforcement control. *Journal of Applied Behavior Analysis*, 1969, *2*, 159-170.
WAHLER, R.G., BERLAND, R.M. and LESKE, G.: Environmental boundaries in behavior modification: Problems in residential treatment of children. Unpublished manuscript, Child Behavior Institute, University of Tennessee, 1975.
WAHLER, R.G. and CORMIER, W.H.: The ecological interview: A first step in outpatient child behavior therapy. *Journal of Behavior Therapy and Experimental Psychiatry*, 1970, *1*, 293-303.
WAHLER, R.G., HOUSE, A.E. and STAMBAUGH, E.E.: *Ecological Assessment of Child Problem Behavior*. New York: Pergamon Press, 1976.
WAHLER, R.G., LESKE, G. and BERLAND, R.M.: Phenomenological reports: An empirical model. In *New Developments in Behavioral Research: Theory, Methods and Application*. D. Baer and B. Etzel (Eds.), Hillsdale, New Jersey: Lawrence Erlbaum Associates. 1977.
WALKER, H.M. and BUCKLEY, N.K.: Programming generalization and maintenance of treatment effects across time and across settings. *Journal of Applied Behavior Analysis*. 1972, *5*, 209-224.

7
The Early Education Project

GERARD M. KYSELA, KATHLEEN DALY,
MARTHA DOXSEY-WHITFIELD, ALEX HILLYARD,
LINDA MCDONALD, SUSAN
MCDONALD and JULIE TAYLOR

INTRODUCTION

Within the Early Education Project, home and school intervention programs utilizing an applied behavioral analysis strategy have been developed in an attempt to enhance the growth of moderate to severely handicapped children between the ages of birth and six years. The application of learning principles in this intervention process utilizes the most current knowledge of human learning to assist developmentally delayed children in the attainment of more normal growth patterns. Recently, many investigators have initiated programs in the early infant and preschool years with handicapped persons, attempting to attenuate or eliminate the extensive retardation which has occurred with moderate to severely handicapping conditions (Bricker & Bricker, 1976; Fredericks et al., 1976; Guess, Sailor, & Baer, 1976; Hayden & Haring, 1976). However, along with establishing the

---

The University of Alberta through the Centre for the Study of Mental Retardation provided the sponsorship for this contract.

The Department of Education of the Province of Alberta through the Departments of Early Childhood Services and Planning and Research provided the fiscal as well as personal support to us in conducting and completing this project. The authors express their appreciation to these institutions, who supported the necessity of early intervention and educational support for handicapped children and their families.

applied behavior analysis intervention program, the Early Education Project is providing unique data on direct and incidental teaching models employable across a broad range of behaviors, skills, and concepts, as well as the development of a novel criterion-referenced assessment device. This chapter will attempt to elaborate these unique characteristics of the Early Education Project and the application of the procedures within the context of the home- and school-based programs.

The intervention orientation employing an applied behavior analysis approach is characterized by the following five steps outlined by Bijou (1976):

(1) specifying the goals of teaching and learning in observable terms;
(2) beginning teaching at the child's level of competence;
(3) arranging the teaching situation to facilitate learning (instructional procedures, materials, setting factors and contingencies);
(4) monitoring learning progress and making changes to advance learning;
(5) following practices that generalize, elaborate, and maintain the behaviors acquired.

To achieve these five basic steps the Early Education staff employs a behaviorally based developmental curriculum, a criterion-referenced test-teach method of instruction, a standard program construction and implementation procedure, a systematic data collection format for behaviors being taught, and an incidental teaching framework (Hart & Risley, 1975) for maintenance and generalization.

Developmental Curriculum

The developmental curriculum is a sequence of behaviors in five areas of development: language, motor, cognition, self-help, and socialization skills (see Table 1). The content of the curriculum originated initially from the Portage Guide (Shearer et al., 1972); however, considerable modifications of this original framework have been made by adopting materials from other curricula, especially in the areas of motor development, language, self-help and cognition; in addition, a different sequencing procedure is employed. Each developmental area consists of a sequence of strands or clusters of behaviors which represent a progression from simple to complex behaviors leading to a terminal behavioral objective (see Table 2). The curriculum modified from the Portage Guide (Shearer et al., 1972) attempts to represent functional behavioral goals, skills, and knowledge in each area of development such that, once acquired, these skills and knowledge will aid in more typical developmental progress for the delayed child.

The Test-Teach Method:
Criterion-Referenced Assessment

Employing this curriculum, the next phase includes an assessment of the competencies or behaviors the child possesses; such information indicates to the teacher or parent where to being programming and subsequent instruction.

The criterion-referenced assessment format provides a behavioral assessment of the child's knowledge and skills in several areas of development. This criterion-referenced format differs significantly from normative assessment procedures as well as standard criterion-referenced assessment procedures. Normative assessments compare a child's performance against other students' performance on the same test or norms established from a large group of students; criterion-referenced assessments measure student's progress in terms of accomplishing specific tasks which are sampled from the domain of tasks which indicate mastery of the behavioral objective (Snelbecker, 1974).

Table 1
Five Areas of the Developmental Curriculum

Cognition:	ability to remember, see, or hear likeness and difference, and to determine relationships between ideas and things.
Self-help:	behaviors enabling child to care for himself in areas of eating, dressing, bathing, and toileting.
Motor:	concerned with coordinated movements of large and small muscles.
Language:	ability to receive and understand information-showing meaning through speech and gestures.
Socialization:	concerned with appropriate interpersonal behaviors with adults and peers.

Table 2

Strands of Terminal Objectives and Subskills for Early Motor Development

Criterion Referenced Assessment Guide

Motor Development

1. Controlled Eye Movements

   A. Looks at object in hands (P15A)
      (1) eye movements on back (P5)
      (2) looks and holds (P7A)
      (3) looks at hands (P14)

2. Head Control Prone

   A. Holds head and chest up 15 seconds prone on elbows (P13)
      (1) holds head up 5 seconds (P6)

   B. Lifts head - prone on elbows
      (1) raises head within 10 seconds (P2)
      (2) raises head within 5 seconds prone on elbows (P8)

   C. Turns head and reaches for toy prone on elbows
      (1) head turning (P3)
      (2) raises head (P8)

3. Head Control Supine

   A. Holds head up 15 seconds

   B. Lifts head within 10 seconds
      (1) lifts head momentarily within 1 minute (P11A)

   C. Turns head
      (1) moves head side to side (P4)

4. Rolling

   A. Rolls back to stomach
      (1) rolls side to stomach

   B. Rolls stomach to back (P21)
      (1) rolls side to back (P10B)

5. Sitting

   A. Sits with back unsupported on floor and chair (P29)
      (1) head erect.

The important difference lies in the criterion-referenced assessment's comparison of a student's performance to an externally established standard or criterion rather than to the performance of other students. This assessment procedure provides directly relevant and functional information regarding a child's level of developmental competencies and as a result has direct implications for instruction.

The test-teach method of criterion-referenced assessment differs from standard formats through the sequential introduction of prompts and guidance to assess the child's skills even if the child is nonresponsive at a spontaneous level; that is, prompts and physical assistance are gradually introduced attempting to determine how extensive intervention must be in order to obtain a response from the child. Thus, the level of remedial input required if the child is not responding at a spontaneous level is determined in the assessment procedure.

During the initial assessment each terminal behavior of the strand is assessed to determine if it is within the teaching range of the student. The terminal behavioral objective is the final most complex behavior for that strand. Spontaneously responding at this level indicates competency in that skill or understanding of the particular concept or set of concepts. For example, in the language area, a terminal behavioral objective might read as follows:

> Child achieves 80% or more correct responses in a session of 32 trials or 12 correct responses in a row when asked "What's that?" and presented with the following 16 stimuli singly: cookie, pants, ball, nose, chair, pop, shoe, car, tummy, table, apple, cup, top, mouth, spoon, drum.

Another objective in the cognitive development area would be as follows:

> The student will reach for, grasp, and retain a small object using a pincer grasp within five seconds of the teacher presenting that object to the child and saying "*(child's name)*, you take."

The testing procedure for the criterion-referenced assessment incorporates the testing of each terminal behavior for successive strands starting with the strand for each developmental area or at a point that seems appropriate for that child. First, for each behavioral objective, *instructions, conditions* for performance, *standards* of behavior and product, and the *observable behavior* required indicating competencies on that skill or concept have been established (Anderson & Faust, 1973).

These components of the behavioral objective are essential in order to have consistent assessment of mastery of the objective across examiners. Table 3 provides a series of behavioral objectives in the area of motor development.

Thus, for each terminal behavioral objective, as well as for each sub-objective, a criterion or standard is established to determine the

Table 3
Behavioral Objectives in the Motor Skill Areas

1. Controlled Eye Movements
   A. After placing an object in the child's hand, he will focus his eyes on it within 5 seconds for a duration of 2 seconds (15A)
      (1) Eye movements on back
          Child will, while lying on his back, follow a moving object or a light held 15-20 cm. with his eyes from the center two inches to the left and right side of his head.
      (2) Looks and holds
          Child will stare at tester's face for 5 seconds if it is within 15-25 cm. of child's eyes.
      (3) Looks at hands
          Child will bring his hands to his face and look at them for 2 seconds at least once during a one-minute observation session preceded by the tester touching the child's hands and bringing them in front of child's face.

2. Head Control Prone (on abdomen)
   A. Child will hold his head in full face forward position for 15 seconds if child is placed prone on elbows with head up within 5 seconds of being told to "look" and offered a toy within view.
      (1) Hold head up 5 seconds
          Child will hold his head in full face forward position for 5 seconds while prone if told to "look" and offered a toy held 1 foot from child at a height of 15 cm. within 5 seconds of command.

   B. If child is placed prone on elbows, he will lift his head up to full face forward position within 5 seconds if told to "look" and offered a toy within view.
      (1) Raises Head
          Child will raise his head 8 cm. off floor within 5 seconds of rattle sound made 15 cm. above head.
      (2) Raises Head
          Child will raise his head at least 15 cm. off mat to full face forward position while prone within 5 seconds of being told to "look" and offered a toy within view.

   C. If child is placed on elbows with head up, he will turn his head from side to side within 5 seconds of being told to "look" and offered a toy within view.
      (1) Head turning
          Child will turn his head from center of body to right and left while prone within 5 seconds of rattle sound being presented.

presence of the skill or concept in the child's repertoire. This procedure insures that the child's performance either through direct assessment or natural observation reliably meets or exceeds a preestablished criterion. For each objective assessed, *a set of instructions* for task completion is presented to the child; this may be a verbal instruction alone or it may be a verbal instruction with the addition of a model by the teacher. The *conditions* for assessing performance are set out by the examiners as specified in the objective. This procedure thus constitutes the assessment portion of the competency-based instructional model as discussed by Baine (1977).

Secondly, the amount of prompting or assistance required to complete the behavioral objective is assessed within one of the following six levels. At each successive level there is the introduction of an increasing amount of prompting (cueing) and/or guidance given to the child.

> *Level 5*—The behavior is performed appropriately following the instruction without further prompting or guidance of any kind.
>
> *Level 4*—The behavior is performed appropriately following a repeat of the instruction and one or two additional verbal prompts after no response by the child or an incorrect response within five seconds of the initial instruction. Verbal prompts are repeated instructions or statements designed to initiate the behavior or focus the child's attention on salient or relevant aspects of the material (Becker, Engelmann, & Thomas, 1975a).
>
> *Level 3*—The behavior is performed appropriately in all respects after repetition of the instruction and the provision of one or two physical prompts or a model; this occurs if the child makes no response or an incorrect response after five seconds following level 4 instruction. Physical prompts are teacher-gestures or a model following the instruction or command which provide further prompts to the child in order to elicit the appropriate behavior (Becker et al., 1975a). Model cues are defined as the teacher or another child actually modeling or demonstrating the desired task. There is no physical contact between the teacher and child at this point.
>
> *Level 2*—The behavior is performed after instructional repetition and provision of minimum physical guidance if the child makes no response or an incorrect response after five seconds following level 3 instruction. Minimum physical guidance is defined as a teacher-initiated behavior where there is physical contact with the child—the degree of physical contact is assisting the child with one finger for a maximum of 5 seconds (Martin et al., 1975).

Level 1—The behavior is performed appropriately after the teacher again repeats the instruction and provides more physical guidance following the lack of a child's response within five seconds or an incorrect response to level 2 guidance. More physical guidance refers to anything more than that defined at level 2 including hands-on guidance for a period of five seconds or leading the child through the behavior (Becker et al., 1975a; Martin et al., 1975).

Level 0—Behavior is not performed in any respect following the physical guidance of level 1 for at least five seconds.

Procedures extend over a possible period of 25 seconds of assessment depending upon the child's responsiveness. This procedure is conducted three times for each objective to indicate the stability of the behavioral objective and determine the teaching level of the objective. The stability of the terminal behavioral objective is assessed as the lowest or most frequent level of assessment exhibited by the child on these three trials.

Upon completion of assessment, a terminal objective is considered to be within a child's teaching range if the child responds to minimum physical guidance or physical and/or verbal prompts by the teacher; that is, if the child's assessment is summarized as level 2, 3, or 4. The important point here is that the child's performance at levels 2, 3, or 4 indicates that the prerequisite skills are present but the child is not completely competent.

However, if the child is totally unable to perform the actions required to meet the terminal objective or requires maximum guidance from the teacher (i.e., levels 0 to 1 on the assessment), then some subskills within the strand are assumed to be lacking and therefore should be further assessed and eventually taught. If the child performs at level 0 or 1 over three trials, within-strand assessment is required for the subskills (see Table 4 for examples).

If subskills within a strand are to be assessed, two possible procedures are employed: (1) a baseline is taken once a day for a five-day period for each subskill; (2) at the time of assessment for the terminal behavior or before program implementation, each subskill is probed three times. With this method, the three probes are carried out at level 5 and no additional levels of testing are employed. The child's performance is recorded as 5 or 0, which indicates either mastery of the skill or concept, or no response or incorrect response. In both of these instances teaching will begin with the lowest behavior scored

Table 4

Completed Example of Infant Criterion-Referenced Assessment in Motor Development

Criterion Referenced Assessment Guide

NAME ____
D.O.B. ____
TEACHER ____
DATE ____

Motor Development

*S1 - summarized stability index

1. **Controlled Eye Movements**

S1	1	2	3
5	5	5	5

A. Looks at object in hands (P15A)
  (1) eye movements on back (P5)
  (2) looks and holds (P7A)
  (3) looks at hands (P14)

2. **Head Control Prone**

	1	2	3
	5	5	5
5	5	5	

A. Holds head and chest up 15 seconds prone on elbows (P13)
  (1) holds head up 5 seconds (P6)

		5	
5	5	5	

B. Lifts head - prone on elbows
  (1) raises head within 10 seconds (P2)
  (2) raises head within 5 seconds prone on elbows (P8)

		5	
5	5	5	

C. Turns head and reaches for toy prone on elbows
  (1) head turning (P3)
  (2) raises head (P8)

3. **Head Control Sipine**

	1	2	3
	0	0	0
0	0	0	

A. Holds head up 15 seconds

0	0	0	
0	0	0	

B. Lifts head within 10 seconds
  (1) lifts head momentarily within 1 minute (P1A)

0	0	0	
0	0	0	

C. Turns head
  (1) moves head side to side (P4)

4. **Rolling**

	1	2	3
	1	1	1
0	0	1	

A. Rolls back to stomach
  (1) rolls side to stomach

0	0	0	
0	0	0	

B. Rolls stomach to back (P21)
  (1) rolls side to back (P10B)

5. **Sitting**

	1	2	3
	0	0	0
5	5	5	

A. Sits with back unsupported on floor and chair (P29)
  (1) head erect

at a zero level in the sequence and work up the strand teaching all of the behaviors the child was unable to perform at level 5 when assessed on baseline; subskills on which the child was competent would be placed on review to maintain them in the child's repertoire. The summary assessment grid for several terminal objectives and subobjectives given in Table 4 illustrates several behavioral objectives assessed in the motor area of development. Behaviors 1A, 2A, 2B, and 2C all represent terminal objectives in each strand assessed at level 5. Level 5 was the lowest and most frequent assessment level over three assessment trials. The stability index is summarized as level 5 for teaching purposes. Objectives 3A, 3B, 3B1, 3C, and 3C1 were all assessed at level 0 for teaching. Objective 4A was at level 1, thus 4A1 was tested; objectives 4B, 4B1, and 5A were assessed at level 0 and 5A1 at level 5. From this assessment data the teacher would begin the planning of teaching programs with the parents in the Head Control Supine area as this is the lowest terminal objective in the strands on which the child did not attain mastery.

In summary, the criterion-referenced procedure indicates to the teacher the what and where to begin instruction for specific objectives and sub-objectives. This assessment procedure is then combined with the teaching model using a consistent program format to provide the instructional design for home or school teaching.

Instructional Program Development

Instructional programs for use by parents at home and teachers in the school are employed from various sources (Anderson, Godson, & Willard, 1976; Fredericks et al., 1976), as well as written by the teachers and staff of the project. The program format contains the following elements:

   a) behavioral objectives—the terminal objective the child must attain for mastery of the skill or concept on completion of the program;
   b) the sequence of steps appropriate to teach the objective—these are derived from a task analysis of the objective;
   c) a procedural section which outlines how to implement the direct teaching model in relation to that specific objective;
   d) review and maintenance components which are implemented following criterion to assist the generalization and maintenance of the behavior over time.

The Test-Teach Method: Direct Teaching Model

The Direct Teaching Model used within the project and in conjunction with the developmental curriculum and criterion referenced assessment procedure provides the teaching format for parents and teachers trying to attenuate developmental delays.

The teaching model is derived from a basic behavioral instructional model developed by Engelmann (Becker, Engelmann, & Thomas, 1975b). The two components of this model include an attention component and an instruction component. Attention signals are used to secure the child's looking and listening and then teaching or task information is provided; if the child responds appropriately, rewards and precise feedback follow; if the child responds incorrectly, correction procedures are provided. Intermittent reinforcement is provided following attention signals in order to build up and maintain persistent attentiveness on the child's part, as this has been a particularly critical area of delay. The antecedent events include task information and instructions, prompts, and teacher guidance; the consequent events include rewards, the use of wrong or "no" as negative feedback, precise feedback regarding accurate responding, corrective feedback, and correction procedures.

This approach emphasizes the importance of both the antecedent events (prior to the child's response) and the consequent events following the child's response; the functional influence and control of these events over the child's behavior are key processes in the teaching model (Skinner, 1953, 1968). Much research evidence (in particular, Becker et al., 1975b; Martin et al., 1975; Zeaman & House, 1963) has suggested that these antecedent instructions (prompts and guidance) and consequent events are particularly important to ensure acquisition of new skills and concepts by the developmentally handicapped child.

The Direct Teaching Model employs prompts and physical guidance procedures to assist the child in responding to the learning situation. This procedure is modified from the work of Martin et al. (1975). The levels of prompting and guidance are the same as those previously described in the assessment procedures with some distinct alterations. Two distinct procedural differences between the assessment procedure and Direct Teaching Model are as follows:

(1) In the teaching model, teaching begins at level 1 and progresses through to level 5. Assessment on the other hand be-

The Early Education Project

gins with level 5 and progressed down to level 1. The teaching model uses an inverse order of the assessment procedure in terms of the introduction of prompts and guidance.

(2) In the assessment model prompts and guidance are not presented together; however, in the Direct Teaching Model the prompts and guidance are employed in a cumulative manner at the lowest levels and gradually faded out as the child progresses.

The prompts and guidance are presented as close as possible after each other or, when appropriate, together. For example, it is not possible to present a verbal instruction and a verbal prompt in any other manner than one following the other. However, physical prompts can be provided at the same time as verbal prompts. Also, physical prompts and physical guidance can be presented together, where one hand guides and one hand prompts.

The cumulative nature of verbal and physical (perceptual) prompts and guidance (motor cue) implies that they serve as mediators for the desired response. This cumulative procedure differs from the model presented by Martin et al. (1975). Within the Direct Teaching Model, prompts are always presented following a discriminative signal (either attention or task instruction) and faded out in a gradual sequential manner as soon as possible. Table 5 shows the sequence and content of each of the five teaching levels.

As can be seen in Table 5, the guidance and prompting are gradually faded out as the teacher or parent moves up the sequence through the teaching levels. Table 6 presents an example of the teaching levels to clarify the specific component sequence for a given trial.

In addition, within a series of several trials at any specific teaching level, the teacher/parent gradually reduces or fades the amount of guidance or prompting such that the transitions on trials between levels, e.g. the last trial of level 1 to the first trial of level 2, is no greater change than the transitions between trials within the teaching level. This fading process is very important in easing the transition to lesser amounts of prompting and guidance while at the same time reducing the child's dependence upon the teacher for assistance.

The criterion for shifting from one level to another is three consecutive correct responses at a given teaching level. If the student displays an incorrect response at any level, the teacher immediately drops back to the previous level of instruction and continues teaching at that level until three consecutive correct responses are obtained at that level again. If, however, the child exhibits the behavior immediately after the instruction without the need for prompting and guidance this is recorded by circling the trial and after five consecutive instances the child is moved from that step in the program or from that particular program into the next step of instruction or program. This procedure allows for skipping rather quickly through the steps of the program if the child does not require prompting and guidance in order to proceed.

Data Collection Format

Teachers and parents record student performance following each instructional trial. Recordings are made on the Training Session Data Sheet developed by Martin et al. (1975). Child correct responses

Table 5
Five Instructional Levels of the Direct Teaching Model

Teaching Levels	Components
Level 1	1. Instruction 2. Model * 3. Verbal prompt 4. Physical prompt 5. Physical guidance — Level 1
Level 2	1. Instruction 2. Model * 3. Verbal prompt 4. Physical prompt 5. Physical guidance — Level 2
Level 3	1. Instruction 2. Model * 3. Verbal prompt 4. Physical prompt
Level 4	1. Instruction 2. Model * 3. Verbal prompt
Level 5	1. Instruction 2. Model *

*May or may not be included depending upon the terminal behavior in the program.

Table 6
Examples of Teaching Levels and Concomitant Scoring Categories

1. Level 2

TEACHER BEHAVIOR	SCORING CATEGORIES
Say "eat"	Instruction model
You say it, Danny, "eat" (gestures to own mouth while saying this)	Verbal prompt model
Use one finger on child's mouth	Physical prompt Physical Guidance — Level 2

In the foregoing example the word eat is scored as a model because the teacher is emitting the sound she wants the child to imitate. If the teacher used both hands to assist in forming the child's mouth to produce the sound, this would have been an example of Level 1 teaching.

2. Level 3

TEACHER BEHAVIOR	SCORING CATEGORIES
Say "ball"	Instruction model
Danny, say "ball." (points to the child while saying this)	Verbal prompt model Physical prompt

Note: "Danny, say" is scored as a verbal prompt because it is a verbal directive following the instruction, directing the child to engage in a specified behavior. In this instance the verbal prompt is an expanded instruction because the teacher includes the child's name. The physical prompt is pointing to the child indicating he should respond.

3. Level 4

TEACHER BEHAVIOR	SCORING CATEGORIES
Say "eat"	Instruction model
Say "eat"	Verbal prompt model

Note: In this example the verbal prompt is a repetition of the initial instruction.

4. Level 5

TEACHER BEHAVIOR	SCORING CATEGORIES
Say "eat"	Instruction model

are recorded by indicating the number of the teaching level. For example, if the child responds correctly at level 1 instruction, a number 1 is recorded in the appropriate box on the data sheet; similar recording procedures are used for all teaching levels. The first row of Table 9 indicates the typical pattern of recording for a particular behavior. Child incorrect responses are recorded by an X or O in the appropriate column for individual trials. This example illustrates criterion shifts up and down which record a child's performance during a teaching session. This recording system is very functional, as it allows for ease of recording and gives an ongoing record of the child's progress through the levels of teaching for programs and steps within programs. Using the criterion for shifting up and down within the 5 levels, the teacher knows exactly where the child is and what to do next.

The results of our criterion-referenced assessment procedure tell us at what level to begin teaching. The parents and teachers then begin the instructional program at this level and gradually increase the level of teaching by the reduction of prompts and guidance until the child is responding spontaneously on his/her own to the natural cues or signals. The reason for starting at the level of assessment is to ensure the greatest success for the child in a teaching situation.

Figure 1 illustrates the graphing format used within the programs. This graph represents the child's progress through each teaching level and for various behaviors in a gross motor imitation teaching program. As can be seen in the graph, days are shown across the bottom and behaviors in the program as successive panels going up the side. As the child's performance reaches criterion at each level it is graphed from the 0-5 level. Review for five days and maintenance once a week are indicated after learning as unconnected dots following level 5. In this example, two actions are taught at once, requiring the child to discriminate between them. When the child imitates one reliably, it is placed on review and another action is incorporated. Review, the time generalization procedure, is taken once a day for five consecutive teaching days; if the child is correct *four of five* or *five of five* trials, the behavior is placed on maintenance. Maintenance, the long-term follow-up procedure, is checked once a week for five weeks. As can be seen in the graph, the second behavior, *clap hands,* was not well maintained so it was re-taught after *tap table* was learned. This graph exemplifies the manner in which one can monitor the child's progress in programs and make helpful changes in program or teaching if a plateau is attained.

The Test-Teach Method: Incidental Teaching Model

An Incidental Teaching Model adapted from Hart and Risley (1975) has also been developed. This procedure is designed to transmit information to the child, practice the development or generalization of a skill or concept, or teach new skills or concepts for language and other areas in naturally occurring situations. The pro-

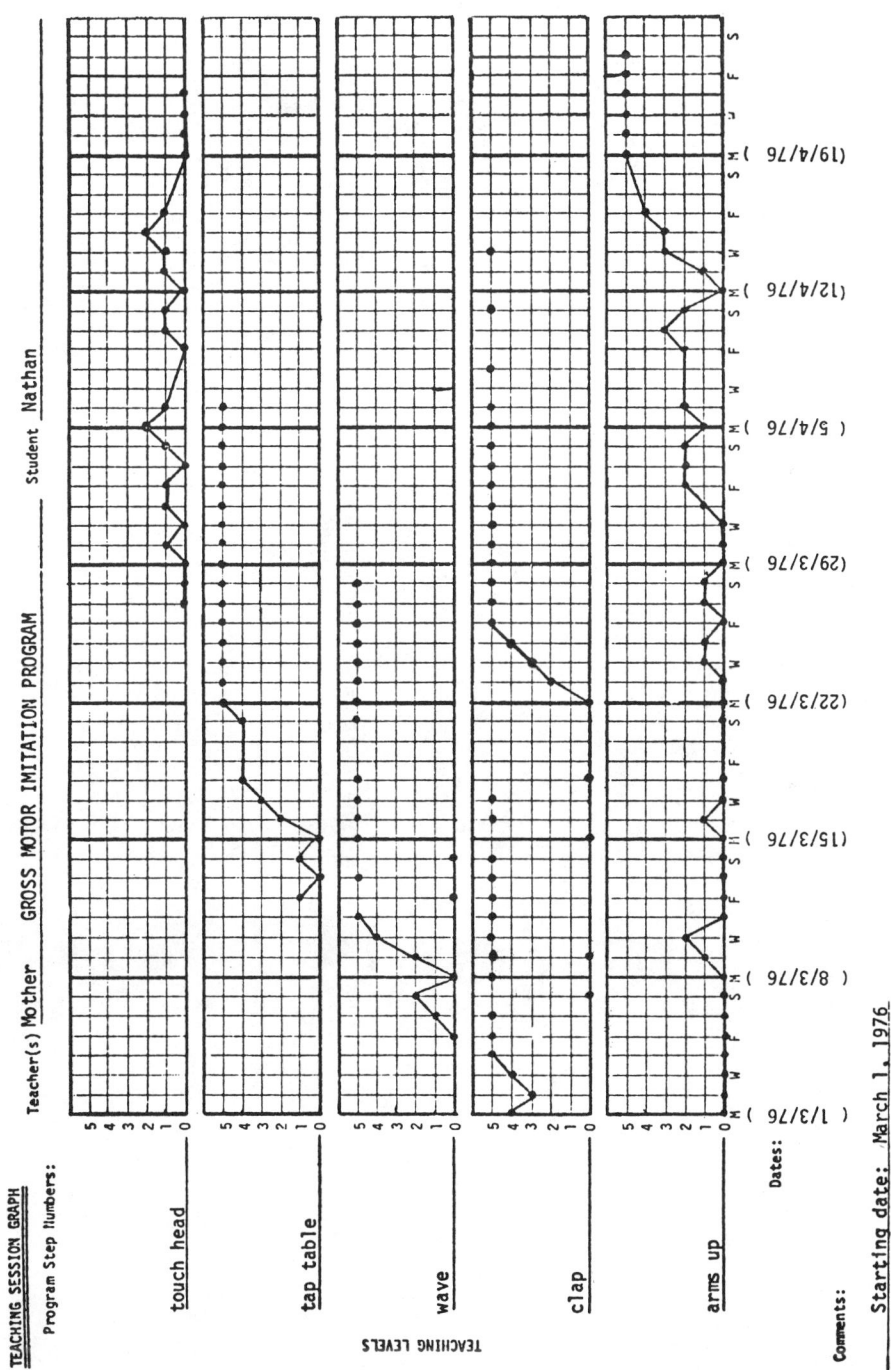

Figure 1. Teaching examples in gross motor imitation in the home program

Table 7

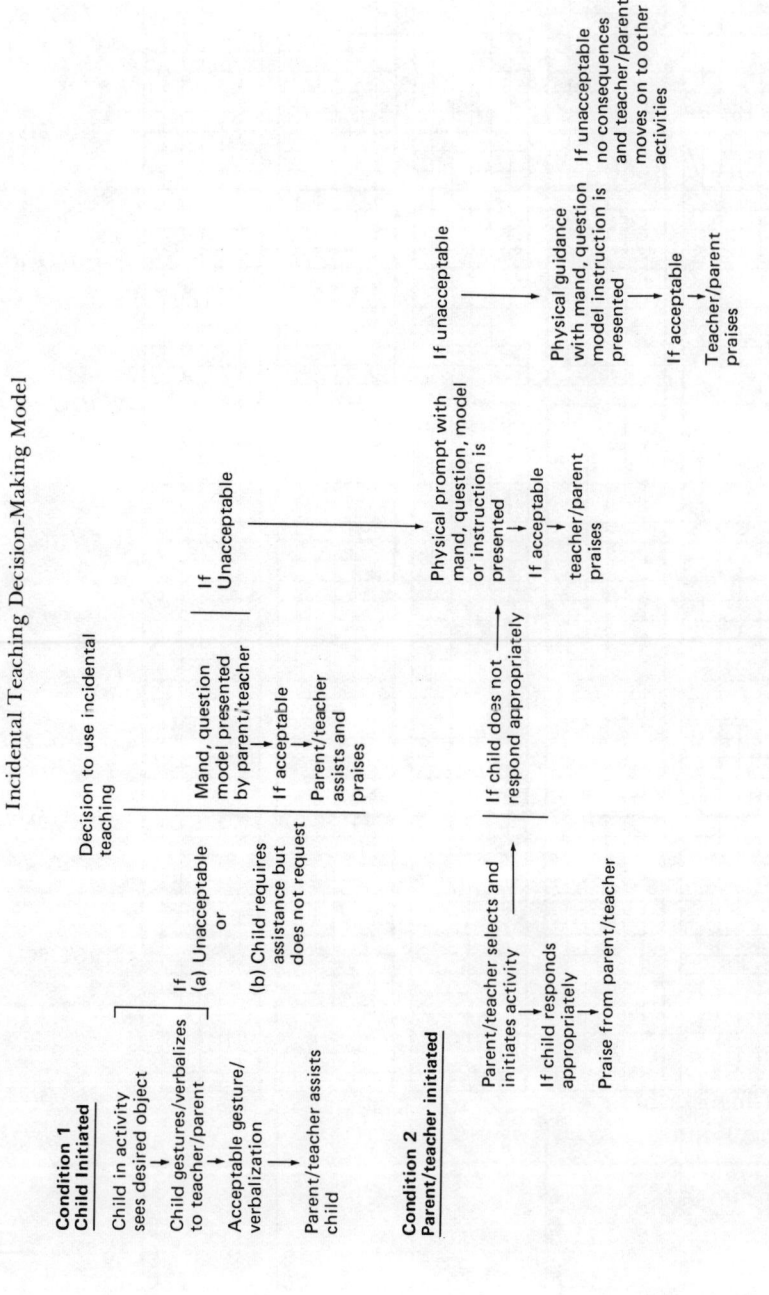

Incidental Teaching Decision-Making Model

**Condition 1
Child Initiated**

Child in activity sees desired object → Child gestures/verbalizes to teacher/parent → If (a) Unacceptable or (b) Child requires assistance but does not request → Decision to use incidental teaching → Mand, question model presented by parent/teacher → If acceptable → Parent/teacher assists and praises

If Unacceptable → Physical prompt with mand, question, model or instruction is presented → If acceptable teacher/parent praises

If unacceptable → Physical guidance with mand, question model instruction is presented → If acceptable Teacher/parent praises

If unacceptable no consequences and teacher/parent moves on to other activities

Acceptable gesture/verbalization → Parent/teacher assists child

**Condition 2
Parent/teacher initiated**

Parent/teacher selects and initiates activity → If child responds appropriately → Praise from parent/teacher

If child does not respond appropriately → (to Physical prompt branch above)

cedure is readily employed by parents, teachers, and volunteers in assisting the child to learn to use language more effectively. Modifications of the procedure outlined by Hart and Risley include the development of parent/teacher-initiated situations, as well as the child-initiated situations, for incidental teaching. Table 7 presents a schematic illustration of both child-initiated and parent/teacher-initiated situations. Parent/teacher-initiated situations, as well as child/initiated situations, are employed because many of our children do not exhibit spontaneous language. This decision-making model includes a series of decisions about which verbal cues and prompts as well as guidance may be used to assist the child in responding. Further explanations of this model with examples will follow.

Home Teaching Program

The general procedures for assessment and teaching are employed both in homes and in the school program. This section presents the process of parent training and teaching in the home program with examples of programs implemented by parents. Following assessment of the child at home, the behavioral objectives in the developmental sequence on which to begin teaching are identified. Programs are then developed using the previously described format. To implement the programs required to teach the objectives, the parents first participate in a parent training program. The three major steps will be briefly outlined.

Parent Training Program

The first step is an explanation of the teaching format and the beginning of teaching at home. The parents are familiarized with how programs are established for specific behavioral objectives within each developmental area and given a brief overview of the "teaching procedure" used to move through the progressive steps in a program. Following this parents are given a behavioral objective assessed at level 5 (this is a behavior or task the child does without prompts or assistance) and a procedure for maintenance. This will give them a week of practice in establishing a behavior under parental instruction, plus time to practice teaching at level 5 until they are confident before proceeding to the more complex teaching required at lower levels. In this way, a method to maintain and generalize newly learned behaviors is provided to the parents from the outset.

In Figure 2, examples are presented for two children's performances at Step 1 of the Parent Training Program over a one-week period, shown along the horizontal axis. Both children maintained a consistent level of performance at a level 5 (shown along the vertical axis). This figure represents one behavior or task performed in three different settings shown in the three panels (the child will follow a moving object with the eyes and head in 180° motion).

The second step in the parent training program requires the parents to implement a sequenced teaching program for a behavioral objective that has been assessed at a level less than 5 but greater than 1. This step gives concentrated practice at teaching using physical and verbal prompts (level 3 and 4). This step also introduces parents to the criteria or procedures used to move the child through the program by gradually reducing the amount of prompting. At this stage, the parents begin to use the data recording procedures. Once the behavior objective is attained at a criterion of level 5, the parent puts the program on maintenance as in the first step of the parent training program.

The first example in Figure 3 on the lower left side illustrates the progress of a 14-month-old child through a put-in program assessed at level 3 (he required a physical prompt or gesture to complete the task). Teaching was started at this level and prompts systematically and gradually reduced until the child performed the task on verbal instructions.

The second example in Figure 3 in the upper right section illustrates the progress of a seven-month-old child through a reach and grasp program assessed at level 3. Teaching continued from this level of the physical and verbal prompts until the child took the object within five seconds of its presentation to him. In both of these examples, the parents were able to move the children through the step in the program to mastery within an eight-day period.

The last step involves having the parent implement a sequenced teaching program for a behavioral objective assessed at level 0 or level 1 (the child required maximum physical guidance, i.e. had to be put through the task or did not respond at all). After supervision and practice in using the teaching procedures at level 2 and level 1 (minimal physical guidance with one finger and maximum physical guidance with hands on, respectively), parents are able to implement a

The Early Education Project 147

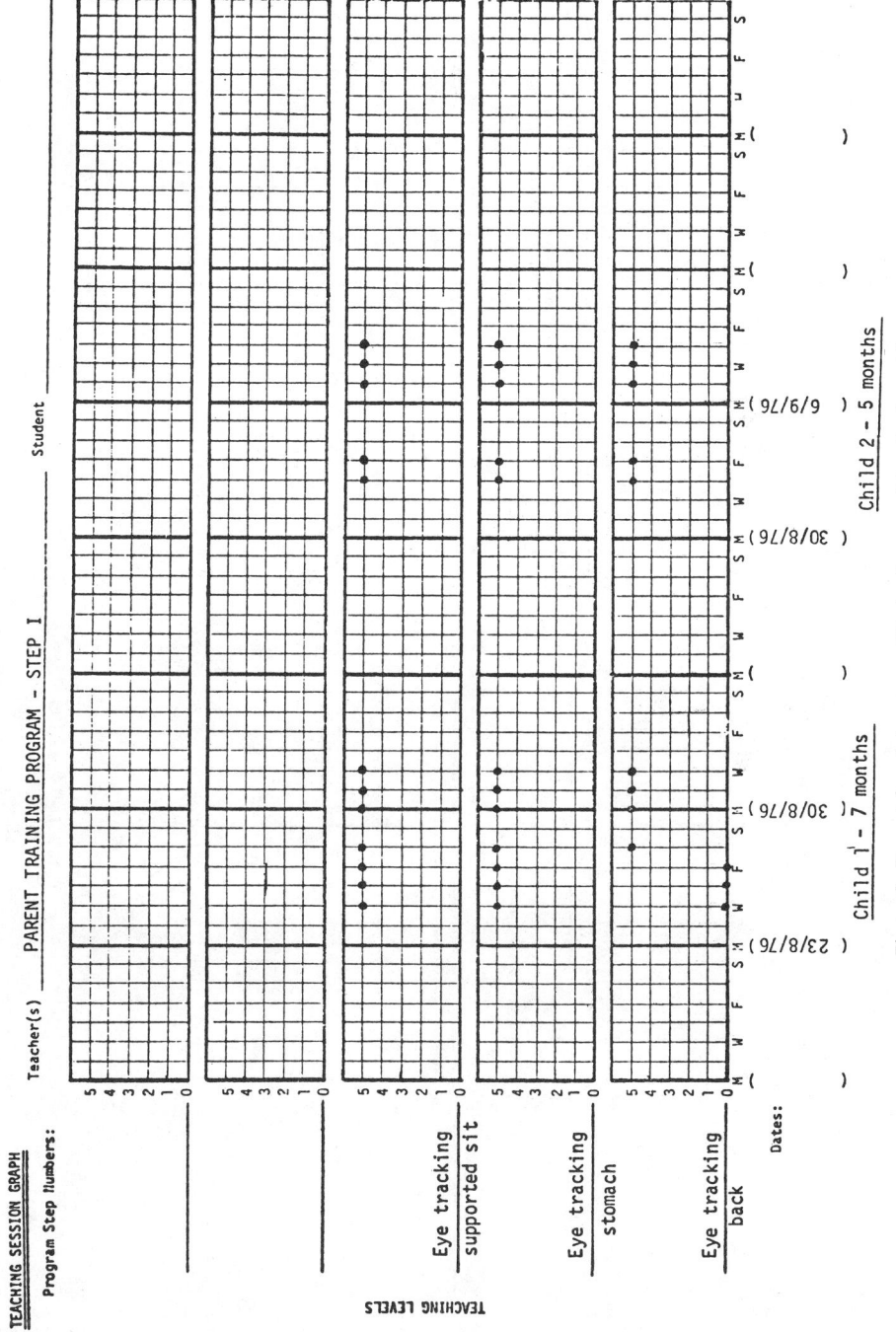

Figure 2. Parental maintenance of behavior at a 5 level of teaching

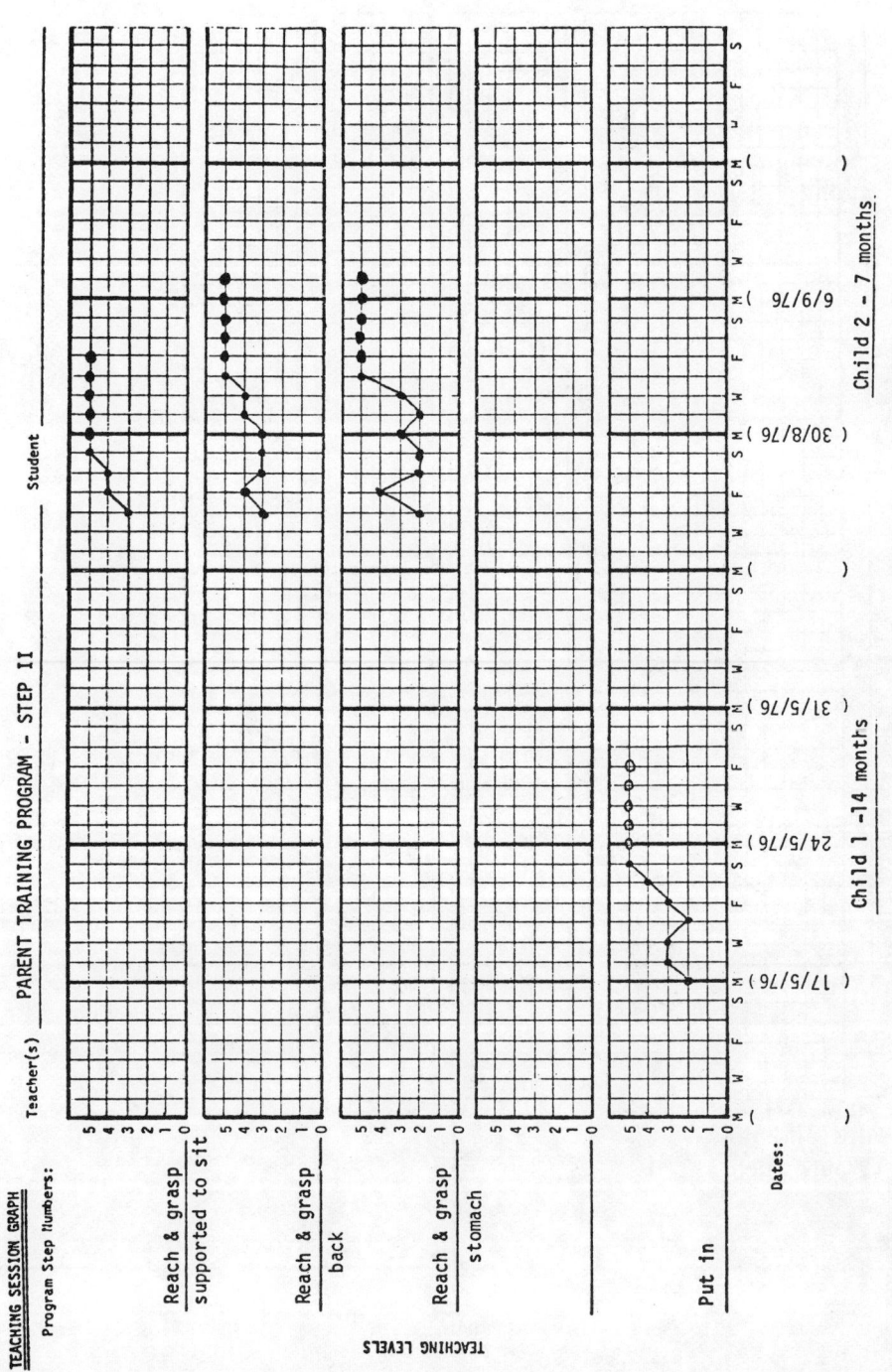

148   *Behavorial Systems for the Developmentally Disabled*

Figure 3. Parental teaching from level 3 to level 5 in the training program

The Early Education Project

program to teach any behavioral objective, move their child through it using the teaching model, maintain the skill or concept on review when it is mastered, and record their results on the MIMR data sheet.

Figure 4 presents an example of a child's progress through one of the language programs. The behavior target includes the child's imitating either motor actions or sounds within five seconds of an instruction and modeled example by the parent. The child learned the actions very quickly but the sounds required more time. However, after several weeks, sounds were acquired as well and the child went on to the next program in the sequence, sounds and words.

To teach parents the procedural implementation of a program at the 5 levels of intervention the home teacher uses a) modeling; b) behavioral rehearsal by the parents; and c) videotape replay. Following the last step of the parent training program the home teacher visits the family on a weekly or biweekly basis. The home teacher may assist the parents in selecting new behavioral objectives which are appropriate to the child's level of development. She will also guide them in improving their teaching procedures and overcoming problems which arise in teaching or with the programs themselves.

Table 8 shows the ages and special characteristics of the children in the infant program. The results from the first and second assessments on the normative tests are also presented showing the extensive changes in the mental and physical areas of the Bailey Scales.

To date specific validation procedures have not been conducted on the parent training program itself, although the parental progress in teaching constitutes a measure of validity. A behavioral analysis system (BAS) for assessing the parents' procedural reliability in implementing programs using the teaching models has been utilized effectively with selected families. The BAS has assisted the home teacher's provision of in-service teaching with the parents to improve their instruction.

In the following sections we will describe some of the programs parents are teaching at home as well as the children's progress in these programs. Even though the parents are visited weekly by a home teacher, they are responsible for teaching their children and recording their response in all of these programs. As with any program, many ups and down are encountered in the implementation of the programs, such as illness or the need to adjust to some teaching procedure. Typical educational or program implementation problems are reflected in a child's progress becoming fixated at one level of the teaching model or at one step in a multi-step program.

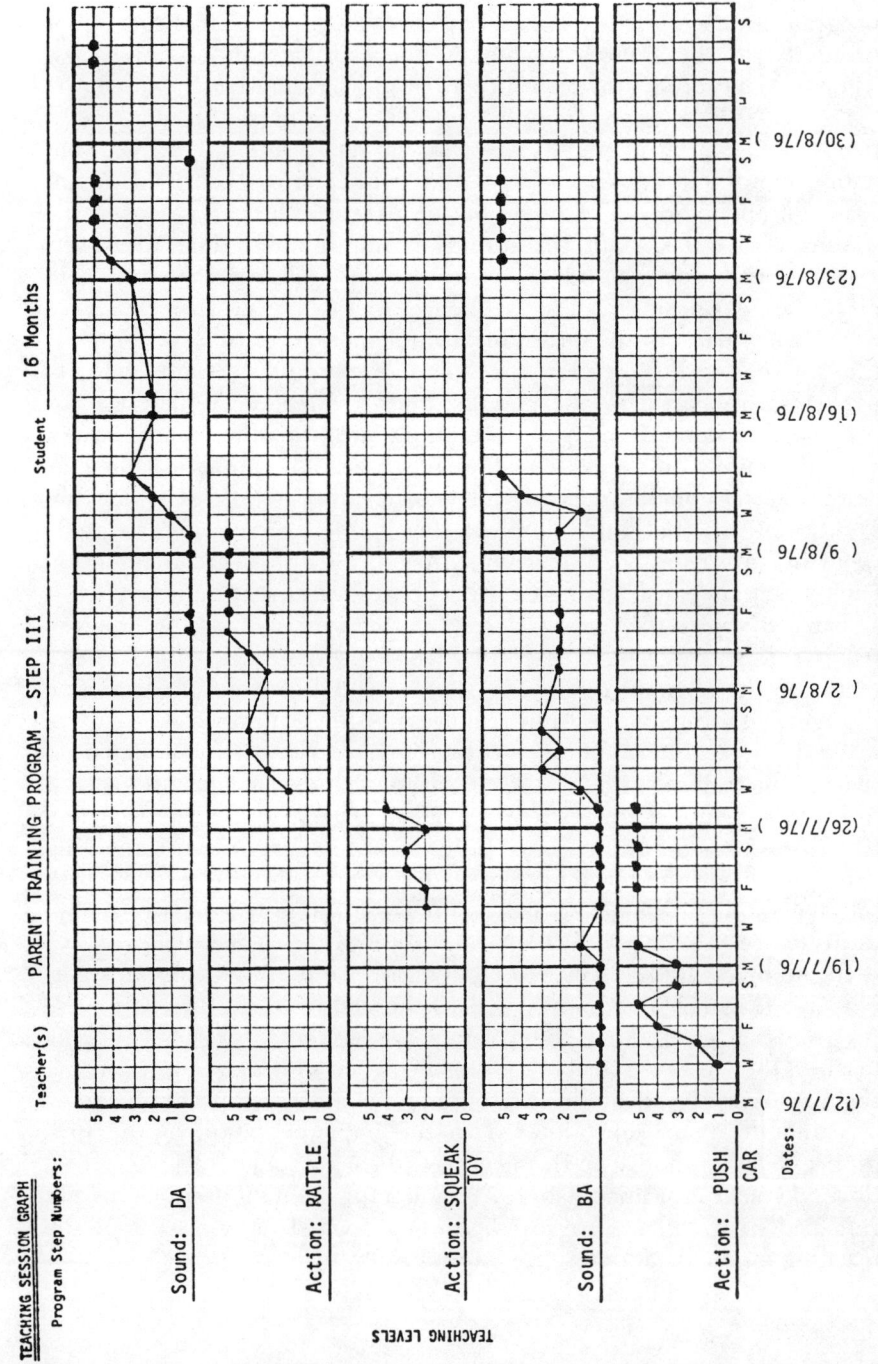

150   *Behavorial Systems for the Developmentally Disabled*

Figure 4. Parent teaching from levels 1 through 5 for the action and sound program

Table 8
Description of Children in the Home Program—Normative Assessment Results

Child	Entry C.A.	Test I MD	PD	VA	EA	Test II MD	PD	VA	EA	Test III MD	PD	VA	EA	C.A. Change	Change Test I – II MD	PD	VA	EA
.	7	7	6	7	6	15	14	13	11	–	–	–	–	9	8	8	6	5
.	15	6	7	7	6	14	8	11	11	–	–	–	–	9	8	–	4	5
.	10	6	7	7	6	11	7	11	9	–	–	–	–	8	5	0	4	3
.	32	20	18	7	11	29	24	26	21	–	–	–	–	8	9	6	15	10
.	10	7	7	7	6	15	11	11	13	17	–	–	15	8	8	4	4	7
.	22	10	9	11	13	19	15	18	18	17	17	14	20	8	9	6	7	5
.	24	9	7	7	*	19	8	7	8	23	16	21	9	7	4	–	–	–
.	12	8	7	7	*	14	9	10	14	15	9	11	–	5	6	2	1	–
.	19	13	9	11	*	12	7	7	9	–	–	–	–	5	7	0	1	–
.	16	3	4	11	*	18	13	19	18	16	10	10	10	5	5	4	8	7
.	5	13	15	12	14	11	8	9	7	–	–	–	–	6	7	4	–	7
.	24	6	6	*	*	–	–	20	21	–	–	–	–	8	5	4	8	7
.	20	6	6	*	*	11	8	11	8	–	–	–	–	6	5	2	–	–
.	9	4	8	*	*	12	10	8	10	–	–	–	–	6	8	2	–	–
x̄	16.07	8.5	8.36	8.89	9.13	14.92	10.92	12.93	12.64	17.6	12.6	15.2	14.6	7	6.92	3.08	7.00	6.13
n	(14)	(14)	(14)	(8)	(8)	(13)	(13)	(14)	(14)	(5)	(5)	(5)	(5)	(13)	(13)	(13)	(8)	(8)
	8	3	5	*	*													
	7	6	6	7	*													
	4	3	3	*	*													
	6	4	5	*	*													
	19	5	7	*	*													
	9	2	2	*	*													
	24	10	9	*	*													
	6	4	4	*	*													
	31	24	11	26	26													
x̄	12.00	6.78	5.78	–	–													
n	(9)	(9)	(9)	–	–													

Legend

* —Indicates Language Age Equivalents are below 6 months
CA—Chronological Age
MD—Mental Development Age Equivalents in months from the Bayley Scales of Infant Development
PD—Psychomotor Development Age Equivalents in months from the Bayley Scales of Infant Development
VA—Verbal Comprehension Age Equivalent in months from the Reynell Developmental Language Scales
EA—Expressive Language Age Equivalent in months from the Reynell Developmental Language Scales

These problems are investigated with the behavioral analysis system (BAS) to analyze parent implementation of the teaching model; in addition, a program component analysis is done employing the program evaluation decision making model. This model allows for a check of various program components such as the size of steps or the standards or conditions of a target objective. Following analysis possible problem areas of either parent teaching or programming are isolated, altered and re-evaluated to note the effectiveness of the remediation. This process of evaluate, analyze, alter, reevaluate, and monitor is continued until the child's developmental progression through the program is positively accelerated.

Language Development

The language portion of our program contains both receptive and expressive components. Receptive language includes parental gestures and verbalizations which the children are able to understand and respond to appropriately. Expressive language includes children's gestures and verbalizations used to make themselves understood.

The language programs have been developed in conjunction with programs employed in the United States and through consultations with a speech specialist. With the children in the home program a sequence of steps towards teaching the child to imitate sounds and words is followed. The teaching programs begin with auditory localizing of sounds and then verbalization, increasing the children's production and repetition of their own sounds and babblings and teaching them to respond to their own names. Once the child responds to his/her own name we begin to teach him/her imitation skills, both for functional motor actions and for sounds leading to words. The imitation programs will be discussed in more depth later in the chapter.

Motor Development

The motor programs were developed in consultation with a physiotherapist who had experience with retarded children and from the publications of Fredericks et al. (1976). With this material and instruction from the physiotherapist, the teachers wrote a series of motor training programs ranging in complexity from controlled eye movements and raising the head in a prone position through sitting

The Early Education Project

and walking to advanced locomotion skills such as hopping. The gross motor items were developmentally sequenced and grouped together into separate strands (see Table 2).

The three components for each motor program—posture, assumption of posture and motion—are considered to ensure that children not only acquire the skill but do so with good posture. Some strands have terminal behaviors in all three components—for example, crawling and walking. When teaching a child to walk it is desirable that the child have the appropriate posture and that he be able to assume the appropriate posture in addition to actually walking. Some strands, like controlled eye movements or sitting, do not have tasks and programming in all three components because of the nature of the skill or objective.

The main concern in the gross motor area is not simply to teach the motor behavior but to ensure that the behavior is carried out with the appropriate posture. These children have learned to sit, stand, and walk with very poor posture. Their head, stomachs and bottoms protrude and their knees are hyperextended or locked. This posture produces the awkward, stiff-legged gait of Down's syndrome children. The motor programs that have been developed are designed to correct some or all of these problems before the damage becomes irreversible.

Children in the home program are working in the rolling, sitting, crawling, and walking strands of the program. Figure 5 presents one child's progress through the motor strands for creeping and reciprocal crawling. When teaching in the motor area was initiated with him, he was able to sit and move around the room by rolling. In five months, he learned to creep along the floor on his abdomen (as shown in the upper panel) and to crawl with a reciprocal pattern on his hands and knees (shown in the second and third panels). Also, he is now going up and down stairs on his hands and knees and can pull to a stand on furniture.

Cognitive Development

In the cognitive area of programming parents in the home program are teaching their children tasks and operations which range from visual tracking, reaching, grasping, and putting in mouth through putting in, taking out and putting on and other general motoric operations.

154 Behavorial Systems for the Developmentally Disabled

Figure 5. Infant's progress in programs for creeping and reciprocal crawling

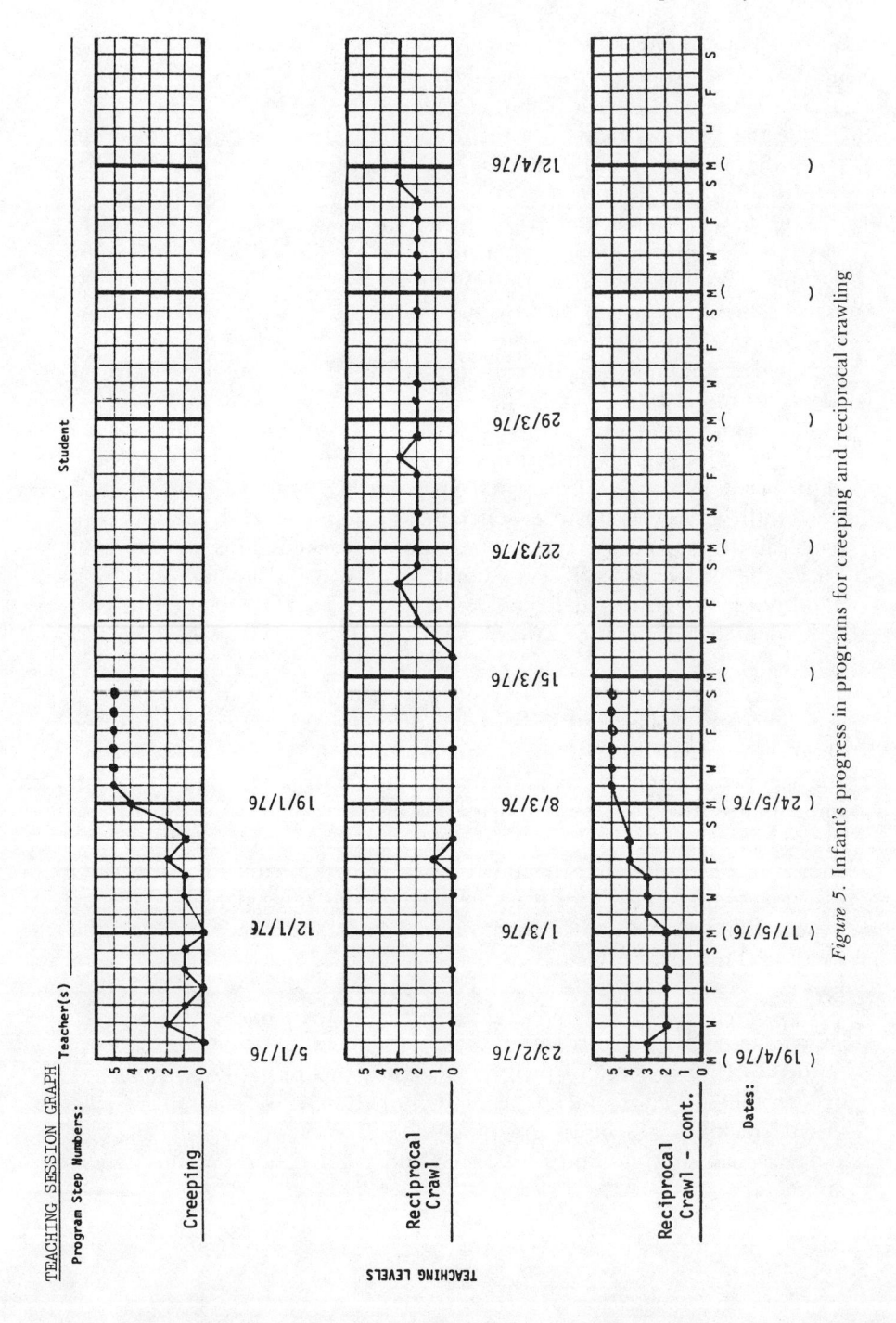

In Figure 6 an example of a child's progress through a variety of these cognitive programs is presented, showing a take out and put in sequence. The behavior targets included the child's being able to take out or put in an object in a container 3" in diameter. The steps in the programs involved gradually decreasing the diameter of the container, thus increasing concentration and dexterity. The child completed the program at a consistent rate until the last step. At this point he experienced difficulty in that he often missed the small container; however, after two weeks this step was mastered.

Self-Help Skills

The children are also working on several programs within the self-help area of development; skills that the children in the home program are working on range from sucking and swallowing, feeding oneself and drinking from a cup to helping and participating in dressing and undressing.

Figure 7 illustrates a 13-month-old child's progress through a program designed to teach him to raise the glass to his mouth using two hands and then to drink unassisted. This program involves several steps as it proved too large a task to teach at once. Since the steps proved to be too small for most children, two steps have been removed. The need for fewer steps is illustrated by the child's rapid movement through the program.

Many of the self-help skills are taught using backward chains and all are taught in the child's environment as the behaviors occur naturally to maintain the ecological validity of the teaching-learning setting.

This description covers the major components of the home program for infant intervention and demonstrates the learning results for these infants when their parents begin instruction at an early age.

The Classroom Project

The classroom segment of the project is located in Mayfield School, an elementary school in the city of Edmonton occupying two classrooms on the ground floor of the school. The toddler classroom has its own toileting facilities and the preschool classroom uses the regular washroom across the corridor. Both classrooms are equipped with toddler-size furniture plus fans and humidifiers because of the upper respiratory problems of many of the children.

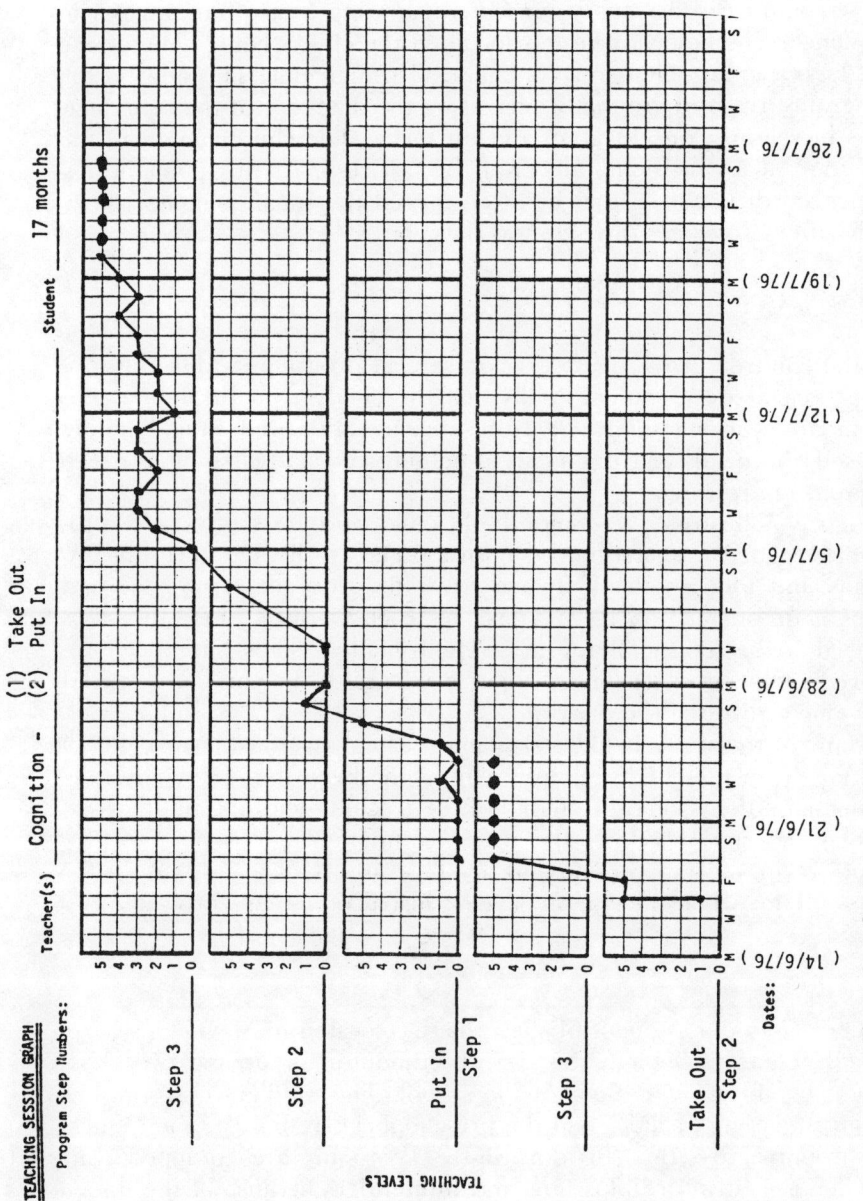

156   *Behavorial Systems for the Developmentally Disabled*

Figure 6. Infant's progress through the first two steps in the motoric operations programs.

The Early Education Project 157

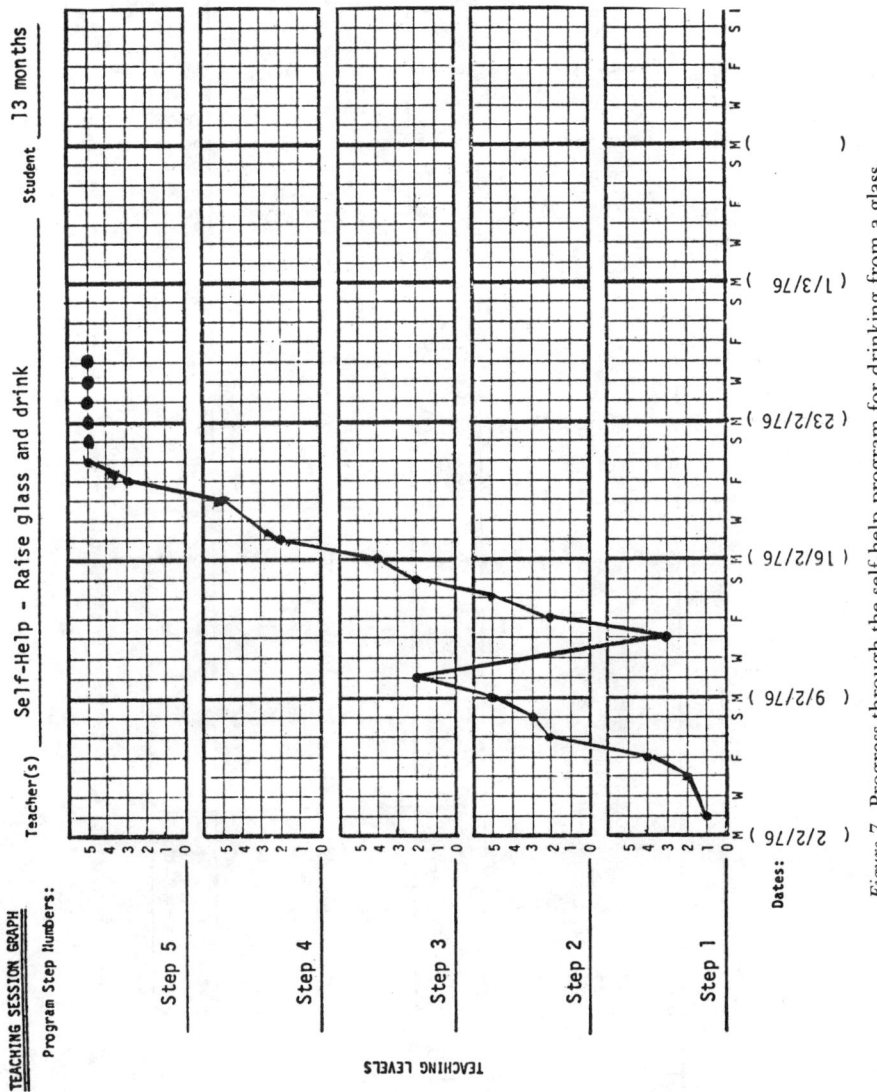

Figure 7. Progress through the self-help program for drinking from a glass.

158

Behaviorial Systems for the Developmentally Disabled

Table 9

Description of Children in the Toddler and Preschool Group—Normative Assessment Results

Child	Entry C.A.	Test I				Test II				Test III				Change I – III				
		MD	PD	VA	EA	MD	PD	VA	EA	MD	PD	VA	EA	C.A. Change	MD	PD	VA	EA
Toddler																		
	20	8	14	*	*	13	21	7	7	17	22	15	14	14	9	8	8	7
	31	14	12	*	6	19	18	7	9	19	20	18	17	11	5	8	–	8
	42	15	12	6	6	13	12	6	9	22**	13	11	–	10	11	–	5	5
	27	14	10	9*	9*	19	13	10	11	21	15	15	18	12	7	5	6	9
	59	14	9	–	–	17	–	–	12	22**	13	13	13	15	8	4	–	–
	21	12	9	11	7	19	–	14	13	24**	–	21	23	16	12	5	–	16
	30	6	9	*	7	18	–	14	13	–	–	–	–	–	–	–	–	–
	22	14	7	7	7	16	–	8	9	19	13	16	17	13	5	6	9	10
	67	11	16	7	7	16	19	5	10	21**	22	11	11	12	7	6	4	4
x̄	35.44	12.00	10.89	8	7.2	16.67	14.11	9.11	10.33	18.13	16.50	15.0	15.5	13.25	8	5.38	7	8.50
(n)	(9)	(9)	(9)	(5)	(5)	(9)	(9)	(9)	(9)	(8)	(8)	(8)	(8)	(8)	(8)	(8)	(6)	(6)
Pre-School																		
	60	–	–	21	15	22	30	24	23	28**	–	–	–	8	6	–	–	–
	39	20	23	21	13	–	–	19	28	34**	–	26	29	14	14	–	15	16
	55	30	24	21	24	32	30	22	23	39**	–	33	36	14	9	–	12	13
	49	–	–	7	19	22	24	14	25	29**	–	22	25	16	7	–	15	6
	35	22	24	17	18	–	–	26	21	36**	–	31	24	14	14	–	14	6
	54	20	24	10	14	20	25	18	17	22**	–	20	22	14	2	–	10	8
	32	20	18	11	11	29	24	26	21	33**	–	29	22	13	13	–	18	–
	35	18	21	–	–	–	–	–	–	27**	–	22	19	12	9	–	–	–
	73	–	–	–	–	31**	–	–	25	–	–	–	–	–	–	–	–	–
	57	41**	–	38	37	–	–	26	–	–	–	–	–	–	–	–	–	–
x̄	43.9	24.43	22.33	17	18.88			19.38	22.8	31	–	19	22.43	13	9.25	–	14	10
(n)	10	(7)	(6)	(8)	(8)			(8)	(8)	(8)	–	(7)	(7)	(8)	(8)	–	(6)	(6)

** – Indicates mental age equivalent from Stanford-Binet Intelligence Scale, L-M, (1960 Norms).

See Table 8 for abbreviation definitions

The Early Education Project

Presently, we have one morning class of seven toddlers, one morning class of eight preschoolers, and an afternoon class of five preschoolers. Table 9 presents a description of the students grouped into preschoolers and toddlers. A student teacher ratio of four to one, with a maximum enrollment of eight students per class, seems to be optimal. Two teachers are assigned to each morning classroom and share responsibility for the afternoon preschool class on a bi-weekly schedule. This scheduling leaves time for each pair of teachers to work on graphs, write programs, and make home visits every second week. Originally, we had anticipated having four classes of eight (two in the morning and two in the afternoon), but the importance of home visits and other classroom duties have made the three classes a full load for the teachers.

The children were originally placed in one classroom or the other according to their functioning level as assessed by the Portage Assessment. Now, new children are placed in the appropriate classroom following assessment on the newly rewritten motor, cognition, self-help and language strands, previously discussed within the developmental curriculum. In general, children placed in the toddler classroom are between two and a half and five years of age (average age three), do not walk without support and have very limited language. Children placed in the preschool classroom are from three to five and a half years of age (average age four), are fully ambulatory and use words and some phrases.

Parents assist teachers with specific programs in the classroom once or twice every two weeks. The teachers have set up parent guidelines in order to aid parent-teacher communication and provide for maximum generalization of our program to the home environment. The guidelines outline parent participation in the classroom, workshops and in-service training, monthly progress reports and home visits.

Initially, the parents participated in a parent training program carried out by a research assistant. Now the teachers themselves are responsible for training of new parents as well as continuation of the program for the original parents. Upon completion of the program, the parents assist the teachers in conducting some of the daily sessions. In addition to parents, volunteers, practicum students and institutional staff help out on a regular basis (three of the children are from a residential institution).

Daily Classroom Schedule

Morning classes run five days a week (9:00 - 11:30 a.m.) and afternoon classes four days a week (1:00 - 3:00 p.m.), with a staff meeting on the fifth afternoon. Most sessions in both morning and afternoon last no more than ten minutes due to the limited attention span of the children. The teachers alternate hourly between individual language and group instruction. While one teacher does individual language sessions in the classroom, the other conducts group motor, cognitive or self-help activities with the remainder of the children. The group sessions have a ratio of one teacher to seven students if there are no parents or volunteers. If a parent or volunteer is present, he or she takes one half of the group session children and conducts incidental teaching sessions.

The children arrive by cab between 9:00 and 9:10 a.m. each morning. Each child is working on a number of undressing behaviors (for example, hat off, zipper down, coat off); each skill is taught at the level of guidance or prompting currently being worked on for that child. Data are recorded on MIMR sheets daily and graphed on a weekly basis.

As can be seen on the schedule, there are several cognitive activities planned each day. During the teaching of these activities the teacher must move from child to child giving trials to only one child at a time. The teacher must move very quickly to keep the attention of the group. In the more advanced preschool cognitive activities, the children learn activities such as drawing a line from dot to dot, one of the early steps in the writing strand.

The children work on individualized motor programs later in the morning, as is shown on the sample schedule. There are two 15-minute toileting sessions in the morning. During this time preschoolers work on getting pants up and down as well as standing up and sitting down on the toilet. The toddlers work on the pants off, pants on program from a sitting position. There is a juice and snack time for about 10-15 minutes after the first toileting. Parents supply snacks for the toddler and preschool class. The preschool class has incorporated socialization and self-help skills into their juice time. Children work on spreading, cutting or passing activities. Children in both classes are expected to gesture, make sounds or words before receiving juice, depending upon the functioning level of the particular child. In addition, the preschoolers are expected to say please or thank you.

The Early Education Project

After juice the preschoolers have an art or music session. Art includes many fine motor activities such as tearing, pasting, picking up small items to be glued and generalization of pencil grasp in drawing tasks. Music sessions include auditory sound discriminations, finger games, and gross motor activities.

Throughout the morning, self-help sessions are done at times when they naturally occur. For example, hand/face washing program is carried out either prior to or just after the juice time. Finally, the children work on undressing behaviors when they arrive each morning and dressing behaviors when they depart. Other self-help programs that cannot be done in a natural setting (e.g. eating with a knife and fork) become home programs to be carried out by the parents. The one exception to this is the fastener program (snaps, buckles, shoe laces, etc.). This program is taught in the classroom because of its complexity.

The children prepare to leave for home at about 11:30 a.m. each day. In the preschool class the children have an informal session on yes/no. The teacher holds up a coat asking, "Is this your coat?" Children are reinforced for answering "yes" if the coat is theirs and "no" if it is not. All children work on dressing items at this time (put on coat, zipper-up, hat on). At about 11:45 a.m. the cab drivers arrive and the children depart for home.

Every Friday probes are given for untrained behaviors and tests for learned behaviors are given to ensure maintenance. The toddlers have crafts or music and the preschoolers go into the kindergarten classroom to sing songs and play games or bake during the last segment of the classroom time.

The cognitive, language and motor programs are presented in detail below.

Cognitive Program

Initially, each of the separate cognitive behaviors that the child did not do four out of five times on initial testing was taught. This approach proved unsatisfactory for a variety of reasons. It was difficult to work with a group of children when one was working on a tower of six blocks, another was working on rings on a peg, a few more were working on stringing activities, etc. In addition, the children were learning a series of isolated motor behaviors rather than operations or concepts. Therefore, the cognitive skills were broken down into a series of strands of behavior much like the motor strands previously described. Each strand has a specific terminal behavior (e.g., puts six pieces in an interlocking puzzle), and a number of subskills (e.g., puts a circle and square in a formboard, puts four pieces in a noninterlocking puzzle). The children work on a number of cognitive strands at the same time, depending upon the classroom they are in and their individual functioning level as determined on baseline criterion-referenced assessment. For example, the toddler children are working on the operations, stringing, stacking, and writing strands. The operation strand is presented in detail to serve as an example of a cognitive activity. Operations taught are "put in," "put on," "take out," "take off," "push," "pull," "open," and "close." Before implementing teaching programs a five-day baseline assessment is taken for each child in each concept or operation to be taught. The instructions remain constant, but the specific materials used to test each operation are changed each day (e.g., a child may be asked to "push" a toy car one day, a toy wagon the next, a block with a button on top the next, and so on). After this assessment each child is taught all of the operations that he/she did not perform to a criterion of at least four of five times correctly on baseline. The baseline assessment procedure (1) indicates the behaviors the child does not know and (2) provides for evaluation of the instructional program. When the child has reached criterion on eight operations, two operations are taught at a time with one distractor item present.

The specific materials used are varied from trial to trial so that the child does not simply learn a specific motor behavior. The preschool children are learning more complex behaviors in the same strands. In addition, the preschool children are learning the body part identification strand and three-word instructions. The story corner session in the preschool classroom involves book and flannel board stories. This period is a time for incidental teaching and generalization of the direct teaching program for cognition.

Language Program

The toddler language program consists of a series of programs that are designed to prepare the children for entry into the language program developed by Guess, Sailor and Baer (1976), which will be de-

The Early Education Project

scribed in more detail later. Before entering the Guess, Sailor and Baer program it is desirable that the children are able to imitate approximately 16 functional words that are easily distinguishable from one another. This requirement is difficult for all the toddlers, since initially none would imitate sounds or words and most children would not consistently imitate motor behaviors.

Integrating the recent research in language training and our own experience following the first eight months of programming, three major points about language training became clear. First, children should be given sound and word imitation as quickly as possible rather than spending inordinate time on motor imitation alone. Secondly, the language training should be as functional as possible. For example, during word imitation, the appropriate object should be present. Thus when teaching the word "ball," the teacher would hold up a ball. In this way, the child receives receptive as well as expressive training. Also, motor imitation should be as functional as possible, if this is a necessary starting point for a language program. Having the child imitate table tapping it not a functional skill; however, it is functional to have a child imitate putting on a hat. Thirdly, manual sign language may be used as a language facilitator to give the child a means of communicating before sounds and words become intelligible.

When establishing the new language sequence, the *attending* component of the program remained the same as originally written. The child is taught to attend to a verbal signal "(Child's name), look," plus a hand signal. When the child is consistently attending, the hand signal prompt of the attending signal is faded out.

In the Gross Motor/Sound Imitation component of the language program, which follows the attending program, imitation of sounds is taught randomly alternating with functional gross motor behaviors. As soon as the child learns to imitate two sounds he/she proceeds with two new sounds and gross motor behaviors are totally eliminated. The gross motor behaviors acquired are all functional, e.g., turning a crank on a jack-in-the-box, putting on a hat, putting penny in a bank slot, and so on. In addition to being functional activities, stimulus materials and resultant activities are chosen which have an inherent naturally reinforcing value in and of themselves. The child is given the object after a correct response and is given some receptive language training when the teacher asks for the object with the word "give" with hand extended when she wants the object back. When a sound is taught the teacher associates the sound with a gross motor behavior. For example, the teacher may say "say ō" while pushing a toy boat across the table. She then gives the boat to the child and prompts him to imitate the gross motor response, at the same time imitating the sound.

The third step in the new sequence is sound/word imitation. Once the child learns two sounds, one sound is randomly alternated with one word or the approximation of the word. Sound imitation proceeds as previously described. During word imitation, the object is always present and is also given to the child as an activity reinforcer if the word is correctly imitated. At this point very gross approximations are accepted.

Once the child can imitate 16 words, he/she moves into the Guess, Sailor and Baer language program.

Guess, Sailor, Baer Language Program

There are six categories in the Guess, Sailor and Baer (1976) program: Persons/Things, Actions with Persons/Things, Possession, Color, Size and Relation/Location. At first the children begin to work on steps 1 through 9 of the category Persons/Things which involve labeling objects, pointing to and asking for objects, asking "what's that?" and answering yes/no questions; they are also working on the initial steps in the Action program. Each day one teacher instructs each child for a 10-15-minute individual language session consisting of 32 trials. For each trial the teacher gives an attending signal, "Lisa, look." The teacher holds up an object (the stimulus for that step) and asks, "What's that?" If the child responds correctly he/she is reinforced with praise, food and feedback about the response, "Good, you said, 'apple'." The teacher marks a plus on the data sheet and goes to the next trial. If a child gives an incorrect response, the correction procedure is employed to teach the correct response. Again the attending signal to get eye contact is presented; the teacher asks, "What's that?" If the child is incorrect, the teacher says "wrong" or "no"—not in a punishing way but to inform the child that the response was incorrect. The teacher immediately models the correct response, "That's a doll." The trial is repeated, "What's that?" If the child is correct, the teacher reinforces the response; if the response is again incorrect the teacher

The Early Education Project 165

says nothing. This trial would be marked minus since only the first response is recorded. Food is used as a reinforcer in language sessions and is always preceded by social reinforcement—smiles and praise. Food is used only when a child is learning a new word or a new step in the program. As soon as the child reaches 30% correct per day, the food is faded to a variable ratio of three correct responses; at 60% accuracy it is eliminated altogether.

Because of the children's age and physical characteristics we do not expect perfect pronunciation. We are primarily concerned with learning functional language. Once a child starts imitating a new word and a high rate of responding is attained, then the best approximation he/she can make is shaped. Approximations are accepted as correct if consistent and distinguishable from the child's other words.

Criterion on each step of the Guess et al. program is 80% correct or 12 consecutive correct answers. Skill tests are given before some steps to determine if the child can perform the behavior, and at specified intervals during the step to determine when the child has met criterion. Figure 8 depicts one child's progression through step 1. The objective of this step is to label 16 common objects. Along the vertical axis is the percent correct trials per session. The days are along the horizontal axis. Initially the teacher gives a skill test on which Kerri was unable to answer any items correctly. The skill test performance is shown as a bar graph periodically in the figure. Kerri was first trained on two words—ball and cup. If she had given any correct responses on the skill test she would have started with one object labeled correctly and one labeled incorrectly so she would have some successes early in the program. In each session the objects are presented in random order for 64 trials, usually over two days. These two words are taught until criterion is reached—marked C in the figure. Another pair of words is taught to criterion in the same way; then all four words are taught in random order. When criterion is reached on all four the skill test is given again—indicated by the bar graph.

Since Kerri did not attain criterion on the skill test she was trained on four new words, two at a time. This sequence is repeated until Kerri reached over 80% correct on the skill test at the right of the graph. At that point she went on to Step 2, pointing to the objects she had learned to label.

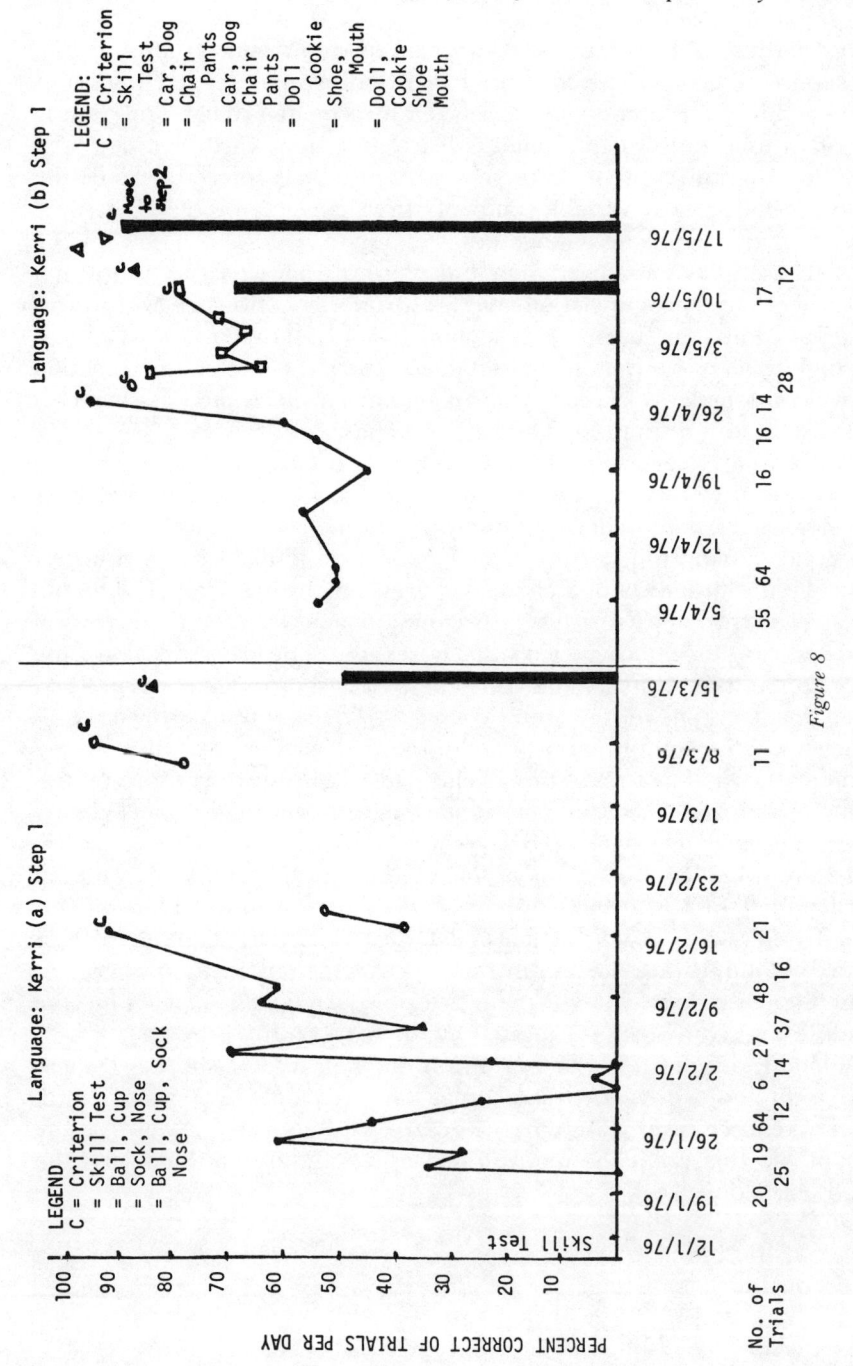

166   *Behavorial Systems for the Developmentally Disabled*

Figure 8

Motor Programs

Motor programs have been developed in several strands, including sitting, crawling, and walking. As an example, we will describe the program for the posture component of the crawling program. At the top of the sheet is the target behavior. Next, the baseline procedure to determine if it is indeed necessary for the child to be working on this program is described. The child is tested five times on the target behavior. If he has the appropriate posture four out of five times, the teacher proceeds to the next program. If the child does not perform adequately on the baseline, the teacher begins the program at the appropriate step. This particular program has four steps. Each step is precisely defined so that all teachers carry out the program in the same way.

The specific procedure to be followed for each step is described, followed by the successive levels of guidance. The guidance is gradually faded out over the trials until the child can assume the posture unassisted (level 5).

At levels 1 and 2 a stretch exercise is given prior to the trial. This procedure involves a quick stretch movement by the teacher that will get the child into the appropriate position through forcing him into a more extreme posture. For example, if the child is sitting with rounded shoulders, the teacher would give give a quick push down (stretch) on the shoulders perpendicular to the floor. The child's immediate response is to resist the push and straighten up—which is the desired posture.

At level 3 the teacher provides the push or resistance during the trial rather than before so the child is working harder to assume the correct posture. This technique is never so forceful as to impede the motion, only to slightly resist it. The resistance is discontinued for the last two teaching levels (levels 4 and 5). Once the child learns the target behavior it is tested over five days to ensure its stability, then the child moves on to the next program. The other motor programs are written in a similar manner.

The children are assessed individually and may be placed on more than one program if necessary. For instance, a child in the toddler class may be working on the posture component of the sitting program to correct for rounded back, the posture component of the walking program to correct hyperextended knees and poor balance, and on the locomotion component of the walking program to teach him to walk with a flexible string as support.

The children in the preschool class are working on the posture and locomotion components of the walking program. A series of exercises accompany the steps of the walking program to develop the control, flexibility, or muscle strength needed to maintain the target posture. Each child has two to three minutes of specific exercises before teaching on the program each day. The exercises include simple activities such as sit-ups, marching, and obstacle courses. A few children are learning more advanced gross motor skills—standing on one foot, hopping, jumping.

Self-Help Skills

As mentioned previously, the children are learning many self-help behaviors, such as undressing/dressing, eating skills, washing themselves, and toileting, during the course of the day and at home. A full discussion of these programs was given in the section on daily schedules.

Incidental Teaching

The incidental teacher procedure (Hart & Risley, 1975) previously outlined is used extensively in the classrooms for skills learned and for teaching new skills and concepts. This procedure has been initiated recently in both the home- and school-based programs and involves teachers, parents, and volunteers. Incidental teaching is carried out in situations in which an opportunity to teach a child something arises and the direct teaching model is not being used.

Table 9 depicts the Incidental Teaching Decision Making Model. There are two possible incidental teaching conditions—child-selected and -initiated or teacher/parent-selected and -initiated.

A child-selected condition occurs when the child indicates either through gesture or verbalization that he/she requires assistance. An example might be struggling to disengage a zipper and gesturing to the teacher. If this was an acceptable means of gaining the teacher's attention for a particular child, the teacher would praise asking for help, then disengage the zipper. Since some children are able to verbalize, this response might be unacceptable; therefore the teacher would model the appropriate request: "What do you want?" "Want help?" If the child said, "Want help" or "Zipper down," the teacher would intervene at this point and help with the zipper, praising the asking for assistance. If the child continued to struggle with the zipper, the teacher would have repeated the question and pointed to the zipper. If the child failed to respond correctly at this point, the teacher would assist without saying anything further. We do not want to discourage the children from asking for help; we simply wish to make a teaching/learning situation out of every possible opportunity.

The second condition is a teacher/parent-selected situation. In this condition the child does not request assistance, but the teacher or parent is able to initiate an intervention designed to facilitate learning. In this condition, a child sitting on the rug, for example, engaging in self-stimulation, not showing any interest in the toys around him, may be approached by the teacher with a peg and some plastic rings and given the instruction, "put on." If the child begins to put the rings on the peg, he/she is praised by the teacher and the teacher moves on to another child. If the child does nothing, the teacher would repeat the instruction and point to the peg. If the child begins to put the rings on the peg, he/she is praised and the teacher moves on. If the child again does not respond, the teacher would physically guide the child's hands to put a ring on the peg, and then move on.

To facilitate incidental teaching, toys have been placed on shelves behind plexi-glass. Preschool children ask for the toy they want. The toddlers are encouraged to gesture or verbalize. In both cases, the child is immediately reinforced for the appropriate response—he/she receives the desired toy. These environmental conditions have been set up in the classroom to help generalize programmed language training and introduce new language skills. For example, the child generalizes object labeling that he/she has learned in language sessions and is encouraged to imitate labels of objects not trained.

At juice time each toddler and preschooler must indicate what he/she wants, the juice or snack, through gesture or verbalization, depending on the level of an acceptable response for that child. For example, toddler Danny says "duce," Stephen points, and preschooler Kerri says, "I want juice." During toileting the children must ask to be put on or taken off the potty. Again Danny points down and Wade says, "want down." Several areas of motor development that could be taught in this manner have been identified with the physiotherapist. The children are encouraged to lift, push or pull whenever something needs to be moved at home or school. For example, the preschoolers can help bring groceries in from the car or pull people in a wagon.

Toddlers can put toys on low shelves. The preschool children have started to take the chairs down from the tables each morning.

SUMMARY

The Early Education Project constitutes a generalizable approach to early intervention with infants and school-aged children likely to exhibit moderate to severe developmental delays. Through the use of criterion-referenced assessment procedures, the child's competencies are established and the objectives for the teaching programs are behaviorally defined. The use of a standard programming method and the Direct Teaching Model provide a format for instruction both at home for parents and infants and in the school-based program for teachers and students. A reliable data recording format provides a continuous monitoring of the child's progress through programs so that helpful changes can be made when plateaus in learning/teaching are reached. Finally, the incidental teaching model reviews, and maintenance procedures ensure the lasting generalization and broad use of the new skills or concepts learned by the children. Hence, the project has implemented the five steps outlined by Bijou (1976) in an attempt to enhance the developmental progress of these developmentally handicapped children and to develop their parents and families as lifelong human resources for their optimal growth and positive living experiences.

REFERENCES

ANDERSON, D.R., GODSON, G.D., and WILLARD, J.G.: *Instructional programming for the handicapped student.* Springfield, Illinois: Charles C. Thomas, 1976.

ANDERSON, R.C. and FAUST, G.W.: *Educational psychology: the science of instruction and learning.* Toronto: Dodd, Mead, and Co., 1973.

BAINE, D.B.: Task analysis and vocational habilitation of the trainable mentally retarded. *Conference proceedings of the WIRTC 1st National Research Conference on Mental Retardation, 1977.*

BECKER, W.C., ENGLEMANN, S., and THOMAS, D.R.: *Teaching 1: Classroom Management.* Toronto: Science Research Associates, 1975a.

BECKER, W.C., ENGLEMANN, S., and THOMAS, D.R.: *Teaching 2: Cognitive learning and instruction.* Toronto: Science Research Associates, 1975b.

BIJOU, S.W., *Child development: the basic stage of early childhood.* Englewood Cliffs, N.J. Prentice-Hall, 1976.

BRICKER, W.A., and BRICKER, D.D.: The infant, toddler and preschool research and intervention project. In T.D. Tjossem (ed.) *Intervention strategies for high-risk infants and young children.* Baltimore: University Park Press 1976, pp. 545-572.

FREDERICKS, H.D., RIGGS, C., FUREY, T., GROVE, D., MOORE, W., McDONNEL, J., JORDAN, E., HANSON, W., BALDWIN, V., and WADLOW, M.: *The teaching research curriculum for moderately and severely handicapped.* Springfield, Illinois: Charles C. Thomas, 1976.

GUESS, D., SAILOR, W., and BAER, D.M.: *Functional speech and language training for the severely handicapped. Part 1: Persons and Things.* Lawrence, Kansas: H. & H. Enterprises, 1976.

HART, B., and RISLEY, T.R.: Incidental teaching of language in the preschool. *Journal of Applied Behavior Analysis,* 1975, *8,* 411-420.

HAYDEN, A.H. and HARING, N.G.: Early intervention for high-risk infants and young children: programs for Down's Syndrome children. In T.D. Tijossen (ed.) *Intervention strategies for high risk infants and young children.* Baltimore: University Park Press 1976. Pp. 573-607.

MARTIN, G., MURREL, M., NICHOLSON, C., and TALLMAN, B.: *Teaching basic skills to the severely and profoundly retarded: The MIMR Basic Behavior Test, Curriculum Guide and Programming Strategy.* Printed in Portage La Prairie by Vopii Press, Ltd., 1975.

SHEARER, D., BILLINGSLEY, J., FROHMAN, A., HILLIARD, J., JOHNSON, F. and SHEARER, M.: *The Portage Guide to Early Education* (Experimental Edition). The Portage Project, 412 East Slifer, Portage, Wisconsin, 53901, 1972.

SKINNER, B.F.: *Science and human behavior.* New York: Macmillan, 1953.

SKINNER, B.F.: *The technology of teaching.* New York: Appleton-Century Crofts, 1968.

SNELBECKER, G.E.: *Learning theory, instructional theory, and psycho-educational design.* New York: McGraw-Hill Book Co., 1974.

ZEAMAN, D. and HOUSE, B.J.: The role of attention in retarded discrimination learning. *In N.R. Ellis (ed.) Handbook of mental deficiency,* New York McGraw-Hill, 1963 pp. 159-223.

8
A Behavioral Analysis of the Home Environment of Austistic Children

SANDER MARTIN
and
BRUCE GRAUNKE

INTRODUCTION

The symptoms of early infantile autism were first isolated by Kanner (1943) in his description of 11 children who shared a specific constellation of psychotic behavior. The primary characteristics of autism noted by Kanner (1971) are: (1) the child's inability, from the beginning of the life cycle, to relate to people and situations in an ordinary way, and (2) the child's desire for the preservation of sameness. Other typical behaviors noted are a delay or lack of speech acquisition, language abnormalities, manneristic behaviors characterized by highly repetitious and stylized movements, and a preoccupation with objects.

Since Kanner's original article in 1943, attempts have been made to apply operant learning principles to the study of autism. One of the first research studies was completed by Ferster (1961), who investigated the amount of positive reinforcement the autistic child receives from his environment. Over the past 15 years, behaviorally oriented therapists and researchers have successfully applied their techniques to a variety of autistic behaviors: a) *social skill building* (Metz, 1965;

This research is based on a thesis submitted by the second author to the University of Houston in partial fulfillment for the requirements of the Master of Arts degree.

(5) echolalic and psychotic speech, and (6) behavioral deficiencies. Lichstein and Wahler (1976) believe that there is agreement, regardless of one's theoretical position, that a child who does not find humans positively reinforcing, engages in stereotypic and ritualistic behavior, and does not develop meaningful verbal communication will be diagnosed as autistic.

Limitations of Behavioral Research

Though there have been many behavioral studies which demonstrate that autistic children are responsive to environmental manipulation, their analysis and description of autism may be limited due to: a) a lack of naturalistic studies and an excessive abundance of laboratory or analog research; b) the tendency for researchers to collect data on only single behaviors (e.g., headbanging, self-stimulation, discrimination learning), or c) the tendency to focus on a specific cluster of behaviors (e.g., speech, imitative behaviors).

A number of authors have suggested that an attempt to understand a subject's behavior requires observations of the subject in his natural environment and the generation of reliable descriptive data (Wright, 1960; Williams & Raush, 1969). Furthermore, the results of current research indicate that there may be little relationship between behavioral data obtained from subjects in laboratory settings and that data obtained in home settings (Dysart, 1973; Martin, Johnson, Johannson, & Wahl, 1976). Lichstein and Wahler (1976) call for naturalistic observations of autistic children and provide descriptive behavioral data on a single autistic child in his home and school environments.

Goals of the Present Study

Few published studies have examined the behavior of autistic children in the home environment. These types of data are essential for providing meaning to the diagnostic category of autism. The present study attempts: (1) to provide a catalog of normative behavior based on the naturalistic observations of a relatively substantial sample of autistic children by using a data system which affords the coding of multiple behaviors, and (2) to describe the types of interactions that par-

McConnell, 1967), b) *decreasing self-stimulation* (Koegel & C
Foxx & Azrin, 1973), c) *decreasing tantrums and self-mutilat*
Freitag, Gold, & Kassorla, 1965; Tate and Baroff, 196
1970), d) *speech development* (Hewett, 1965; Lovaas, 196(
Wolf, 1967), e) *self-help skills* (Marshall, 1966; Lovaas, Frei
& Whalen, 1967), and f) *discrimination learning* (Lovaas, S
Koegel, & Rehm, 1971). As well as applying behavioral i
techniques to clinically alter autistic behavior, a number of
have been interested in describing those critical behaviors t
sociated with the diagnosis of autism.

A major concern to all clinicians, regardless of theoretic
tion, is the problem of differential diagnosis. Many authors
that an autistic child examined by two separate diagnost
most likely receive two separate diagnoses (DesLauriers &
1969; DeMyer, Churchill, Puntius, & Gilkey, 1971; Lovaas
1972; Rimland, 1971). The first attempts to understand auti
a variety of descriptive studies in demographic factors. For e
variety of opinions exist about parental characteristics. Some
ers describe parents as members of the upper socioeconomic
being affectively "cold" (Lotter, 1967; Rutter & Lockyer, 196
fert, 1970; Kolvin, Ounsted, Richardson, & Farside, 1971), wh
researchers find these characteristics not related to autism (
Chess, 1964; Levine & Olson, 1968; McDermott, 1968
Cantwell, Johnson, Clements, Benbrook, Slagel, Kelly, & Ritz
Similar equivocal findings characterize the research on the
ship between birth order and autism (Creek & Ini, 1960; Pi
Oppenheim, 1964; Rutter & Lockyer, 1967; Wing, O'Connor,
ter, 1967). Scientists do agree on the incidence of autism (2/10
4.5/10,000) and the fact that there are at least twice as many
males as females (Kanner, 1954; Rimland, 1964; Lotter, 1966;
1966; Ritvo et al., 1971). Due to the lack of success with demog
factors in aiding differential diagnosis, many behaviorally orien
searchers have developed descriptive checklists and other pape
pencil tests. Unfortunately, checklists have not proven to be ver
able (Rimland, 1971; DeMyer et al., 1971). A more recent tre
understanding autistic behavior has been to restrict diagnosis t
havioral descriptions of the children.

Lovaas and Koegal (1972) list several critical behaviors related
diagnosis of autism: (1) apparent sensory deficit, (2) severe affec
lation, (3) self-stimulation, (4) tantrums and self-mutilatory beha

ents have with their autistic children by coding interactions between children and parents.

METHOD

Subjects

Fifteen autistic children between the ages of five and 13 were recruited from family membership lists of the Houston Chapter of the National Society for Autistic Children. Typically, each child had been diagnosed as autistic by a family physician and a mental health professional (e.g., a psychologist or psychiatrist). The present study did not examine the quality of these diagnoses or develop a standardized procedure for re-diagnosing the children.

In return for their participation, each family received feedback on their family interactions and a written summary of the study's results. A total of 27 families were contacted; however, 12 declined to participate in the study. Reasons for not participating included the following: lack of time, illness in their family, placement of the autistic child outside the home, being tired of participation in research projects, and not wanting observers in their homes.

Procedures

Prior to the home observations, all participating parents were asked to complete biographical questionnaires on themselves and all their children. Parents were also given forms which defined the observational rules and confirmed their right to withdraw from participation at any time.

Each family was observed for five 45-minute periods at times arranged by the family and the observer. Typically, four sessions were during weekday evenings, with one session during a weekend morning. During these sessions, all families were asked to minimize outside visitors and to avoid interactions with the observer. Observational studies often require that all family members remain in one designated area; however, the present study did not have this observational rule. Although such a rule increases the probability of parent-child interactions, it decreases the typicalness of the obtained data. The present study required the target child to remain within the house or yard.

Observers

Observers were nine undergraduate students who received course credit for participation in this research project. The training schedule contained the following steps: introduction, group consensus, individual observer agreement, and coding pair agreement. The introductory phase consisted of the philosophy behind behavioral coding, individual written code descriptions, having each coder memorize the code list, and having the researchers present examples for each code. The group consensus stage consisted of coding role-playing sessions and resolving differences of opinion about coding categories. During the individual observer agreement stage, each coder computed her agreement against standard criterion tapes. Prior to entering the final stage, each observer was required to achieve two agreement scores of at least 85%. The final stage consisted of observer pairs coding in families' homes. The training was completed when the observers obtained at least an 85% inter-observer agreement score during a 45-minute session.

During home observations, one out of the five family sessions was checked for observer reliability. If any observer had dropped below a 75% observer agreement, she discontinued coding until recompleting training steps three and four. For each of the above agreement tests, an agreement was scored whenever the same behavior was coded for the same agent in the same 10-second interaction block. Agreement percentages were computed by dividing the number of agreements by the number of agreements plus disagreements.

Observational System

Observers used a coding system developed by the authors which resembles family observation codes developed by Patterson, Ray, Shaw, and Cobb (1969), but which is modified to be sensitive to the behavior of autistic children. The coding system is composed of 30 distinct behavioral categories and records 29 target child behaviors and 23 behavioral responses from other family members. The system is designed for rapid sequential coding of the target's behavior and his relationship to other family members. For purposes of calculating observer agreement, all interactions are coded at 10-second intervals. All observers were equipped with reading pacers which indicated the beginning of each 10-second interaction period.

After data collection, the codes were collapsed into the following categories (see Appendix A for the specific codes in each category): Deviant, Non-Deviant, and Pro-Social for the target child, and Positive, Negative, and Neutral for family member's responses. The sum of Positive and Negative Response codes was defined as Active Response.

Results

The present study utilized two methods of data collection: questionnaires that generated descriptive data, and behavioral coding which directly recorded family interactions. Each method obtained data for a target autistic child and his family.

Descriptive Data

Autistic child. Table 1 describes characteristics of the autistic children in the present sample. The children ranged from five to 13 years of age, with a mean age of eight. The sample included 10 males and five females. The typical child was a first born male, receiving medication, and attending a special education class. All of the children had engaged in self-destructive behaviors such as biting, hitting, scratching, or headbanging; and in repetitive behaviors such as rocking, hand wringing, or repetitive speech. Most of the children had received a diagnosis other than autism, typically either mental retardation or a speech problem.

The parents reported that their children speak in sentences, interact "quite often" with family members, and "quite often" understand directions. The parents indicated that the mothers have been primarily responsible for raising the autistic children.

Family data. Table 2 describes the family characteristics of the present sample: All of the parents are married, all of the husbands employed, and none of the parents have received psychotherapy. The vast majority have attended college and have incomes in excess of $15,000. The wives had a mean age of 37 years, with a range of ages from 30 to 44. The husbands had a mean age of 40, with a range of ages from 31 to 49.

Table 1
Descriptive Characteristics of the 15 Autistic Children

Characteristic	Number of Children Qualifying	Percent of Total Sample
First born in Family	9	60%
Males	10	66%
Receiving Psychological Services	5	33%
Receiving medication	10	66%
Having been in Residential Treatment	5	33%
Attending a Special Education Class	11	73%
Having Completed Rimland's E-2 form	10	66%
Having received Rimland's E-2 score	0	0%
Having Received a Diagnosis other than Autism	9	60%
Having Engaged in Self-Destructive Behavior	15	100%
Having Engaged in Repetitive Behavior	15	100%

Table 2
Parental Characteristics of the Families

Characteristic	Number	Percent of Total Sample
Families with Both Parents Living at Home	15	100%
Caucasians	12	80%
Wives who had Attended College	13	87%
Husbands who had Attended College	11	73%
Wives Employed	5	33%
Husbands Employed	15	100%
Family Income of over $15,000	12	80%
Parents having Received Therapy	0	0%
Parents having Received Parent-Training	2	13%

Behavioral Coding Data

Description of the autistic child. As previously mentioned, there are 29 autistic child behavior codes which are clustered into Deviant, Non-Deviant, and Pro-Social categories. Tables 3, 4, and 5 present the mean rate by percent, the range, and the standard deviation for each of the observed behaviors.

Table 3 presents the frequency with which the autistic children engaged in the 15 behaviors (e.g., Self-Stimulation, Physical Negative, or Crying) that are categorized as Deviant by the coding systems. It is of interest to note that the children's overall percentage of Deviant behavior was relatively low (6%). The most frequent behaviors observed within the Deviant category were Deviant Behavior (1.6%), Whining (1.2%), and Self-Stimulation (1.2%).

Table 4 indicates how frequently the autistic children engaged in the six behaviors (e.g., Verbal Neutral, Physical Contact, or Independent Activity) that are categorized as Non-Deviant by the coding system. These six behaviors made up the majority of behaviors that were coded during the observational periods (60%). The most common

Table 3

Rate of Deviant Behaviors of the Target Children by Percent of the Observational Period

Behavior	Percent	Range	S.D.
Aversive Command	0	–	–
Non-Compliance	.45	0 – 2.5	.92
Verbal-Disapproval	.13	0 – 1.3	.37
Dependency	.01	0 – .08	.02
Tease	.1	0 – 1.0	.29
Demand Attention	.08	0 – .5	.18
Turn Off	.01	0 – .1	.03
Physical Negative	.22	0 – .67	.33
Destructiveness	.12	0 – 1.0	.29
Self-Stimulation	1.2	0 – 9.2	2.62
Whine	1.24	0 – 8.3	2.60
Deviant Behavior	1.59	0 – 14.	3.95
Ignore	.03	0 – .16	.05
Cry	.76	0 – 5.6	1.57
Self-Destructive	.41	0 – .41	.13
TOTAL	6.01	.2 – 19.1	6.04

Non-Deviant behaviors were Independent Activity (44.9%) and Verbal Neutral (19.5%).

Table 5 shows the frequency of autistic child behavior on the eight codes (e.g., Laugh, Physical Positive, or Play) that are categorized as Pro-Social by the observational system. The total rate for the Pro-Social category was 34%, with Attention (15%) and Play (11.2%) being the most frequent behaviors.

Behaviors Typically Associated with Autism. In addition to providing a topography for the autistic child's home behavior, the present study examined several behaviors that are commonly associated with autism. These behaviors included Self-Stimulation, Self-Destructiveness, Independent Activity, and Verbal Neutral.

Table 4
Rate of Non-Deviant Behaviors of the Target Children by Percent of the Observational Period

Behavior	Percent	Range	S.D.
Command	.07	0 - .43	.16
Verbal Compliance	.01	0 - .07	.02
Verbal Neutral	10.45	0 - 20.4	6.54
Physical Contact	2.06	0 - 6.5	2.35
Independent Activity	44.85	20.4 - 73.0	17.50
Leave	1.54	0 - 8.3	2.31
TOTAL	60.06	41.77 - 85.77	14.32

Table 5
Rate of Pro-Social Behaviors of the Target Children by Percent of the Observation Period

Behavior	Percent	Range	S.D.
Compliance	1.04	0 – 2.1	.74
Verbal Approval	.04	0 – .22	.08
Laugh	1.62	0 – 8.5	2.30
Attention	14.97	0 – 32.5	9.13
Physical Positive	2.86	0 – 3.9	3.11
Work	2.16	0 – 9.2	2.99
Play	11.21	0 – 26.8	9.57
Request	.01	0 – .07	.02
TOTAL	33.96	12.97 - 52.65	12.36

If one were to cluster the deviant behaviors associated with autism, he would find that these behaviors occurred at relatively low rates: Self-Stimulation (1.2%), Self-Destructiveness (.05%), and Tantrums (2.69%). Tantrums were defined as the sum of the following codes: Physical Negative, Destructiveness, Deviant Behavior, and Cry.

An examination of the extent to which the autistic children were socially isolated, according to the observation system, reveals that Independent Activity (44.9%) and Non-Interaction (43.3%) behaviors occurred at relatively high rates. Non-Interaction was defined as the sum of the percent of time that the autistic child was alone and the percent of time that he was in the presence of other family members but had no interactions. The rate of Non-Interaction ranged from 19% to 81.3%, with the standard deviation of 23.1%.

Because the existence of speech is an important prognostic indicator for autistic children, it is interesting to note that 14 of the 15 autistic children engaged in some form of verbal behavior (Request, Verbal Approval, Verbal Neutral, Verbal Compliance, Command, Aversive Command, and Verbal Disapproval). These verbal behaviors composed 10.7% of the children's total behavior. The primary verbal behavior was Verbal Neutral (10.5%). In addition, the relationships between Verbal Neutral and the three general behavior categories, Deviant, Non-Deviant, and Pro-Social, were examined by calculating the correlations between Verbal Neutral and the Deviant Behavior category ($r = .22$), between Verbal Neutral and the Non-Deviant Behavior category ($r = .36$), and between Verbal Neutral and the Pro-Social category ($r = .70$). The third correlation was significant at the .01 level.

Family Response Data. Table 6 shows the percent of Negative, Neutral, and Positive responses made by fathers, mothers, and siblings to the target's behavior. The table also includes the actual number of responses for each cell. A survey of Table 6 reveals that all family members consequated all behavior categories in a positive manner far more frequently than in a negative manner. All family members were most positive when the autistic child engaged in Deviant Behavior, but siblings had the highest percent of Negative responses.

Differences Between Mothers and Fathers. The most striking difference between mothers and fathers was the mothers' greater number of responses within every cell of Table 6. Individual case analyses show that for 14 of the 15 families, mothers responded at a higher rate across all behavior categories than any other family member. The

Table 6

Child	MOTHERS Positive	MOTHERS Negative	MOTHERS Neutral	FATHERS Positive	FATHERS Negative	FATHERS Neutral	SIBLINGS Positive	SIBLINGS Negative	SIBLINGS Neutral
Deviant (1046) 6%	(528) 59%	(89) 4%	(315) 37%	(181) 48%	(10) 1%	(139) 51%	(39) 21%	(26) 13%	(80) 66%
Non-Deviant (11217) 60%	(3310) 44%	(83) 3%	(4168) 53%	(1296) 31%	(26) 2%	(3461) 67%	(645) 25%	(18) 2%	(2936) 73%
Pro-Social (6346) 34%	(2791) 67%	(89) 2%	(1489) 31%	(1680) 56%	(14) 1%	(868) 43%	(850) 60%	(10) 1%	(496) 39%
Total (18609) 100%	(6629) 52%	(291) 2%	(5972) 46%	(3157) 41%	(50) 1%	(4468) 58%	(1533) 30%	(54) 1%	(3512) 69%

range of the mother to father response ratio was from 1: 1.1 to 3.5: 1, with a mean of 1.7: 1. When parents were interacting with their autistic child, mothers most frequently responded in a positive manner and fathers in a neutral manner.

Because the Neutral Response category implies minimal interaction with the austistic child (e.g., the No Response code), it would be of interest to highlight the mother-father differences while omitting this category. An examination of Active Responses (defined as the Positive and Negative Responses) finds the ratio of mother to father interactions increased from the mean of 1.7: 1 to a mean of 2.1: 1 (with a range of 1.1: 1 to 17.3: 1).

Observer Reliability

Observer reliability was checked by having a calibrator observer join the trained observer during one session for each participating family. The level of observer reliability was measured by an overall agreement percentage and by correlating the calibrator's codes and the observer's codes. As previously mentioned, the agreement percentages were computed by dividing the number of agreements by the number of agreements plus disagreements. For individual families the agreement percentage ranged from 83% to 94%, with a mean of 89%.

Table 7 presents three lists of correlations that provide data for the following questions: (1) To what extent did the observers code the same behavior at the same time? (2) To what extent did the observers record the same category of behavior at the same time (e.g., Deviant, Non-Deviant, or Pro-Social)? (3) To what extent did the observers agree upon the overall frequency for each of the codes? An examination of Table 7 indicates that the correlations were significant at the .01 level. These data suggest that the coding system was highly reliable.

Summary of the Main Results

The present section briefly summarizes seven primary findings:

(1) A relatively small percentage of the autistic children's behaviors were deviant (6%). In addition, the three following behaviors that are commonly associated with autism occurred at low rates: Self-Stimulation (1.2%), Self-Destructiveness (.05%), and Tantrums (2.7%).

(2) The autistic children were frequently isolated or not interacting with other family members. Independent Activity accounted for 44.9% of the children's behaviors. In addition, the rate of Non-Interaction was 43.24%. As previously mentioned, this rate was obtained by summing the percent of time that family members were present but had no interactions with the subject.

(3) There was a significant correlation ($p < .01$) between the percent of time that the autistic children exhibited Pro-Social behaviors and the percent of time that the children engaged in Verbal Neutral ($r = .70$).

(4) There were major differences between the autistic children, as indicated by the ranges and standard deviations in Tables 4, 5, and 6. The rate for Deviant behaviors ranged from .2% to 19.1%, with a standard deviation of 6.04%, and a mean of 6.01%. The rate for Non-Deviant behaviors ranged from 41.8% to 85.8%, with a standard deviation of 14.32%, and a mean of 60.06%. The rate for Pro-Social behaviors ranged from 13% to 52.7%, with a standard deviation of 12.4%, and a mean of 33.96%.

(5) As indicated in Table 6, the parents in the present sample were typically positive in responding to their autistic children. Of the mothers' responses, 67% were positive for their children's Pro-Social

Table 7
Correlations* Between the Calibrator's Codes and the Observer's Codes for the Codes, Coding Categories, and Overall Frequencies

Coding Categories	Codes	Coding Categories	Overall Frequency
Tease	1.00	1.00	1.00
Turn Off	1.00	1.00	1.00
Non-Compliance	1.00	1.00	1.00
Whine	1.00	1.00	1.00
Ignore	.79	.79	.79
Physical Negative	1.00	1.00	1.00
Self Stimulation	1.00	1.00	1.00
Verbal Disapproval	1.00	1.00	1.00
Cry	1.00	1.00	1.00
Verbal Neutral	.97	.98	.96
Physical Contact	.95	.95	1.00
Independent Activity	.99	.99	.98
Leave	1.00	1.00	1.00
Compliance	.85	.92	.85
Verbal Approval	1.00	1.00	1.00
Laugh	1.00	1.00	1.00
Attention	.98	.98	.92
Physical Positive	.92	1.00	.92
Work	1.00	1.00	1.00
Play	1.00	1.00	1.00

*Calculated Spearman Rank Correlation Coefficients
(For the present sample)
$p \leq .01$ FOR r's $\leq .71$

behaviors, and 52% were positive for the children's overall behavior. Of the fathers' responses, 56% were positive for their children's Pro-Social behaviors, and 41% were positive for the children's overall behavior. The overall ratio of Positive to Negative responses was 25:1 for the mothers and 63:1 for the fathers.

(6) The mothers were involved far more frequently with the autistic children than fathers. Table 6 shows that the mothers had a greater number of responses within every response category. In comparing the mothers' and fathers' Active Responses (the Positive and Negative responses), the mother to father responses ratio ranged from 1.1:1 to 17.3:1, with a mean of 2.1:1. On the average, the mothers had over

twice as many Active Responses, with a greater number in all 15 families.

(7) The siblings were more contingent in responding to the target children than either the fathers or mothers. The siblings had the highest percentage of negative responses to the targets' Deviant behaviors (13%) and had the highest ratio of Positive to Negative responses for the targets' Pro-Social behaviors (60:1).

Discussion

As previously mentioned, a primary goal of the present study was to initiate the collection of naturalistic data. The results describe the home behavior of autistic children and demonstrate the ability of behavioral coding systems to generate highly reliable and descriptive information on autistic children and their families.

Observational data indicate that autistic children engage in many socially appropriate activities (e.g., Play and Attention) and suggest that theorists overemphasize the children's deviant behavior (e.g., Tantrums and Self-Stimulation). The autistic child's withdrawal or low rate of interaction appears to be his primary behavioral characteristic. The importance of this interaction variable suggests that researchers may lose valuable data if they require families to remain within a confined area (e.g., requiring a family to remain within a living room). For example, it might be important to observe that an aggressive youth spends 60% of each day being alone in his room. In the present study, much of the Independent Activity and Non-Interaction might have been missed by designating a specific observational room.

The data demonstrate the importance of verbal behavior for autistic children and support its use as a prognostic indicator. The high correlation between Verbal Neutral and the Pro-Social category suggests that researchers might focus on developing speech training programs for autistic children. While implementing speech programs, it might be beneficial to monitor other socially appropriate behaviors for possible improvements. It seems plausible that speech development might allow the autistic child to obtain a higher level of external reinforcement, which might facilitate the development of other socially desired behaviors.

The data indicate that there are individual differences among autistic children and discredit the notion that there is only "one type" of autistic child. The autistic children in the present sample exhibited diverse rates for each observed behavior and for each of the behavioral categories.

Analysis of parent responses reveals that parents of autistic children are typically positive and somewhat contingent in responding to their children, and fails to support the psychogenic theory of autism. The authors suggest that parents might benefit from training in contingency management techniques.

Comparisons with Related Research

Several behavioral studies of child interaction have used observational systems similar to that of the present research but with populations of "acting out" children or children defined as "normal" (Patterson & Cobb, 1971; Johnson, Wahl, Martin, & Johannson, 1973). Results indicate a high level of agreement with present findings that mothers have higher rates of interaction with their children than fathers, and that siblings are more contingent in their responses to the target child's behavior than are adults. Closer inspection of the Johnson et al. study, which reports home observations of 33 "normal" children aged four to six years and their families, affords interesting comparisons between "normal" and "autistic" children in the amount of: deviant behavior observed (3.6% vs. 6.0%); independent activity exhibited (26.5% vs. 44.9%); and verbal behavior coded (26.9% vs. 10.7%). Though there appear to be major differences between both groups, the meaning and stability of such differences are yet to be demonstrated.

A recent study by Lichstein and Wahler (1976) provides an opportunity to compare the results of the present study with data obtained from the home observation of a single autistic child, aged five years. Though the behavioral coding systems used are very different, it is interesting to note that when behavioral categories are ranked in order of percent occurrence, there seems to be a high degree of similarity on the type of behavior observed. For example, both studies agree that the autistic child spends much of his time by himself or not interacting with others. Secondly, both studies observe the child relating to objects rather than people. Finally, there is strong agreement that vocalizations occur at a relatively high rate. Table 8 presents a comparison of the five most frequent behaviors seen in both studies. The main area of disagreement is the occurrence of self-stimulation, ranked fourth by Lichstein and Wahler (1976) and twelfth in the present study.

Table 8
Five Autistic Child Behaviors Ranked in Order of Percent Occurrence

Lichstein and Wahler, 1976	Martin and Graunke, 1978
1. Sustained non-verbal interaction(NI)	1. Independent Activity (IA)
2. Object Play (OP)	2. Attention (AT)
3. Vocalization (V)	3. Play (PL)
4. Self-Stimulation (S)	4. Verbal Neutral (VN)
5. Unusual Self-Stimulation (US)	5. Physical Positive (PP)

The authors are aware that attempts to create comparison groups by examining, post hoc, research which utilizes like coding systems in natural environments are tenuous at best. Differences in design, subject characteristics and selection, coding procedures, and coding definitions weaken relationships between studies. Comparisons are included for speculative purposes, to generate discussion, and to seek out areas of congruence. The authors also suggest that several additional features will increase the external validity of future research: a) a comprehensive and reliable diagnosis of autism, b) random subject selection, c) random observation times, d) an assessment of observer reactivity, and e) creation of a standardized behavioral coding system for autistic behavior.

The present study was designed to examine a relatively substantial sample of autistic children and their families through naturalistic observations in their homes. In contrast to previous naturalistic behavioral research, the present study includes a larger sample of autistic children, examines a wider range of child behaviors, and provides a detailed description of the interactions between the children and family members.

Appendix A
Observation Codes and Definitions

This appendix contains a list of the codes used in this study with their definitions. Many of the codes were taken from the Patterson coding system (Patterson, Ray, Shaw, & Cobb, 1969).

1. CM Command. This category is used when a direct, reasonable and clearly stated request or command is made to another person. The statement must be sufficiently specific to indicate clearly the behavior which is expected from the person to whom the command is directed.
2. AV Aversive command. This is a command very different in "attitude" from the above command. It demands immediate compliance, and aversive consequences are implicitly or explicitly threatened for non-compliance.
3. CO Compliance. Use this category when a person does what is asked of him in a CM or AV.
4. NC Non-compliance. This is used when a person doesn't do what is asked by a CM or AV. This non-compliance can be of a verbal or non-verbal nature. If the command is not to be done until some later time, but the person says he won't do it later, NC is the appropriate code. Care must be taken to distinguish NC from VD in some situations. If an individual says "I hate this work," but complies, the appropriate codes are 1VD 1CO.
5. VC Verbal-compliance. This code is used when the observer can't know if the target will comply with a AV or CM. For example, if a parent says "Take the dog out before you go to bed" and the target says "okay."
6. VA Verbal-approval. Used when a person gives approval verbally, such as "thanks" or "that looks good." Can be to one's self.
7. VD Verbal-disapproval. Used when a person gives verbal disapproval of another's behavior or characteristics. Includes self-derogatory statements.
8. VN Verbal-neutral. Use this category when a person gives verbal statements which are neither VD or VA, such as reading aloud. If an observer is uncertain whether a statement is VA or VN, always code it VN.
9. DP Dependency. Behavior is coded DP when the target requests assistance in doing some task which he is clearly capable of doing himself and when the request is an imposition on another.
10. TE Tease. This is used for "challenge" behavior. For example, "you can't make me take out the garbage" or the parents holding an object just out of the child's reach. This doesn't include name-calling, which is VD.
11. DA Demand-attention. Includes all non-hurting physical gestures or physical contact which attempt to get another's attention. Also includes non-word noises.
12. TO Turn off. Are non-word cues, such as giving someone the finger, acting like your going to spit at someone. Also includes sounds such as "ech," or humiliating laughter.
13. LA Laugh. Used whenever a person laughs in a non-humiliating way. If an observer is uncertain if a person is attempting to humiliate, code as LA.
14. AT Attention. Used whenever a person is watching, listening, or obviously aware of another person. Is not coded with other codes which imply AT, such as play or VA.
15. PP Physical positive. Used whenever a person touches another person in a friendly or affectionate manner, i.e., hug, pat, or holding hands.
16. PN Physical negative. Used whenever a person physically attacks, attempts to attack, or hurts another person. The attack must be of sufficient intensity to potentially inflict pain. The circumstances around the act need not concern the observer.
17. PC Physical Contact. Used whenever there is physical contact or a person hands an object to another person. Only use this code if some other code isn't appropriate, such as AT or PL.
18. DS Destructiveness. This is used when a person destroys, damages, or attempts to damage an object. The damage need not actually occur, but the potential for

damage must exist, i.e., a child starts to throw a glass, but is stopped by his father. The value of the object or amount of damage is of no concern.
19. WK Work. Used when a person is doing a chore, homework, or an extended, assigned task. Can be with others or alone.
20. PL Play. Used when a person is playing a game, playing with puzzles, or playing with blocks. The child can't be just shoving the blocks around but must be directed or involve others.
21. IA Independent-activity. Used when the target is involved in some solitary activity; for example, watching television, looking into space, or aimlessly shoving blocks around.
22. SS Self-stimulation. Used when the target does something at a higher than normal rate and repeatedly. For example, rocking, finger waving, or hyperventilating.
23. Wh Whine. Used when a person is making a verbal request and the tone is annoying, such as pleadings or whines.
24. DB Deviant behavior. Used when the target is engaged in some behavior which is inappropriate for the situation and no other codes cover the behavior.
25. LE Leave. Used when the target leaves the observer's viewpoint.
26. IG Ignore. Used when a person is aware of another's behavior but decides not to respond. For example, a child is screaming and the parents hear, but don't respond. The observer must be certain the individual had heard or is aware of the other's behavior.
27. NR No response. This category is to be used when a person does not respond to another person. This category is applicable when a behavior does not require a response or when behavior is directed at another person, but the person to whom the behavior is directed fails to perceive the behavior.
28. SD Self-destructiveness. When the child harms himself or attempts to harm himself, such as headbanging or biting his arm.
29. CR Cry. Used when the subject cries.
30. TO Time-out. Used when a family member places the target in some designated area, such as in his room or in a chair for punishment.

CHILD BEHAVIOR CATEGORIES

Deviant
aversive command
non-compliance
verbal disapproval
dependency
tease
demand attention
turn off
physical negative
destructiveness
self-stimulation
whine
deviant behavior
ignore
cry
self-destructiveness

Nondeviant
command
verbal-compliance
verbal neutral
physical contact
independent activity
leave

Pro-social
compliance
verbal approval
laugh
attention
physical positive
work
play
request

PARENT RESPONSE CATEGORIES

Positive	Neutral	Negative
compliance	command	aversive command
verbal approval	verbal	verbal disapproval
laugh	physical contact	demand attention
attention	no response	turn off
verbal neutral		physical negative
physical positive		destructiveness
work		ignore
play		cry
request		non-compliance
		tease

REFERENCES

CREEK, M., and INI, S.: Families of psychotic children. *Journal of Child Psychology and Psychiatry*, 1960, *1*, 156-175.

DeMYER, M., CHURCHILL, K. W., PUNTIUS, W. and GILKEY, K. M.: A comparison of five diagnostic systems for childhood schizophrenia and infantile autism. *Journal of Autism and Schizophrenia*, 1971, *1*, 175-189.

DESLAURIERS, A., and CARLSON, C.: *Your child is asleep.* Homewood, Ill.: The Dorsey Press, 1969.

DYSART, R.: A behavioral description of family interactions in the home and the clinic: Inter and intra setting analysis. Unpublished doctoral dissertation, University of Houston, 1973.

FERSTER, C. B.: Positive reinforcement and behavioral deficits of autistic children. *Child Development*, 1961, *32*, 437-456.

FOXX, R. M., and AZRIN, N. H.: The elimination of autistic self-stimulatory behavior by overcorrection. *Journal of Applied Behavior Analysis*, 1973, *6*, 1-14.

HEWETT, F. M.: Teaching speech to an autistic child through operant conditioning. *American Journal of Orthopsychiatry*, 1965, *35*, 927-936.

JOHNSON, S. M., WAHL, G., MARTIN, S., and JOHANNSON, S.: How deviant is the normal child: A behavioral analysis of the pre-school child and his family. *Advances in Behavior Therapy*, 1973.

KANNER, L.: Autistic disturbances of affective contact. *Nervous Child*, 1943, *2*, 217-250.

KANNER, L.: To what extent is early infantile autism determined by constitutional inadequacies? In D. Hooker and C. C. Hare (Eds.), *Genetics and inheritance of integrated neurological and psychiatric patterns.* Baltimore: Williams and Wilkins, 1954.

KANNER, L.: Follow-up study of eleven autistic children originally reported in 1943. *Journal of Autism and Childhood Schizophrenia*, 1971, *1*, 119-145.

KOEGEL, R. L., and COVERT, A.: The relationship of self-stimulation to learning in autistic children. *Journal of Applied Behavior Analysis*, 1972, *5*, 381-388.

KOLVIN, I., OUNSTED, C., RICHARDSON, L. M., and FARSIDE, R. F.: The family and social background in childhood psychoses: III. *British Journal of Psychiatry*, 1971, *118*, 396-402.

LEVINE, M., and OLSON, R. P.: Intelligence of parents of autistic children. *Journal of Abnormal Psychology*, 1968, *73*, 215-217.

LICHSTEIN, K., and WAHLER, R.: The ecological assessment of an autistic child. *Journal of Abnormal Child Psychology*, 1976, *4*, 31-54.

LOTTER, V.: Epidemiology of autistic conditions in young children: I. prevalence. *Social Psychiatry,* 1966, *1,* 124-137.
LOTTER, V.: Epidemiology of autistic conditions in young children: II. Some characteristics of the parents and children. *Social Psychiatry,* 1967, *1,* 163-173.
LOVAAS, O. I.: A program for the establishment of speech in psychotic children. In J. K. Wing (Ed.), *Early childhood autism: Clinical, educational, and social aspects.* London: Pergamon Press, Inc., 1966.
LOVAAS, O. I., and KOEGEL R. L.: Behavior therapy with autistic children. In C. E. Thoresen (Ed.), *Behavior modification in education.* Chicago: National Society for the Study of Education, 1972, 230-258.
LOVAAS, O. I., FREITAG, G., GOLD, V. J., and KASSORLA, I. C.: Experimental studies in childhood schizophrenia: Analysis of self-destructive behavior. *Journal of Experimental Child Psychology,* 1965, *2,* 67-84.
LOVAAS, O. I., FREITAS, L., NELSON, K., and WHALEN, C.: The establishment of imitation and its use for the development of complex behavior in schizophrenic children. *Behavior Research and Therapy,* 1967, *5,* 171-181.
LOVAAS, O. I., SCHREIBMAN, L., KOEGEL, R., and REHM, R.: Selective responding by autistic children to multiple sensory input. *Journal of Abnormal Psychology,* 1971, *77,* 211-222.
MARTIN, S., JOHNSON, S. M., JOHANNSON, S., and WAHL, G.: The comparability of behavioral data in laboratory and natural settings. In E. Mash, L. Hamerlynck, and L. C. Handy (Eds.) *Behavior modification and families* New York: Brunner/Mazel, 1976, 189-203.
MARSHALL, G. R.: Toilet-training of an autistic eight-year-old through conditioning therapy: A case report. *Behavior Research and Therapy,* 1966, *4,* 242-245.
McCONNELL, O. L.: Control of eye contact in an autistic child. *Journal of Child Psychology and Psychiatry,* 1967, *8,* 249-255.
McDERMOTT, E.: Social class and mental illness in children: The question of childhood psychosis. In S. Chess and A. Thomas (Eds.), *Annual progress in child psychiatry and child development.* New York: Brunner/Mazel, 1968.
METZ, J. R.: Conditioning generalized imitation in autistic children. *Journal of Special Education,* 1965, *2,* 389-399.
PATTERSON, G. R., and COBB, J. A.: A dyadic analysis of aggressive behaviors. In J. P. Hill (Ed.), *Minnesota symposium on child psychology, Vol. 5.* Minneapolis: University of Minnesota Press, 1971, pp. 72-129.
PATTERSON, G. R., RAY, R. S., SHAW, D. A., and COBB, J. A.: Family observation code. Unpublished manuscript, University of Oregon, 1969.
PITFIELD, M., and OPPENHEIM, A. N.: Child rearing attitudes of mothers of psychotic children. *Journal of Child Psychology and Psychiatry,* 1964, *5,* 51-57.
RIMLAND, B.: *Infantile autism.* New York: Appleton-Century-Crofts, 1964.
RIMLAND, B.: The differentiation of childhood psychoses: An analysis of checklists for 2,218 psychotic children. *Journal of Autism and Childhood Schizophrenia,* 1971, *1,* 161-174.
RISLEY, T., and WOLF, M.: Establishing functional speech in echolalic children. *Behavior Research and Therapy,* 1967, *5,* 73-88.
RITVO, E., CANTWELL, D., JOHNSON, E., CLEMENTS, M., BENBROOK, F., SLAGEL, S., KELLY, P., and RITZ, M.: Social class factors in autism. *Journal of Autism and Schizophrenia,* 1971, *1,* 297-310.
RUTTER, M., and LOCKYER, L.: A five to fifteen-year follow-up study of infantile psychosis: I. Description of the sample. *British Journal of Psychiatry,* 1967, *113,* 1169-1182.
TATE, B. G., and BAROFF, G. S.: Aversive control of self-injurious behavior in a psychotic boy. *Behavior Research and Therapy,* 1966, *4,* 281-287.

TREFFERT, D. A.: The epidemiology of autistic conditions in young children: I. prevalence. *Social Psychiatry,* 1970, *22,* 431-438.

TURNER, R.: A method of working with disturbed children. *American Journal of Nursing,* 1970, *70,* 2146-2151.

WING, J. K.: Diagnosis, epidemiology, and etiology. In. J. K. Wing (Ed.), *Early childhood autism.* Oxford: Pergamon Press, 1966.

WING, J. K., O'CONNOR, N., and LOTTER, V.: Autistic conditions in early childhood: A survey in Middlesex. *British Medical Journal,* 1967, *3,* 389-392.

WILLIAMS, E. P., and RAUSH, H. L.: *Naturalistic viewpoints in psychological research.* New York: Holt, Rinehart and Winston, 1969.

WOLFF, S., and CHESS, S.: A behavioral study of schizophrenic children. *Acta Psychiatricia Scandinavica,* 1964, *40,* 438-466.

WRIGHT, H. F. Observation child study.: In P. H. Mussen (Ed.), *Handbook of research methods in child development.* New York: Wiley, 1960, pp. 71-139.

Index

Boldface page numbers indicate material in tables and figures.

Achievement Place model, 52
Acquisition, behavioral, 7
Acting-out, 54, 80, 186
Allen, K.E., 51, 64, 65, 82*n*.
American Psychological Association (APA), 11
Amidon, E., 48, 82*n*.
Amphetamines, 34, 38, 41, 45
Anderson, D.R., 132, 137, 170*n*.
Anxiety:
　management of, conference on, ix
　and sensory memory, 24–25
　and verbal tics, 41
　and work difficulty, 45
Apolloni, T., 48, 49, 50, 51, 53, 70, 82*n*., 85*n*.
Applied Behavior Analysis (ABA), 3, 6–10
　compared, 16, **17,** 18
　Curriculum Research, 10
　and future trends, 19–20
　and Science of Instruction, 15
Arithmetic performance, and tic control, 42–44, **42, 43**
Arnold, C., 7, 20*n*.
Asher, S., 50, 51, 82*n*., 85*n*.
Atkeson, B.M., 105, 126*n*.
Atkinson, R.C., 14, 18, 20*n*.
Attention, and environment, 14
Attitude Scale Ratings (ASR), 114
Auditory discriminations, 161
Autistic children, home environment, xiii, 172ff.
　behavior rates data, 177ff., **179, 180**
　characteristics of, 172, **178, 187**
　family aspects, **178,** 181–82, **182**
　incident of, 173
　and observation codes, 176–83, **184,** 187–90
　operant study of, general, 7

and psychogenic theory, 186
and reinforcement, 65
research limitations, 174
study of:
　discussion of, 185–87
　goals, 174–75
　method, 175–77
　results, 177ff.
　therapy of, 172–73
Ayd, F.J., 33, 46*n*.
Ayllon, T., xiv, xvii*n*.
Azrin, N.H., xiv, xvii*n*., 7, 20*n*., 173, 190*n*.

Baer, D.M., 7, 15, 20*n*., 21*n*., 51, 64, 71, 79, 81, 82*n*., 85*n*., 92, 100*n*., 102, 104, 105, 126*n*., 128, 162, 163, 164–65, 171*n*.
Bailey Scales, 149
Baine, D.B., 134, 170*n*.
Bandura, A., 23, 24, 30*n*.
Banff International Conferences on Behavior Modification, vii–x
Banff School of Fine Arts, x
Barlow, D.H., 41, 46*n*.
Barnard, J.D., 90, 92, 100, 100*n*., 101*n*.
Barnard, S.R., 92, 100*n*.
Baroff, G.S., 173, 192*n*.
Becker, W.C., 7, 20*n*., 134, 135, 138, 170*n*.
Behavioral Analysis System (BAS), 149, 152
Behavioral coding, of autistic behavior, 176ff., **184,** 187–90. *See also* Autistic children, home environment
Behavioral ecology stage, of behavioral modification, xiii–xvii
Behavioral management packages, 52ff. *See also* Program for Establishing Effective Relationship Skills
Behavioral Systems for the Developmentally Disabled: II. Institutional, Clinic and Community Environments, xiii

193

Behavior Analysis Follow Through Programs, 9–10
Behavior modification, general. *See also* Operant psychology
 on classroom behavior, 7–10
 conferences on, viii–ix
 flaws in, xiv
 as methodology, 7–8
Beickel, S., 52, 53, 83*n*.
Benbrook, F., 173, 191*n*.
Benztropine mesylate, 38
Berland, R.M., 105, 110, 111, 126*n*., 127*n*.
Bijou, S.W., 7, 16, **17**, 18, 21*n*., 102, 126*n*., 129, 170, 170*n*.
Birnbrauer, J.S., 8, 21*n*.
Birth order, and autism, 173
Blind:
 schools for, 4
 sensory aid for, 19
"Blind contact" procedure, 93
Bloom, B.S., 18, 21*n*.
Bonney, M.E., 48, 82*n*.
Boren, J.J., 32, 45, 47*n*.
Brain stem, 33
Brauer, W., 33, 46*n*.
Brenner, J., 48, 85*n*.
Bricker, D., 15, 21*n*., 128, 170*n*.
Bricker, W.A., 128, 170*n*.
Brison, D.W., 48, 82*n*.
Bronfenbrenner, U., 49, 82*n*., 89, 100, 100*n*.
Buckley, N.K., 105, 127*n*.
Budd, K.S., 104, 126*n*.
Buell, J.S., 51, 65, 82*n*.
Bureau of Child Research, University of Kansas, 89*n*.
Bureau of Education for the Handicapped, 32*n*., 48*n*.
Burrus, G., 50, 84*n*.
Bushell, D., JR., 8, 10, 16, **17**, 18, 21*n*., 22*n*.
Bushwell, M.M., 49, 82*n*.
Butterfield, W.H., 9, 22*n*.
Butyrophenone tranquilizers, 38. *See also* Haloperidol

Cameron, R., 70, 84*n*.
Cantwell, D., 173, 191*n*.
Carlson, C., 173, 190*n*.
Cartelli, L.M., 104, 126*n*.
Center at Oregon for Research in the Behavioral Education of the Handicapped (CORBEH), 48*n*., 51, 52, 53–54, 66*n*., 79, 81

Centre for the Study of Mental Retardation, 128*n*.
Cerebral palsy, xiii, 19
Challas, G., 33, 46*n*.
Charlesworth, R., 49, 82*n*., 83*n*.
Chess, S., 173, 192*n*.
Child Behavior Institute (CBI), 106ff., 114, 116, 117
Christensen, A., 105, 126*n*.
Christopher Robin, in analogy, 12
Christophersen, E.R., 89ff., 92, 99, 100*n*., 101*n*.
Churchill, K.W., 173, 190*n*.
Clark, D.F., 33, 45, 46*n*.
CLASS Program, 52, 80
Cleft palate, 90
Clement, P.W., 51, 82*n*.
Clements, M., 173, 191*n*.
Cobb, J.A., 52, 53, 82*n*., 83*n*., 103, 127*n*., 176, 186, 187, 191*n*.
Coding. *See* Behavioral coding, of autistic behavior
Coe, T.D., 111, 126*n*.
Cogentin, and tics, 38. *See also* Benztropine mesylate
Cognition:
 and science of instruction, 16
 skills of, teaching of, 129, **130**, 132, 153–55, **156**, 161–62
Cognitive psychology, and learning, 18
Community-based programs, 3
Community Interaction Checklist (CIC), 117, 118, 122–23
Competence, analysis of, 18
Computer assisted instruction, 19. *See also* Program for Establishing Effective Relationship Skills
Concept performance, and environment, 14
Conger, R.E., 52, 85*n*.
Conrad, R.J., 9, 21*n*.
Consultant Trainer's Manual, 80
Contingency management, 186
Cook, H., 49, 82*n*.
Cooke, T.P., 48, 49, 50, 51, 53, 70, 82*n*., 85*n*.
Coprolalia, 33, 34
CORBEH. *See* Center at Oregon for Research in the Behavioral Education of the Handicapped
Cordua, G., 104, 126*n*.
Cormier, W.H., 103, 127*n*.
Corpus striatum, 33
Corson, J.A., 51, 86*n*.
Corson, T.A., 33, 46*n*.

Index

Cossairt, A., 8, 21*n.*, 60, 82*n.*
Counter-control, xv
Covert, A., 173, 190*n.*
Coyle, J.T., 33, 46*n.*
Creek, M., 173, 190*n.*
Criterion-referenced assessment, and teach-test method, 129ff., **130, 131, 136,** 142, 170

Daly, K., 128ff.
Deaf:
    schools for, 4
    sensory aid for, 19
Delquadri, J., 52, 53, 83*n.*
DeMyer, M., 173, 190*n.*
Department of Education, Province of Alberta, 128*n.*
Depression, management of, conference on, ix
Desensitization, and social withdrawal, 51
DesLauriers, A., 173, 190*n.*
Developmentally-delayed children, home-based program:
    discussion of, 99–100
    family training program for, 89ff.
    method of, 90–93
    results of, 93–99
        command compliance, **98**
        command occurrence, **97**
        parent-child interactions, **94, 95**
        parental non-attendance, **96**
Dewey, J., 11, 21*n.*
Dextro-amphetamine, 38
Didactic verbal interchanges, 103
DiGiancomo, J.N., 33, 46*n.*
Dilley, M.G., 23, 24, 30*n.*
Direct and Individualized Instruction Procedures, 10
Direct Teaching Model, 138–40, **140, 141**
Discrimination:
    and autism, 173, 174
    and environment, 14
    stimuli, 73
Doleys, D.M., 104, 126*n.*
Dopaminergic brain mechanisms, 38
Dopaminergic pathways, and verbal tics, 33
Double vision, and family training program, 90
Down's syndrome, 153
Doxsey-Whitfield, M., 128ff.
Dysart, R., 174, 190*n.*

Early Education Project, 128ff.
    classroom project, 155ff., **158**
    criterion referencing, 130–37
    data collection format, 140–42, **143, 158**
    Direct Teaching Mode, 138–40, **140, 141**
    developmental curriculum, 129–30, **130, 131**
    home teaching program, 145ff., **147, 148, 150, 151, 154, 156, 157, 158**
    Incidental Teaching Model, 142–45, **144**
    instructional program development, 137
    intervention orientation, steps listed, 129
    scope of, 128–29
    summarized, 170
Echolalic speech, 174
Edmonton School, 155
Empey, L.T., 107, 126*n.*
Englemann, S., 74, 82*n.*, 134, 138, 170*n.*
Epilepsy, xiii
Episode report data (ERD), 109–110, 114
Exceptional children:
    conference on, vii
    school toleration of, 11–12
Experimental analysis of behavior (EAB), 18
Experimental Education Unit (EEU), 10, 34
Extinction, observed, 7
Extrafamily insularity, 116

Fahn, S., 33, 46*n.*
Family Training Program Model, 99, 100
Farside, R.F., 173, 190*n.*
Faust, G.W., 132, 170*n.*
Feedback:
    on parent performance, 103, 112
    in teaching, 15, 138
Feldman, R.B., 33, 46*n.*
Ferster, C.B., 172, 190*n.*
Findley, J.R., 9, 22*n.*
Fixsen, D.L., 52, 53, 85*n.*
Fleischman, D.H., 53, 62, 79, 80, 83*n.*, 84*n.*
Flumen, A.B., 48, 83*n.*
Ford, D., 90, 92, 100*n.*
Forehand, R., 103, 104, 105, 126*n.*
Formative evaluation, 11, **17,** 18
Foxx, R.M., 173, 190*n.*
Fredericks, H.D., 128, 137, 152, 171*n.*
Freitag, G., 7, 21*n.*, 173, 191*n.*
Freitas, L., 173, 191*n.*
Fry readability levels, 35, 36

Garrett, B., 55, 56, 61, 82*n.*, 84*n.*
Generalization:
    and environment, 14
    and instruction, 137
    of pencil grasp, in art instruction, 161

and recess behavior, 78
and treatment durability, 106ff.
Gentry, N.D., 10, 21n.
Gilkey, K.M., 173, 190n.
Gilles de la Tourette syndrome, 33–34, 38, 45
Glaser, R., 10, 12, 13, 16, **17**, 18, 21n.
Glass, J.B., 33, 46n.
Glazer, J.A., 49, 83n.
Godson, G.D., 137, 170n.
Goetz, E.M., 64, 84n.
Gold, V.J., 173, 191n.
Gottman, J.M., 50, 51, 82n., 83n.
Grabowski, J., xvi, xviin.
Graunke, B., 172ff.
Green, D.R., 64, 84n., 104, 126n.
Greenwood, C.R., 48ff., 49, 51, 52, 53, 54, 56, 62, 79, 83n., 84n., 86n.
Grinstead, J.D., 100, 101n.
Guerney, B.F., jr., 48, 83n.
Guess, D., 15, 21n., 128, 162, 163, 164–65, 171n.
Guild, J., 53, 79, 80, 83n., 84n.

Haldol, 38. *See also* Haloperidol
Hall, R.V., 8, 9, 21n., 60, 82n.
Haloperidol, 33, 34, 35, 37, 38, 41, 44, 45
Halverson, C.F., 50, 86n.
Hamerlynck, L.A., xv
Hand clapping behaviors, autistic-like, 91
Handicapped children:
 school toleration of, 11–12
 status of, 3–6
Hanf, C., 103, 126n.
Haring, N.G., 10, 16, **17**, 18, 21n., 128, 171n.
Harris, F.R., 7, 21n., 51, 82n.
Hart, B., 51, 71, 82n., 85n., 129, 142, 145, 168, 171n.
Hartup, W.W., 49, 82n., 83n.
Hastings, J.T., 18, 21n.
Haus, B.F., 89, 101n.
Hawkins, N., 51, 52, 85n.
Hayden, A.H., 128, 171n.
Hayden, M.L., 104, 126n.
Healy, C.E., 33, 46n.
Help-Seeking Interview (HSI), 117–18, 123–26, **124, 125**
Headbanging, of autistic, 174
Hendriks, A.F.C.J., xv, xviin.
Herbert, E.W., 104, 105, 126n.
Hersen, M., 41, 46n.
Hewett, F.M., 173, 190n.
Hillyard, A., 128ff.

Hirschi, T., 107, 126n.
Hobbs, S.A., 104, 126n.
Hoffman, C.B., 48, 82n.
Home-based family training program. *See* Developmentally-delayed children, home-based family training program for
Home Teaching Program, 145ff.
Hopkins, B.L., 8, 9, 21n., 60, 82n.
Hops, H., 48, 49, 51, 52, 53, 54, 55, 56, 61, 62, 64, 66, 79, 80, 82n., 83n., 84n., 86n.
House, A.E., 109, 117, 127n.
House, B.J., 138, 171n.
Hoyt, R.K., jr., 19, 22n.
Hyperactivity, reduction of, 23–30, **28, 29**. *See also* Self-modeling, photographic mediated

Imitation:
 generalized, 7
 sensory feedback theory of, 24
Incidental Teaching Decision Making Model, 168
Incidental teaching procedure, 168–70
Individual Interaction Code (IIC), 55
Ini, S., 173, 190n.
Insular family, deviance support system, 102ff.
 conclusions on, 123–26, **124, 125**
 family structure, 119, **119**
 insularity hypothesis, 115–16, 124–25
 research on, general, 102–106, 107ff.
 social networks of, 116–23, **119, 120, 121, 122, 123**
 socioeconomic aspects, 118
 treatment durability, risk aspects, 107ff., **108, 109, 112, 113**, 120, **120**, 124, **124, 125**
Intelligence tests, 33
Interaction skills, generalization of, 51
Israel, A.C., 71, 84n.
"Issues Relating to the Future of Special Education," 19n.

Jackson, C., 104, 126n.
Jackson, D., 8, 21n.
Jackson, P.W., 49, 84n.
Jarvik, M.E., 34, 35, 46n.
Jason, L., 89, 101n.
Johannson, S., 174, 186, 190n., 191n.
Johnson, E., 173, 191n.
Johnson, S.M., 23, 25, 30n., 105, 126n., 174, 186, 190n., 191n.

Index

Johnson, T.L., 64, 84*n*.
Joint Task Procedure, in PEERS, 65–68, 70, 71, 79, 80
Jones, R.R., 52, 85*n*.

Kanner, L., 172, 173, 190*n*.
Kassorla, I.C., 173, 191*n*.
Keasy, C.B., 49, 84*n*.
Kelley, W.R., 24, 30*n*.
Kelley, P., 173, 191*n*.
Kerr, M.A., 51, 85*n*.
Keutzer, C., 51, 85*n*.
Kidder, J.D., 8, 21*n*.
Kinder, M.I., 7, 21*n*.
Kirby, F.D., 51, 84*n*.
Knopp, W., 33, 46*n*.
Koegel, R.L., 173, 191*n*.
Kolvin, I., 173, 190*n*.
Kuehn, B.S., 100, 101*n*.
Kuehn, F.E., 100, 101*n*.
Kuhn, T.S., 68, 84*n*.
Kysela, G.M. 128ff.

Lahaderne, H.M., 49, 84*n*.
Lahey, B., 33, 46*n*.
Language skills:
  and autism, 172
  functional, 165
  Gross Motor/Sound Imitation Component, 163–64
  Guess program for, 164–65, **166**
  teaching of, 129, **130,** 152, 162–66
Law of Effect, xiv
Lawrence, Kansas, school study in, 9
Learning, conditions fostering, 16, **17**
Least restrictive alternatives, 4, 5
Leske, G., 102ff., 105, 110, 127*n*.
Levin, J.R., 24, 31*n*.
Levine, M., 173, 190*n*.
Levoamphetamine, 38
Lewis, M., 49, 50, 84*n*.
Liberty, K.A., 32ff.
Lichstein, K., 174, 186, 187, 190*n*.
Liddle, W., 35, 36, 46*n*.
Limbic mid-brain area, 33
Lindsley, O.R., xiv, xvii*n*., 7, 9, 20*n*., 21*n*., 45
Lippitt, R., 49, 84*n*.
Lockyer, L., 173, 191*n*.
Lotter, V., 173, 191*n*., 192*n*.
Lovaas, O.I., 7, 21*n*., 48, 65, 84*n*., 173, 191*n*.
Lovitt, T.C., 16, **17,** 18, 21*n*.
Lubeck, S.G., 107, 126*n*.
Lund, D., 8, 21*n*.

Madaus, G.F., 18, 21*n*.
Madsen, C.H., 7, 20*n*.
Mahoney, M.J., 15, 21*n*.
Mainstreaming, in school, xv, xvi, 4, 5
Maintenance, behavioral, 7
Marshall, G.R., 173, 191*n*.
Martin, G., 134, 135, 138, 139, 140, 171*n*.
Martin, S., 25, 30*n*., 172ff., 174, 186, 190*n*., 191*n*.
Mash, E.J., 104, 126*n*.
Maternal and Child Health Service, of HEW, 32*n*.
Maternal discriminative cue pattern, 103
Mayfield School, 155
McAllister, L., xvi, xvii*n*.
McConahey, O.L., 33, 46*n*.
McConnell, O.L., 173, 191*n*.
McDermott, E., 173, 191*n*.
McDonald, L., 128ff.
McDonald, S., 128ff.
McKay, H.D., 107, 127*n*.
McKenzie, H.S., 80, 84*n*.
McNeal, S., 51, 52, 85*n*.
McNees, M.C., 33, 46*n*.
McNees, P.M., 33, 46*n*.
Medication, and verbal tics, 32ff. *See also* Tics, verbal, medication, and school performance
Mees, H.L., 7, 22*n*., 51, 85*n*.
Meichenbaum, D.H., 70, 84*n*.
Memory, and environment, 14
Mental health services, ideal, conference on, vii
Mental retardation, xiii, 4, 6, 91ff.
Messiha, F.S., 33, 46*n*.
Methodology Stage, of behavioral modification, xiv
Methylphenidate, 45
Metz, J.R., 172, 191*n*.
Meyerhoff, J.L., 33, 46*n*.
Michael, C.M., 50, 84*n*.
Miller, J., 15, 21*n*.
Milne, D.C., 51, 82*n*.
MIMR data sheets, 149, 160
Minke, K.A., 9, 22*n*.
Model cues, 134
Modeling. *See also* Self-modeling and learning, 14
  and parent instruction, 103
  in teacher training, 149
Morris, D.P., 50, 84*n*.
Motor skills, teaching of, 129, **130, 131,** 132, 152–53, **154**

in art instruction, 161
behavioral objectives, 133, **133**
deficit in, 79
infant criterion-referenced, **136**
and language instruction, 163
programs for, 167–68
Mowrer, O.H., 23, 24, 30n.
Mueller, E., 48, 49, 84n., 85n.

Nagoshi, J.T., 53, 84n.
National Institute of Child Health and Human Development, 89n.
National Institute of Mental Health (NIMH), 102n., 106
National Society for Autistic Children, Houston Chapter, 175
Needs analyses, 11
Nelson, K., 173, 191n.
Nicholes, J.S., 55, 84n.

O'Brien, V., 33, 46n.
Observational learning, 14, 23
O'Connor, N., 173, 192n.
O'Connor, R.D., 51, 85n.
Oden, S., 50, 51, 82n., 85n.
O'Leary, K.D., 7, 22n., 70, 71, 84n., 85n.
O'Leary, S.G., 70, 71, 85n.
Olson, K.A., 23–30, 30n.
Olson, R.P., 173, 190n.
Omura, R.T., 53, 84n.
Operant psychology. *See also* Behavior modification, general
child studies of, 6–7
experimental branches of, 6
and behavior modification, 7–8
school studies of, 7
Oppenheim, A.N., 173, 191n.
Oppositional children, in insular family, 102ff. *See also* Insular family, deviance support system
noncompliance of, 104
rule violations of, 110–11, **111**
socioeconomic characteristics, 107
therapy of, durability, 104–106
treatment, general, 107ff.
Optimization models, 14
Oregon Social Learning Center, 52
Ounsted, C., 173, 190n.

Pain, management of, conference on, ix
Paine, S., 79, 80, 83n., 84n.
Paivio, A., 23, 24, 30n.

Parent re-education strategies, 110–11
Parent Training Program, 145ff., **147, 148**. *See also* Early Education Project
Parker, C.A., 80, 85n.
PASS programs, 52, 80
Patterson, G.R., xiv, xv, xviin., 23, 26, 29, 30n., 31n., 49, 52, 53, 85n., 102, 103, 105, 115, 127n., 176, 186, 187, 191n.
Peed, S., 104, 126n.
Peer groups, children in, 29, 48–49, 73–75. *See also* Program for Establishing Effective Relationship Skills
Peer Interaction Recording System (PIRS), 55, 61, 63
PEERS. *See* Program for Establishing Effective Relationship Skills
Peer Tally Code (PTC), 55, 56
Pharmacology, operant behavioral, basic strategy, 32–33
Phelps, R., 51, 52, 85n.
Phillips, E.A., 52, 53, 85n.
Phillips, E.L., 52, 53, 85n.
Physical prompts, in teaching, 134
Physiotherapy, for motor development skills, 152–53
Piaget, J., 12
Pictorial mediated self-modeling. *See* Self-modeling, photographic mediated
Piglet, in analogy, 12
Pinkston, E.M., 104, 126n.
Pinkston, S., 104, 126n.
PIRS codes. *See* Peer Interaction Recording System
Pitfield, M., 173, 191n.
Placebos, in tic study, 41
Play:
in autism, 180, 185, 187
peer interaction in, 69ff., **76, 77**
Portage Assessment, 159
Portage Guide, 129, 130
Porter, D., 36, 46n.
Pragmatism, philosophical, 11
Praise statements, parental, in global rating system, 91
Premack, D., 18, 22n.
Prescription teaching, 11. *See also* Prescriptive Science of Instruction
Prescriptive Science of Instruction, 12
and cognition, 15
competence performance, 13
environment, 14
initial state aspects, 13–14
instructional effects, 14–15

Program for Establishing Effective Relationship (PEERS)
  and behavioral management packages, 52–54
  conclusions on, 79–81
  experimental classroom research on, 54–60, **58, 59**
  generalized behavior gains, 74–75
  procedures tested, 64ff.
  program package, 51–52
  regular educational setting research, 60ff., **62, 63, 64, 65, 72**
Programmed learning, 11
Progressive inclusion, 4, 5
Psychosis. *See also* Autistic children, home environment
  and operant conditioning, 6
  and social withdrawal, 50
Psychotherapy, of parents of autistic, 177
Psychotic speech, 174
Puberty, tics in, 33
Punishment:
  and environment, 14
  of oppositional children, 104
Puntius, W., 173, 190*n*.

Quilitch, H.R., 92, 101*n*.

Rafi, A.B., 33, 46*n*.
Rainey, S.K., 100, 101*n*.
Ramp, E.A., 10, 21*n*.
Ranier School, 8
Rardin, M.W., 23ff.
Raush, H.L., 174, 192*n*.
Ray, R.S., 103, 127*n*., 176, 187, 191*n*.
Reading behavior, reinforcement contingencies on, 8–9
Reading for Concepts (Liddle), 35, 36
Reading skills, and tic treatment, 35–36
Recess, school. *See* Play
Re-education model, of family intervention, 102–103
Rehm, R., 173, 191*n*.
Reid, J.B., xv, xvii*n*., 49, 51, 52, 85*n*., 102, 115, 127*n*.
Reid, K.M., 51, 85*n*.
Reinforcement:
  and autism, 65
  in behavioral management package, 57
  and classroom, 32
  contingent, and self-regulation, 25
  in home-based study, 91, 93
  of insular family, and community, 116
  natural 79–80
  of oppositional children, 104, 115–16
  and peer groups, 49, 71, 78
  and PEERS, 64–66, 70
  of reading behavior, 8–9
  in self-monitoring study, 27
  and sensory memory, 24
  social, and language, 165
  in teaching, 138
Resch, E.E., 111, 126*n*.
Residential Community Corrections Programs, 105, 127*n*.
Residential schools, 3, 4
Response frequency, as measure, 6
Responsive Teaching, 9
Reynolds, M., 3, 22*n*.
Richardson, L.M., 173, 190*n*.
Rimland, B., 173, 191*n*.
Risley, T.R., 7, 22*n*., 71, 81, 82*n*., 85*n*., 92, 100*n*., 129, 142, 145, 168, 171*n*., 173, 191*n*.
Ritvo, E., 173, 191*n*.
Ritz, M., 173, 191*n*.
Riverbend program, 105, 106
Roberts, H.W., 104, 126*n*.
Roberts, M., 104, 126*n*.
Robins, L.N., 103, 127*n*.
Roff, M., 103, 127*n*.
Rogers, E.S., 102ff.
Rogers-Warren, A., 71, 85*n*.
Rohwer, W.D., 24, 31*n*.
Rosenblum, L.A., 49, 50, 84*n*.
Rosenthal, R., 93, 101*n*.
Ross, D., 23, 24, 30*n*.
Ross, S.A., 24, 30*n*.
Rubenstein, B.D., 7, 21*n*.
Ruder, K., 15, 21*n*.
Rutter, M., 173, 191*n*.

Sailor, W., 15, 21*n*., 128, 162, 163, 164–65, 171*n*.
Sajwaj, T.E., 104, 126*n*.
Schaeffer, B., 7, 21*n*.
Schiefelbusch, R.L., 3ff., 16, **17,** 18, 19, 22*n*.
Schreibman, L., 173, 191*n*.
Schultz, R.E., 9, 22*n*.
Schuster, C.R., 32, 47*n*.
Schweid, E., 102, 126*n*.
Science of education:
  components of, 13–18
  philosophical aspects, 11–13
Schizophrenia, xiv, 7, 48

Self-control procedures, and social interaction, 70–71
Self-help skills, 129, **130**, 155, **157**, 160–61, 168, 173, 187
Self-modeling, photographic mediated, 23ff. *See also* Modeling
  experiment on, 25–30
  discussion, 29–30
  method, 25–28
  results, 28, **28, 29**
  research related to, 23–25
Self-mutilation, in autism, treated, 173
Self-report, and social interaction, 75–78, 80
Self-stimulation, in autism, 173, 174, 179, 181, 185
Sensory aids, and education, 19
Shafto, F., 33, 46n.
Shaping, and social withdrawal, 51
Shapiro, A.K., 33, 34, 46n., 47n.
Shapiro, E., 33, 34, 46n., 47n.
Shaw, C.R., 107, 127n.
Shaw, D.A., 176, 187, 191n.
Shearer, D., 129, 130, 171n.
Sherman, J.A., 7, 8, 20n., 22n.
Shores, R.E., 49, 51, 85n.
Simmons, J.Q., 7, 21n.
Skindrud, K., 53, 84n.
Skinner, B.F., 6, 138, 171n.
Slagel, S., 173, 191n.
Snelbecker, G.E., 130, 171n.
Snyder, S.H., 33, 46n.
SOC. *See* Standardized coding system
Socialization skills, and self-help, 129, **130**, 160
Social Learning Approach to Family Intervention, A (Patterson, et. al.), 52
Social learning theory, principles of, 23
Social withdrawal:
  behavioral management packages on, 52ff.
  conclusion on, 79–81
  long-term, 50
  research, general, 48–52
  and skill tutoring, 74–75
  teacher identification of, 62
Solomon, G.E., 34, 47n.
Soroker, E., 50, 84n.
Special class model, 3
Special education, history of, 5–6.
  See also Mental retardation
SRA Power Builders IIb, 36
Staats, A.W., 9, 15, 22n.
Staats, C.K., 9, 22n.

Stambaugh, E.E., 109, 117, 127n.
Standardized coding system (SOC), 109–110, 113–14
Stanton School, 30n.
Stevens, T., 61, 82n.
Stingle, S., 49, 82n.
Stotland, E., 23, 25, 31n.
Strain, P.S., 48, 49, 50, 51, 53, 70, 73, 85n.
Street, A., 62, 79, 84n.
Suicide, and early social isolation, 50
Sulzbacher, S.I., 32ff., 32, 33, 45, 46n., 47n.
Super School, 9
Sweet, R.D., 34, 47n.
Sykes, B.W., 89ff.
Symbolic modeling, and social withdrawal, 51. *See also* Modeling

Tague, C.A., 8, 21n.
Tapia, F., 33, 47n.
Taplin, P.S., 102, 127n.
Tate, B.G., 173, 192n.
Taylor, J., 53, 84n., 128ff.
Taylor, K.M., 33, 46n.
Teacher-consultant model, efficiency, 80
Teacher praise, and peer group interaction, 64–65
Teaching Family Handbook, The (Phillips, et al.), 52
Teaching machines, 19
Terdal, L., 104, 126n.
Test-teach method, of instruction, 130–37, **130, 131, 133, 136.** *See also* Early Education Project
Tharp, R.G., 52, 85n.
Thomas, D.R., 7, 20n., 134, 138, 170n.
Thompson, S., 89, 101n.
Thompson, T., xvi, xviin., 32, 45, 47n.
"Three Years Past 1984" (Schiefelbusch and Hoyt), 19
Tics, verbal, medication, and school performance, 32ff.
  discussion of, 44–46
  methods of study, 34–38
  results on, 38–44, **39, 40, 42, 43**
Timm, M.A., 51, 85n.
Tjossem, T.D., 89, 101n.
Todd, N.M., 49, 55, 56, 62, 82n., 83n., 84n., 86n.
Token systems, xiv, 8, 51, 64
Toler, H.C., 51, 84n.
Transfer, and instruction, 15
Treffert, D.A., 173, 192n.
Turner, R., 173, 192n.

Index 201

Tyler, J.L., 52, 85*n*.
Tyler, R.W., 11, 22*n*.

University of Alberta, 128*n*.
University of Calgary, x
University of Chicago, 11
University of Houston, 172*n*.
University of Kansas, 9, 89*n*.
University of Washington, 7, 10, 34

Vanecko, S., 33, 46*n*.
Verbal behavior, and social interaction, 75, 78, 80
Verbal cues, in teaching, 145
Verbal discrimination, and self-modeling, 30
Verbal prompting, 134, 135
Verbal tics. *See* Tics, verbal, medication, and school performance
Videotapes:
 in home life, 92
 in teacher training, 149
Vincent, L., 15, 21*n*.
Vocalization, and autism, 180ff.

Wahl, G., 174, 186, 190*n*., 191*n*.
Wahler, R.G., 51, 85*n*., 102ff., 102, 103, 104, 105, 109, 110, 111, 115, 117, 126*n*., 127*n*., 174, 186, 187, 190*n*.
Waldrop, M.G., 50, 86*n*.
Walker, H.M., 48ff., 49, 51, 52, 53, 54, 55, 56, 61, 62, 64, 66, 79, 82*n*., 83*n*., 84*n*., 86*n*., 105, 127*n*.
Walker Problem Behavior Identification Checklist, 55

Walters, R.H., 23, 30*n*.
Wayne, H., 33, 34, 46*n*., 47*n*.
Weinrott, M.R., 51, 86*n*.
Welfare agencies, and insulated families, 120–22, **122**
Wells, K.C., 104, 126*n*.
Werry, J.S., 33, 46*n*.
Westlake, R.J., 33, 46*n*.
Wetzel, R.J., 52, 85*n*.
Whalen, C., 173, 191*n*.
Whalen, K., 103, 127*n*.
White, O.R., 41, 47*n*.
Whoopee Stage, xiii–xiv, xvi
Wilchesky, M., 51, 86*n*.
Willard, J.G., 137, 170*n*.
Williams, E.P., 174, 192*n*.
Wing, J.K., 173, 192*n*.
Winnie-the-Pooh, 12
Withdrawal. *See* Social withdrawal
Wohwill, J.F., 12, 22*n*.
Wolf, M.M., 7, 8, 9, 21*n*., 22*n*., 51, 52, 53, 79, 81, 82*n*., 85*n*., 90, 92, 100*n*.
Wolf, W., 173, 191*n*.
Wolff, S., 173, 192*n*.
Woozle hunt, as analogy, 12
Wright, H.F., 174, 192*n*.

Yates, A.J., 33, 45, 47*n*.
Yawns:
 and boredom, 45
 as drug side effect, 35, 36, 38, **40**, 41–42
Yoder, D., 15, 21*n*.

Zeaman, D., 138, 171*n*.